Praise for *Fal...*

"Made me want to run away to a Greek island."

—Helena Frith Powell, author of
All You Need to Be Impossibly French

"This inspiring true story made us laugh and cry."

—*Heat Magazine*, five out of five stars

"Remarkable story…a moving book."

—*Daily Express*

"One woman's rat race escape."

—*You* magazine, *Mail on Sunday*

"This book will make you laugh and cry and laugh again. I didn't want it to end."

—Emma Woolf, author of *An Apple a Day*

"What makes *Falling in Honey* so gripping is the clear adoration that Jennifer feels for the country she now calls home. Through exquisite descriptions and very honest revelations, soon she's not the only one falling head over heels. One way ticket to Greece anyone?"

—*Wanderlust* magazine

"Deceptively simple prose…at times as breathtaking as the landscape it describes…beautiful book."

—Richard Clark, author of *Rhodes: A Notebook*

falling
in
honey

How a Tiny Greek Island
Stole My Heart

Jennifer Barclay

This book is a memoir. It reflects the author's present recollections of her experiences over a period of years. Some names and characteristics have been changed, some events have been compressed, and some dialogue has been re-created.

Published by Sourcebooks, Inc.

P.O. Box 4410, Naperville, Illinois 60567-4410

(630) 961-3900

Fax: (630) 961-2168

www.sourcebooks.com

Library of Congress Cataloging-in-Publication Data

Barclay, Jennifer.

Falling in Honey : How a Tiny Greek Island Stole My Heart / Jennifer Barclay.
    pages cm

Includes bibliographical references and index.

(pbk. : alk. paper) 1. Barclay, Jennifer—Travel—Greece—Telos Island. 2. English—Greece—Telos Island—Biography. 3. Telos Island (Greece)—Description and travel. I. Title.

DF901.T59B37 2014

914.9587--dc23

2013031146

Printed and bound in the United States of America.

VP 10 9 8 7 6 5 4 3 2 1

I felt once more how simple a thing is happiness: a glass of wine…the sound of the sea.

—*Zorba the Greek*, Nikos Kazantzakis

When you set out on your journey to Ithaka,
Pray that the road is long,
Full of adventure…

—*Ithaka*, Constantine P. Cavafy

Note

I t's difficult to find a system of spelling Greek words in English letters, but in general I've spelled words pretty much as they sound, except where it would look too unusual. So, for example, Yorgos, because that's how it's pronounced, not Georgos. Male Greek names usually end in -s when they are the subject of a sentence (Yiannis) but drop the -s when you are addressing the person (Yianni!) or they are the object of the sentence (talking about Yianni). For simplicity, when I'm writing in English, I've used the -s form throughout, except in speech.

This is a true story, so I've altered some names and changed identities to protect people's privacy.

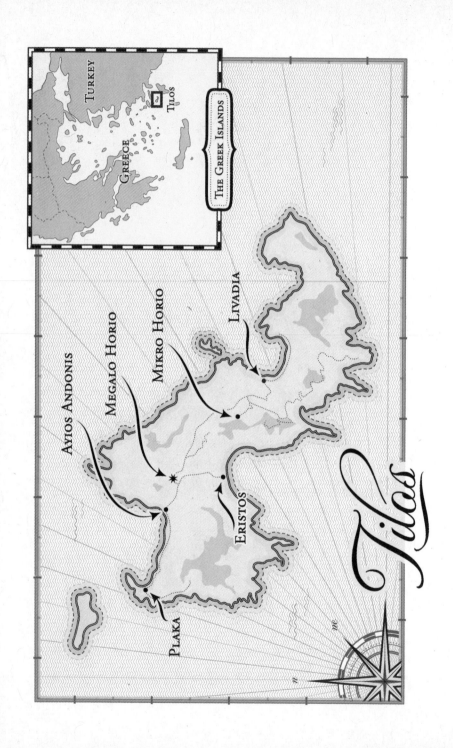

TURKEY

GREECE

TILOS

THE GREEK ISLANDS

AYIOS ANDONIS

MEGALO HORIO

MIKRO HORIO

LIVADIA

ERISTOS

PLAKA

Tilos

Prologue

~~~~~~

There's a bee on my arm. I've gotten used to having bees around, hovering in the flowers and basil bushes, sometimes coming for a curious look in my kitchen when I'm working with the doors open. I can't see or hear my nearest neighbors in this valley, but I like to think of it as a buzzing place...

Inside the honey factory, Pavlos removes the wooden frames from the hives. "I'm just the worker!" he says, but without the worker bees, there'd be no honey. The frames are like hanging folders in a filing cabinet, and each holds an uneven slab of honeycomb. The best ones are almost covered in sealed wax cells. Pavlos takes a heated knife and skims off the outer edge of wax, releasing the clear golden liquid. It gleams as it pours off thickly. "Here, taste," he says, and hands me pieces of oozing soft honeycomb.

It amazes me that it's ready to eat straight out of the hive, this perfect food full of goodness—it needs nothing from us. What we're doing here is just releasing and gathering it, cleaning it and putting it in jars. The actual making of honey has all been done by the bees. As Pooh Bear said to the bee: the only reason for making honey is so I can eat it.

The smell of warm honey is intoxicating. It's thirty-plus degrees outside and the hives were standing out there not long ago, the bees happily coming and going, blissfully unaware. When there are flowers in the fields, the bees can fill up a honeycomb in as little as a week.

"Here, take some more," says Pavlos, scooping up spoonfuls of honeycomb onto a plate. My hands are getting sticky.

"This honey is made from herbs, votana, flowers that are healthy for your body, and thyme. We don't use any chemicals."

Tilos has always been famous for its herbs that grow wild everywhere, and its mountainsides are mostly empty except for tiny chapels, goats, and beehives. Pavlos and his family grow a lot of food and are passionate about never using chemical pesticides or fertilizers in their gardens and fields: it's not only bad for you, but for the birds and the bees as well.

As each frame is opened up, it is slid into a compartment in the centrifuge, which will extract all the honey. When all the compartments are full, the machine is closed and starts spinning.

It circles to the left for a few minutes, to the right for a few minutes, slowly at first to protect the delicate honeycomb from breaking as it empties. If you were on one of those fairground rides that spin you round, you'd be saying: that wasn't too bad, was it? Then it starts to the left again but fast this time, causing the honey to start pouring, thick and caramel-colored, into the *vat. And then it stops and spins fast to the right, at which point if you were on the fairground ride you'd be thinking this was a bad idea.*

But it's only a bee or two that was on the ride, having been asleep perhaps in one of the honeycombs, and now they've fallen in the honey and are perhaps thinking, "But what a way to go…"

CHAPTER ONE

Pick an Island, Any Island

I am looking for a Greek island.

If I were going on my own, maybe I'd just take a backpack and trust to serendipity. I've fallen in love with so many islands over the years just by hopping on the next ferry: islands that smelled of herbs and pine trees, whose villages had whitewashed alleys overhung with magenta bougainvillea, stalked by cats and chickens. Islands where pigs roamed on the wild beaches and cows wandered through the ruins of ancient hilltop castles; where people gathered in the village square at least once a day to gossip and play backgammon; where the hills were filled with olive trees and thyme and dropped away to a deep sparkling blue.

Once, island-hopping with another traveler, we'd arrived on the night of a big local festival. All the rooms were booked up, but sometimes you could sleep on someone's rooftop. It had been too late to ask permission, and I was slightly nervous the next morning when I heard a window opening by our heads, expecting a sharp telling off. Instead, we got an amused "*Kalimera!*" or good morning, and a coffee and biscuits.

Later, we found a room to rent at the back of someone's house; our landlady, Eleni, gave us plates heaped with ripe fresh fruit from her garden every day. In the mornings I had a coffee and homemade biscuits on the balcony with her, and one day we went to help the family with the grape harvest. We followed stony tracks all over the island, accompanied by the sound of birds and crickets, but mostly to the empty beach where Eleni's mother used to go when she was courting. As the sun was going down, we sometimes stopped at a farm where a jolly man would fill up our water bottle with slightly fizzy homemade wine that we sipped on the way back to the pretty port, and we sat on the quayside watching brightly painted fishing boats bobbing in deep blue water, their nets laid out to dry.

The spontaneous hospitality, the color, the traditional, rural island life, the shimmering blue sea, the sheer, sunny beauty of it all—that's what I'm looking for again.

This time John and I are going together, so I've offered to book somewhere in advance. It feels like the grown-up thing to do, and a good compromise. I want him to get hooked on Greece too. I want to find somewhere new so that we can discover it together.

Guidebook nearby, I look at some beautiful places to rent on various websites, but keep going back to a big villa with a swimming pool available for a reasonable last-minute deal on Tilos, halfway between Rhodes and Kos. It's an island I've somehow missed before, even though I've traveled up and down the Dodecanese. The villa looks fantastic. It's within walking distance of a village and two beaches.

"Hey, Jen," mumbles John, who's been dozing in front of the Grand Prix in his sunny, cozy flat; he's been working some crazy shifts. Nestling into the couch for a while with him, I sift through the options, tell him about the villa and what little I've managed to find out about Tilos.

"Book it! It's huge. We can bring Kate and Chris over. I owe her a birthday present—I'll pay for her flight."

I smile. What a lovely, generous idea. "Are you sure?"

"Yeah, why not? I'll leave the decision to you—you're the expert on Greece, Jen! But it sounds great to me. Let's do it."

I go back to book the villa with a big smile on my face, remembering how I met John and his sister Kate the first time.

Almost a year ago, I was sitting at the bar of the Park Tavern one evening with a glass of wine and got into conversation with Kate, who was visiting from Vancouver. That's the kind of place the Park Tavern is. When I first moved to this town near the south coast of England for my work, the Park was a welcoming place to stop on my way home, look over some paperwork, and eat a sandwich. Soon, I got to know the landlord and he'd introduce me to people. I might end up talking to the local judge, a builder, a city planning officer, or a sausage maker. When John took on managing a local restaurant, he was welcomed into the special club of the Park Tavern too. He and his sister Kate were half English and half Canadian; I knew Vancouver, had stayed there with friends and visited the islands. We all swapped notes on favorite places. Kate wore vintage clothes, was a music producer, and had a mischievous grin. John looked very clean-cut with his suit and tie and baby-blond hair, but there was much more than met the eye; he had a wicked sense of humor, and the more I learned about him, the more I was fascinated. There was good chemistry between us. Before long, we started seeing each other.

I don't mind that John's job involves working long and unusual hours. I happily spend the early parts of the evenings seeing friends or reading or catching up at the office; it's good having a bit of downtime for myself. I go for challenging bike rides or walks on the weekends while he works. I don't have to faff around in supermarkets making sure we have something for dinner; if we're hungry, he'll make us something later. When he finishes work, he comes to meet me wherever I am and we exchange news of our days on his sofa over a good bottle of wine or listen to music. We talk about our experiences and our dreams. I'm drawn to his passion for his work, the way he throws himself into what he loves doing, the way I do; I'm inspired by the way he nurtures his staff. And finally he's found a way to take a week away from work in the summer, a super-busy time of year for him, and spend it with me in the place I love, Greece.

My dad sometimes says his happiest memories are of family holidays we took when my brother and I were young. I'm pretty sure he's not thinking of the holidays when we drove to the south of France and he swore a lot trying to put up a seventies-style three-bedroom tent made of scaffolding and canvas during a torrential thunderstorm; or of the holiday where the old station wagon broke down carrying that tent through the Alps, and all my mum's clothes were stolen at a campsite in Italy while Hare Krishnas chanted next door. I expect he's mainly thinking about the later holidays when we ditched the tent and started going to Greece.

I still have a diary from when we first went to Corfu—I was eleven:

After a few seconds of waking up I literally jumped out of bed and dressed immediately.

Apparently I enjoyed every minute of the three-hour flight (including the meal, described in great detail right down to the sachets). Then arrival in Corfu: the heat, the drive through quaint villages, the Greek folk songs, the vines and olive trees, washing hanging outside the whitewashed or stone houses.

We step off the coach and the holiday really begins. We were on the beach after 15 minutes. The sea was blue and warm and the sand hot, white, and soft, even if it was a bit dirty with sticks and seaweed.

I ate souvlaki and chips and Greek salad, and drank Greek lemonade, "which is more like fruit juice, and much nicer than English."

If the first day is anything to go by, I think the holiday is going to be wonderful. Already by two o'clock we have sunbathed, swum, played in the dinghy... The sweets like Turkish delight are so cheap and sesame bars are only 8.50 dmx which is the same as 8½ p. We did some Greek dancing at a hotel.

I'm afraid we did bring back a record of Greek dance music. I remember all of us dancing around our house in Saddleworth to "Zorba."

In case you're not familiar with it, you hold your left arm around the shoulders of the person to the left of you, and your right arm around the shoulders of the person to the right; you kick one leg out gently in front, then the other, then take steps to the side and repeat, slowly at first, but getting faster in time with the music until you think you can't keep going another minute and collapse, laughing, at the end (at least in our house we did).

But I also remember the solo dances by the men: shows

of grace, agility, and strength to slow songs about pain and heartache that were utterly mesmerizing.

Miss Hatch, Hulme Grammar School for Girls' most eccentric teacher, with a passion for playing the violin and tending her tropical fish, scared most students off the classics during first-year Latin by making us all jump around the edges of the classroom carrying a ruler and shouting, "Um, am, em—object," a lesson most of us will never forget. But a few of us who were also perhaps eccentric went on to do Ancient Greek and memorized long monologues from classical plays, to be rewarded with powdery Greek coffee brewed in a metal jug and biscuits made from sesame seeds and honey. It's partly Miss Hatch's fault, too, that Greece got under my skin.

By the time I was seventeen, I was the only student at my school still studying Ancient Greek, and Miss Hatch gave me extra lessons in my free periods if I wanted to finish reading and translating a text. She taught me how the ancient roots were reflected in Modern Greek, instilling in me a fascination with words. Over my teenage years, there were holidays to Rhodes and Crete, Cephalonia and Ithaca, and then with a university friend around the Greek mainland.

After graduation from university, I'd had no idea what to do. I'd been applying for all sorts of graduate jobs, but with no clear goals (just big dreams), I wasn't getting very far at all. Then I saw an ad in the paper: an agency looking for graduates to be English teachers in private language schools in Athens. I thought of warm sunshine and blue sea, dancing and ancient amphitheaters. Maybe it was time to stay for longer. So I went to Greece.

Athens, when I first arrived that autumn, was not much like those dreamy holidays I'd been on before. My new home as an English teacher—it came with the job that the agency assigned to me in a *frontistirion*, or language school, in the district of Galatsi—was beside a six-lane highway that never seemed to sleep, among an endless stretch of gray concrete apartment buildings. But in the afternoons, I went up to the roof of my building where people hung their laundry, and high above the noise of street level I marked papers or read books in the sun, looking beyond the jumble of faded apartments to the gleaming silver sea. On Saturday mornings I'd hurry to the port of Piraeus. The clocks on the back of each ferry showed what time they would leave for which islands, and that would determine my adventure for the weekend.

On the island of Hydra, with houses clinging to rugged hillsides, there were no cars allowed and no real roads. I followed a footpath to the other, emptier side of the island, past a monastery and fields where mules and goats wandered, until the huge expanse of sea opened out before me. I found a flat rock on a hillside and lay barefoot on it, feeling like an Arcadian shepherdess as I ate my bread and cheese, basking in the warmth of the sun and the gentle breeze.

In the winter, on a ferry to the island of Aegina, I ran into my friend Yiannis, who I'd first met in Hydra. He had just bought a new artist's studio outside the town, and invited me to come and stay. It was a converted stone barn, with thick walls and wooden beams. French doors opened out onto a patio where bougainvillea trailed from a wooden trellis, the fallen leaves and petals swept by the wind into a pretty drift against the wall. The bedroom window looked out across an orchard of frost-covered fig trees and vines. Yiannis looked perfectly at home, transformed in his potter's apron and woolen hat, his bushy black mustache peeping out over the top of a scarf. Unfortunately my attempts at getting a fire going while he got absorbed in his work were useless. So he taught me instead to help him shape the clay and we drank ouzo, the strong Greek aniseed liqueur, to keep warm.

For the Easter holidays, I took the overnight ferry to the huge island of Crete. After another term's teaching in Athens in winter, I needed solitude and the rugged beauty of the wild, west coast. I found a room on a farm, whose big window looked out onto a deserted beach and a clear, pale blue sea. I scrambled high up rocks to vast views of wild scrub and mountains whose tops were enveloped in clouds. I tired myself out and then retreated under the quilts to fall asleep to the sound of birds and waves. Dinner was tomatoes stuffed with rice and herbs, or stews of potatoes, aubergines, broad beans, tomato, and more fresh herbs, with lots of fresh crusty bread. In the evening, I drank brandy and had live music played for me on the *bouzouki*, a Greek stringed instrument like a lute. The simple physical pleasures of sea and fresh air made me feel alive.

The island of Mykonos in early summer was completely different, with its exquisite whitewashed dovecotes, the town a jumble of baffling alleys and painted balconies. Wending my way toward the harbor, I turned a corner and there was a huge bird strutting up toward me: Petros, the resident friendly pelican, with a soft pink quiff that he let me stroke. You couldn't help liking a town that had its own pelican. Later, I made friends with someone who made a living by performing Greek dancing and catching fish; he taught me a few steps of *syrtaki* and directed me to where I could watch locals dancing to traditional music, holding hands together in never-ending lines that snaked around the room, the steps far more complex than they looked to the observer. I danced and I swam at Paradise Beach and soaked up the infectiously free-love atmosphere of the bars and cafés. A beautiful stranger said, "How do you say good-bye in England—kissing? On the lips? Like this?"

Even Athens began to feel like home. I liked the orange trees lining the streets, even if they were straggly and dusty. It was a joy to listen to men standing in the bakery having detailed discussions about different types of bread, or to brave the busy queues in the local market to buy heavy bags of vegetables. Good things happened out of the blue. I would be reading a sign, and an old man would offer assistance; I would end up with incomprehensible instructions in Greek and a foolish smile on my face. I'd go up to the roof of my apartment building in the evening, see the mountains all smoky blue, Athens a hazy white jumble of crystals, and off Piraeus, tankers lying motionless in the sea. One evening, a man from Crete started talking to me as we were walking the same way; he liked Athens, he said, because he didn't need to buy cigarettes anymore—he could breathe bad air for free. "I like the pollution. I like the rubbish. I like fighting people for my position on the bus." I laughed. I knew what he meant. I liked the random, bizarre excitement of my new life too.

It wasn't exactly clear what would happen next. Sometimes I thought I'd stay. Coming to Greece was not just about a job, I knew that. I was having the adventures that life should be about, searching out what my life was supposed to be.

A few years later, I found myself living in Canada. I moved from one neighborhood of Toronto to another until I ended up on the Danforth—the Greek district. The street signs were in both English and Greek, there was a Greek butcher who sold marinated souvlaki, and travel agents catering mostly to Greeks going back home, plus Greek restaurants and a Greek nightclub. I liked just standing in the shops and listening to people speaking the language I missed.

CHAPTER TWO

Tilos

Tilos is a tiny eight miles long and a few miles wide. The population is somewhere around five hundred depending on the season, the people far outnumbered by thousands of goats roaming wild. The dirt bike trails my out-of-date guidebook complained about are gone, if they ever existed: the whole island is a conservation area for wildlife. From the villa the only sounds are crickets, bees, crows, and donkeys. There are little chapels built into otherwise empty hillsides. Walks from the villa to nearby Eristos beach—a long stretch of sand with just a couple of hotels hidden in the trees behind it—go through a lush valley of olive and fig trees.

Our villa is on the edge of Megalo Horio, which means "Big Village." Although it is the administrative capital of the island, these days the name seems amusingly ironic, like calling a basketball player "Shorty." I read in the guidebook that Megalo Horio had a "one-way system" and "supermarket." I'd imagined lots of traffic and a hypermarket on the outskirts of town. The reality is so very different. For "one-way system," read: there is one road through the village, and it's too narrow for more than one car at a time, and even that car has to stop sometimes to let cats and chickens pass; as it goes through the village there's shade created by a huge arch of bougainvillea. As for the supermarket, it's a family-run shop with two rooms. The village is home to about one hundred people, one taverna or restaurant, one café-bar serving drinks and frequented mostly by locals (we seem to be the only tourists staying in the village), and two small grocery stores (one of which is the supermarket). The two cafés listed in the guidebook are clearly closed. Slumbering on a hillside topped by a ruined castle, Megalo Horio isn't exactly a hive of activity.

The island also has a "Small Village," or Mikro Horio, but that was abandoned half a century ago and is now uninhabited. And there's a very small settlement with just a couple of tavernas by the sea at a place a mile north of here called Ayios Andonis. But the main village is the port, Livadia, where we arrived, four miles to the south of Megalo Horio. We visit again on the island bus and find it has about a dozen tavernas, a handful of family-owned mini markets, a butcher's and a bakery, and a few gift shops and low-key bars. We sit on the rooftop terrace of one of the seafront bars and meet a friendly local man who tells us about the sheep and goats he raises when he's not helping his son serve drinks.

Tilos, it seems, hasn't succumbed to mass tourism or become the kind of place that sees visitors only as a source of money, but, thankfully for us, it hasn't developed itself into a "holistic spa yoga retreat" either; it is pure, unreconstructed Greece at its best. The island is also a walker's paradise. Many of its beaches are reached only by restored mule paths or goat tracks through countryside. The islanders, though they might not walk much themselves, encourage visitors from all over Europe who enjoy walking and nature—with the protection of wildlife, rare bird species found here include Eleonora's falcons and Bonelli's eagles and long-legged buzzards.

One morning, alone, I follow a dirt track leading away from Megalo Horio and end up wandering through a deserted valley pungent with thyme, marjoram, and sage, until gradually blue sea appears in the distance. I keep going and find a secluded cove of red sand and clear water: this must be Skafi beach. The others are jealous and the next day we walk there together. I've never seen John walk much farther than the hundred meters from his flat to his car. When he sees the bottom of his feet are blotched with nasty black oil that has washed up on shore, perhaps from a passing tanker cleaning out its hold, instead of losing his temper as he has a tendency to do when stressed back home, he actually laughs and makes me take silly photos.

The four of us have big lunches at a taverna by the sea at Ayios Andonis where they bake their own bread and catch their own fish and add pickled local capers to the salad, and another place where they grow their own vegetables and have friendly cats. At the restaurant in Megalo Horio, where I endear myself to the owner by speaking a few half-remembered words of Greek, they serve dishes of their home-reared goat and pork baked with tomatoes, and mash up their own potatoes and herbs into irresistibly melt-in-the-mouth *keftedes*. I laugh as John eats record-breaking amounts of ice cream.

One evening, walking back from the restaurant toward the villa, we hear live music coming from behind trees at the end of a long garden. "D'you think that's a bar?" asks Chris, walking toward it.

"It might just be someone's house," we whisper.

He keeps going, and we follow a few steps behind. Sure enough, we've walked onto someone's terrace, where a man and a boy are playing traditional dance on a Greek lute and a *lyra*, the three-stringed fiddle. They invite us in to sit down and listen, and the man's wife brings us a plate of melon and apple. I am delighted to have found this island.

⌒

For the last few days, John and Chris decide to go to Livadia to rent scooters so we can explore some more. Kate and I set out to walk to Plaka beach together, a secluded spot beyond Ayios Andonis on the way to the monastery, and they'll catch up to us on the bikes and drive us the rest of the way.

It's a good opportunity to get to know Kate again after so many months. We chat about our careers and how time races ahead from one busy year to another. Gradually she brings the conversation around to the idea of children. Since she turned thirty, the challenge of her work has decreased and she's ready for another stage of life, ready to be a mother. Funny, I'd never thought of her that way—as someone who sells guitars and manages a band and lives in a tiny walk-up apartment furnished with vintage cool, she strikes you as the ultimate rock chick. Although she's a few years younger than me, she feels it's getting to that time when she needs to decide fairly soon about having kids.

"It creeps up on you, this age thing," I say with a sardonic smile. "I still feel barely old enough to look after myself."

I've only recently committed myself to a mortgage after moving back to England and have just about stopped getting hangovers; I've given up a few things that are bad for me over the years, though I'm still prone to a bit of adventure. And yet already my odds of conceiving are diminishing by the year.

"I know John likes the idea of having a family one day," I continue, "though we haven't really discussed yet whether… you know, whether we want to together." It's been less than a year. I don't want to scare him away, but we've talked around

17

it and both know it's a possibility, and something I can't hang about too long to decide. I'm not sure how much I should share with his sister.

Back in my early twenties, I got married in Canada to a man I'd met in the Mediterranean, but back then, having a family was the last thing on my mind—I certainly wasn't ready. After all those years of study, I wanted travel, adventure, and to learn an interesting way to make a living. It turned out, in any case, that deep down we were badly suited and the marriage wasn't destined to last; we didn't see our second wedding anniversary. Throughout my twenties, having kids was far from a priority: even after I recovered from the shock of the bad marriage, I had my own life to build, and finding the right partner wasn't easy. I figured I'd know when the time was right, and only wanted it if I was absolutely certain and in the right relationship.

I was then with a wonderful man for six years, and after traveling and living in different countries together, we started thinking of children, but recurrent problems made me realize it wasn't a stable enough relationship. We spent a year trying to work things out before I sadly ended things between us, aware that I couldn't keep hoping forever that things would fix themselves. I took the risk that I would find something more lasting, a better place to start a family. It hasn't been easy, but with John, things feel strong and positive and like the right time.

To someone who was always fairly practical and unemotional about the topic, it's come as a big surprise that for vast swathes of my mid-thirties all I can think about is children. My body is finally telling me something—loud, if not clear. Babies have become vastly cuter, although I still feel occasional blasts of uncertainty. The pub landlord at the Park Tavern, Richard, got so used to me talking about the issue that he cheekily referred to John, when I started seeing him, as "The Donor." I haven't solved the conundrum of knowing if I'm in the right relationship, heaven knows, but I'm feeling good about this one.

"If it happened by mistake, though, if you got pregnant by mistake now, would you go ahead with it?" asks Kate.

"At this stage—yes!"

I think: *It's pretty unlikely. I've been on the pill my whole adult life.*

"It would seem like it was meant to be and I might not get another chance." Meant to be? It would be a miracle.

"I'm pretty sure I would," says Kate thoughtfully.

When John and Chris catch up with us on the scooters, we all drive together to Plaka, where peacocks roam in a garden behind the deserted beach. We fall asleep on the sand in the shade and awaken to the electric-blue face of a peacock that has hopped over the fence and is staring right at us.

At the end of the summer, I am throwing a party for all our friends and both families to celebrate a little victory in my work, and John kindly foots half the bill and runs around all evening like a mad thing filling up people's champagne glasses. We have lots to celebrate.

Because Kate has announced she's pregnant. She must have had an inkling of it when we were in Tilos. I'm thrilled for her, knowing how ready she is for this. Sadly, Chris says he isn't ready to be a father. But Kate is happy and will go it alone with the help of family and friends; she's sure she wants this baby and perhaps he might come around to the idea later.

John flies to Vancouver for a week to see her toward the end of the year and to look at a business opportunity. The restaurant he runs is going through a change of ownership, and he's been talking seriously about setting up his own bar and restaurant back home. We're thinking of moving to Vancouver together; I could work there, my growing love for the outdoors would be amply catered for on the nearby islands, and the whole new arrangement might be perfect for starting a family if we decide we're ready. It's been an exciting time, looking at places for sale, and business plans, and plots of land in the islands.

I'm in a bookshop in London one day when he calls from Vancouver to let me know how things are looking with this particular business opportunity; it's not as rosy as he thought and he's frustrated with some red tape. He seems to miss having me around to talk to, and I'm touched.

The night after he gets back, a few days before my birthday, we sit on his couch in our usual way with a drink, some of our favorite music playing, while he demolishes a pack of cigarettes, and he tells me he's started to feel troubled. I know he's had a difficult time recently with his grandfather dying—they were very close. With the problems he encountered in Vancouver, it turns out he's suddenly feeling unsure about everything, though. The move back to Canada. Buying a business. *Us.*

I have an awful falling feeling, wanting to rewind the tape and for him never to have said that. This isn't how it's supposed to turn out.

Nothing's gone wrong. Nothing's changed. He just isn't sure anymore, and he knows how important it is for me to know that. He knows how much honesty and trust mean to me. And maybe he's also thinking about an old friend of mine who recently found the courage to leave his unhappy marriage of many years, and his wife accused him of taking away her childbearing years; we don't want to get to that.

The rest is a bit of a blackout. Do we talk about anything, or do I just cry? Am I trying to be cool—he's only said he's "unsure," after all? I see his upset and nervous face as he says those words to me, and then later, "It'll be OK," as I cry next to him that night. What does that mean? The next day, he leaves for work and locks me out of his life. I sit at home in tears. I try to remember the Buddhist philosophy about letting go, and I eat chocolate and send him a funny message about it, which makes him laugh. Later I ring the buzzer of his flat over and over again, with no answer.

Just let me back in to your life, I think. We've made it so far together; we can get through this. It all still feels like a horrible dream. But he is wrestling with his own demons, and suddenly, I am on my own in a very cold, harsh place.

It's a bad night. I learn to smoke cigarettes again, drown my sorrows in red wine until the pubs close, and walk around in the dark on my own until dawn. I call in to work, speak to my boss about what's happened, and arrange to take a day or two off.

~

I spend a lot of time after that just walking through winter countryside during the day and going out every night, drinking and smoking and clinging to friends. He's having a crisis of doubt about everything in his life. Maybe he'll realize that this is what he wants after all. It doesn't look hopeful, but I'm not willing to give up on our relationship just yet. On all those plans we had for the future.

Finally he makes contact, and we agree to meet in a neutral pub to talk. I childishly dress for the occasion in my best seamed stockings and high heels and a short enough skirt that he might notice the tops of the stockings. He arrives and gives me a dull birthday present of a brown wool scarf, which I pretend to like until he confirms it's definitely over between us. He hates the way things have turned out too. We're both in tears with not much left to say.

I can't just go on as normal, and keep taking days off work. I need to do myself a favor and give life a shake.

I start the next day by sending a text to my boss, quitting my job.

Then I call in the cavalry, sending texts to any friends in my phone book who might help me get through the day. Shivering and numb and weeping from time to time, I pass the afternoon in the Park Tavern, drinking whiskey macs; the alcohol and the adrenaline of free fall allow me to get through the day. My friend Mike tries persuading me that giving up my job might be somewhat rash and that things always look bleak in winter.

But I'm insistent. I have to do something drastic and meaningful.

Chapter Three

The Gifts to Self

I get on a train and spend my birthday not being taken away by my beloved to his favorite Spanish city for the weekend, as he'd hinted in what now seems like the distant past, but weeping and shaky with my parents. I feel pathetic, crying on the train. But at least I recognize that my parents are pretty amazing people and I am lucky to enjoy spending time with them.

First stop is my dad's in London, and he takes me for dinner at his local pub. Dad, who knows how hard breakups can be, tells me wisely that sometimes people just fall out of love, just change their minds, and there isn't anything you can do about it. It's horrible but probably true. When a few friends show up at the pub, including his ex-girlfriend, we all laugh and cry about the various traumas we've experienced over huge glasses of red wine. Then, as the searing pain and bewilderment and emptiness kick in again the next day, I take the train to Mum's and do the whole thing all over again: one of the benefits of having divorced parents.

"Don't let him do this to you. You've got so much going for you, so much to give," says my mum, distraught at seeing me still sobbing away.

"I know, Mum… So—*why*? What am I doing wrong?" It isn't just about *him*. It's about what's wrong with *me*—why is it so difficult for me to find someone to share my life with?

When Mum has to go away for a few days, my stepdad looks after me. I take the dog for long walks during the day until dinner time, when we have a chat and laugh and I try not to cry.

At last I feel strong enough to go back home again, and I return to work on a tentative basis. There's only so long my friends and family and colleagues can put up with a miserable me who weeps herself to sleep on their couch. And this isn't what I want either, obviously. I want to go back to being the person who enjoys life. Only I can make myself happier.

And that's how the Gifts to Self begin.

I am suffering from more than just heartbreak. I've been putting up with my work and home situations because I thought they were temporary. I need to replace the plans I had with *him* and come up with new ones. Now that there's truly only me to consider, what do I want to do and where do I want to be? Why wait for someone else to change my life, for goodness sake?

My boss, knowing what I'm going through, has told me to take some time to think before he'll accept my resignation. I still enjoy the work, but as with many interesting jobs, the problem is its intensity, the tendency of the years to roll around fast in a never-ending cycle. I don't want to give it all up, but by cutting back my hours, perhaps I can carve out some time for other projects without surrendering my weekends or letting my work suffer, and ideally then I will appreciate the days at the office more. I consider going down to three days a week, but I don't like worrying about money. Losing just one-fifth of my pay will be easier to take. The first Gift to Self will be not quitting a job I still like, but giving myself Freelance Fridays.

The second Gift to Self is the vow of celibacy.

Let me define my terms here: This isn't really about becoming nunlike. The idea is merely to stay away from a relationship. For six months, I am having a break from emotional involvement, from looking for the right man. Otherwise, I'll meet someone nice as I always seem to (a blessing or a curse?), and it will start all over again—too soon. I need to become myself again before I can meet anyone else.

In the very, very dark days of this winter, it's been hard

not to get confused and let a friend looking after me turn into something more. I often need someone to look after me. It isn't pretty, but it's the truth. I'm scared. I numb the pain with alcohol and cigarettes, and sometimes I can't go to sleep without a friend holding me.

But I'm setting off mines—I'm a danger to myself and others. And physically, emotionally, I just can't go through this again; I'm getting too old for this. Refusing to consider getting romantically involved with anyone for half a year, however good and honorable and warmhearted they seem, gives me a positive power, a force field of protection. And somehow, making this decision really does give me strength. After moping around all sad and victim-like, suddenly I feel like a warrior princess. As the weeks go by and I recover, I wake up in the morning feeling surprisingly happy: no one is going to break my heart today, or tomorrow, or next week, or next month. The vow of celibacy is something positive I can tell people about at last. "If I so much as mention that I've 'met a nice man,'" I explain to friends and family, "give me a stern talking-to."

It turns out, of course, that a vow of celibacy is a great way to meet men, even ones who seem pretty nice. It gives me hope to hear from more than one male friend, "Well, I'm only interested in a serious relationship, so if you change your mind, let me know." But I deflect them with the warrior sword.

After the initial novelty wears off and I feel stronger, it's harder to adhere to the plan—I still believe that good things happen out of the blue, and my biological clock is still ticking aggressively away. I'm not going to beat myself up if I falter. But the aim is to protect myself and focus the mind on other things.

I really need to think some things through—to reflect on where I want to go next. I need to get out of this town that's associated with so many memories for a while. More than that, I want to do something that's purely for me.

So the third and most important Gift to Self is a month in Greece.

Greece was the answer before, and now maybe Greece is the answer again. During this cold, dark winter, I feel a need for warm sunshine, and plenty of it. I am drawn to the idea of giving up my job entirely and moving to Greece, maybe working in a hotel for the summer as I did once before. But I also wonder if I might go for a long break without giving up my job.

And where? I've found what might be the perfect Greek island for me at this stage in my life. I discovered it with the man I once saw my future with. Trouble is, he's changed his mind. Can I go back there?

Oddly, I don't need to think too long about returning to Tilos. That island is a special place, I think, and I'm not finished with it yet; maybe I even need to reclaim it for myself. Over a couple of months, I've come to terms with what happened with John and have tried to move on. Clearly I can't rent the same place again (it's a big, luxurious villa, too expensive to rent for a month, and going back to the same place I stayed with John would be silly)—but the owners were friendly, and I reckon there's nothing to lose by writing to them. So one evening in February after work, I send an email saying I'm thinking of coming back to the island, and if they hear of a cheap room available could they perhaps let me know? I go off to the gym, and when I come back two hours later to drop stuff at my office, there's a response.

Hi Jen! I just happened to be online and got your email. I don't know if it's what you're looking for but the flat above our bar in Livadia is free until July. I'm attaching some photos and let me know—we can give you a good price if you're staying for a month and can do your own cleaning...

My heart's already beating fast as I read on... I open the attached photos and see a large terrace covered with vines, a mountain in the background, and a table where I can already picture myself working. Other pictures show a bathroom with washing machine, bedroom, and kitchen. I look at the email again. Did it really say wireless Internet? Yes. Above their bar in Livadia, just minutes from the sea.

The following day, I explain my idea to spend a month in Greece to my boss.

"I can take two weeks' holiday and work from there for the other two weeks. Easy! I'll take a laptop, and there's wireless Internet and Skype. It'll be fine!"

He isn't as thrilled with the idea as I am, clearly. But then he's sympathetic to what I've been through in the last little while. He knows I was willing to quit; I know I have to fight for what I need and not compromise again. It isn't a huge amount to ask, I hope; I've been working hard for the company for five years.

"Let me think about it," he says.

"OK," I respond with an irritated impatience that is completely unjustified, "but I have to decide really soon as the flat may not be available for long, and I'll need to book a flight before the prices go up…"

He sighs. Point taken. But I am excited about my plan. I believe in it and don't want to see it slip out of my hands. Eventually, he says yes.

Greece for the month of May: the moment I book it, I dance around the room. It's my talisman. Whenever things look bleak, I think about my month in Greece and smile.

And in fact the vow of celibacy seems a particularly good plan when going to a Greek island for a month. The problem with Greece is that it's so damn romantic. Let's just say it's not an obvious choice for a cure for love. Every holiday in Greece, ever since my teens, yielded new opportunities for kissing dreamily against the backdrop of ancient ruins.

When I was fifteen in Rhodes, the young man who worked in the souvlaki takeaway in Lindos took me to the ancient amphitheater one evening, and I was semi-smitten. At sixteen I fell for a biker in Crete with wavy black hair down to his shoulders, and we sat on the beach at night watching the moon rising over the sea, much to the consternation of my parents. Pretty much the same happened the next year in Cephalonia. Then, of course, there were all the scrapes I got myself into that year after university... I have a distinct memory of showering a dark-haired, olive-skinned stranger's white sheets with a handful of bougainvillea blossoms.

Is Greece really the answer? Can a Greek island be a good cure for love? There's only one way to find out.

"Do you know people in Tilos?" a friend asks when I say I'll be spending a month alone on this island no one has heard of with a population of a few hundred.

Well, there's the couple I'm renting from, and the lady who runs the restaurant in Megalo Horio. There's Vangelis, who I met in the bar in the port, when he was serving drinks there. And the bus driver. Oh, and the neighbors who invited us to sit in their garden when they were playing music...

I don't think I'll be too lonely. But I'll stay away from relationships—in any case, I'm not a sylph-like twenty-one-year-old anymore—and give all my attention to the island. In Greece.

Bye-Bye Love, Kalimera Happiness

*I*n early May, I am waiting outside Rhodes airport at dusk. The next bus into town, according to the timetable, is not for over an hour, surprisingly. A taxi is only twenty euros, but the bus is only two euros and I have nothing in particular to get to Rhodes town for earlier, since my boat to Tilos is not until tomorrow morning. It's warm and I have a book, and I have all the time in the world (well, a month). It's a good feeling. There's a young chap in army uniform also waiting, smoking a cigarette, and he stops a bus driver to check that it really is an hour until the next bus. From the bags at his feet, I guess he's doing his military service and either going home on leave or going back to base. I try out my rusty Greek and check with him about the bus. I tell him I'm going to Tilos for a month, and he seems amused.

I'm beginning to wish it had taken a bit longer to get

through the airport, to kill some time. It was such a short walk into the terminal to show my passport and pick up my rucksack. You have to wonder why airports pride themselves on being the busiest, the biggest. Small airports are so much better. I sit and wait. It's all part of the adventure.

The bus arrives at last, and I grin all the way into town as I pass the gyros joints, the outdoor bars, all the bakeries and little shops. When the bus stops in the center of Rhodes town, familiar to me from many times of passing through this island, often on the way to another, I hoist my rucksack onto my back and walk through the medieval city gate.

Rhodes Old Town was founded a few centuries before the birth of Christ and served as party central for half a dozen colorful civilizations. Restorations of old buildings tend to unearth ancient Doric columns, Roman roads, Byzantine walls built over by medieval Crusaders and improved in the sixteenth century by the Ottoman invaders; the walls were rebuilt by the Italians under Mussolini in the 1930s. The whole of the old town is fascinating and beautiful but far from undiscovered. Tour groups of various nationalities march up and down the cobbled streets on their modern-day crusades.

Last year, passing through on that June afternoon, the old town had seemed a mess of endless shops selling garish paintings and beach towels and other paraphernalia emblazoned with freakish Colossi to cruise-ship tourists wearing fanny packs.

I'd forgotten how beautiful it can be.

At night in early May, it's quiet, deserted mostly, the old walls floodlit, stone columns and fountains lying modest and unassuming in the shadows. I wander for a while, looking for a room to rent, surprised to see so few. I stop in a corner shop to ask and end up outside Eudoxia, a pretty pension up a steep staircase covered in flowers. At the top of the stairs, there's no one about and the door's closed. I go back down to the street and dither for a while, until a young woman comes along.

"*Theleis voeethia?*" Do you need help?

Oh, indeed I do—how much time has she got? But let's start with looking for a room.

She leads me upstairs and knocks on the door for me. The man inside seems delighted to see the attractive young Greek woman and engages in some friendly banter, completely ignoring me, even though I'm standing here with a backpack still sporting its easyJet handling tag, which might as well read, "Your first customer of the season has arrived, sir." Eventually the woman leaves and I thank her and smile expectantly at the man. He goes back to what he was doing before, shuffling some papers on a desk, until gradually he seems to have forgotten me again.

"*Echete dhomatio?*" I ask hesitantly. Do you have a room?

He seems extremely uncertain about this. Am I using the wrong word and asking for a fish or a hamster by mistake? But no, the woman understood me. Eventually he is forced reluctantly to pick up the phone, argues for a while, then shows me upstairs, opens a door, and shrugs. It's a nice room with a bathroom and a balcony. How much? He looks defeated: he clearly has no idea. Well, I can guess roughly. And besides, my balcony has a view of minarets and old fortress walls. I'll be staying.

I settle in, freshen up, and am just heading back out for the evening when the rest of his family returns. It seems they've been out for dinner somewhere, leaving the grumpy one behind. They are certainly in better spirits, and suddenly I am being introduced to everyone, shaking hands with the mother and the father and the uncle and the brother, and I remember the word *harika*, pleased to meet you. They ask about my holiday and I explain I am en route to Tilos for a month.

"Ah, Tilos, wonderful…"

The father apologetically asks for thirty euros for the room, and they say I must come back and see them when I return.

Welcome back to Greece.

I walk outside to a narrow street cobbled decoratively with gray and white pebbles, passing a large stone doorway housing an elegant plant pot, and the old synagogue; past a man paid to invite tourists up to a rooftop restaurant, who smiles when I wish him good evening, *kalispera*; and down to the square with the fountain. Last June, when John had tried to get money from the bank machine here on the first day and it swallowed his card, it put him in a foul mood. This time, I don't have to worry about anyone's mood.

I find a bar with funky modern chandeliers and not a tourist in sight, venture into the glossy dark interior, and order a beer. A middle-aged Greek man in glasses, expensively but casually dressed, tells the bartender it's on him. I thank him and we exchange pleasantries, and I end up sitting at the bar with the charming Nikos and his pal Stergos, who has just won a court case and is celebrating. I tell them about my month in Tilos, and Stergos says when he was a child his father used to take him along on hunting trips there for *perdika*, which I think must be partridge, before hunting was banned on Tilos. Another time they went there in one hour on someone's speed boat for ouzos and came straight back again. Nikos orders *sfinakia*, shots, and smoked salmon canapés, and we end up laughing a lot. The beautiful girls and boys behind the bar play great music as the crowd livens up even though it's eleven thirty on a Wednesday evening, and I feel a million miles from England.

"*Ti oreia parea*," says Nikos to Stergos, and I smile, understanding: "What good company!" There's joking and teasing and harmless fun, and it reminds me of so many nights in Greece. Suddenly I am transported back to being twenty-one again. When they leave to go to a bouzouki club, I finish my beer, listening to Greek love songs and looking out toward the square. I really didn't expect it to be hard to leave Rhodes town, didn't expect it to be so charming. The tables continue to fill up with well-dressed Greeks. When I leave and amble across the square, I follow a side street where chill-out music spills from a dozen bars with old stone-vaulted ceilings, most of them empty still. But I am off home for an early night. I am going to the small island of tranquillity, *isichia*.

~

Back when I was twenty-one, I had gradually begun to feel very much at home in Greece. In Athens I met Vassilis, a sweet young biker with wavy brown hair and long eyelashes, a bandanna round his neck and his leg in a cast from a motorbike accident. We met in a bar in my neighborhood of Galatsi, one night when the city lights were shimmering below like a cave full of jewels. He pouted when I said I wouldn't be his girl.

"I like you," said Vassilis.

"Really?" I laughed.

"Very-very." He gave me his bandanna and a little skull for a necklace, and I was enjoying the attention of those big brown eyes. I started to wonder how I would ever tear myself away from the beautiful people of Greece.

The next month, his leg was out of the cast, and he asked if I wanted to come to a nightclub on the other side of Athens. It was dark and sweaty and they played heavy metal loud, and

I loved it. We got so hot dancing until the early hours that we poured beer on ourselves to cool down, then we roared back down the highway on the back of his bike, me trying not to think of legs in casts. Back at my flat we fried up eggs and salty cheese for breakfast, and he stayed over. And that was that. I was his girl. We couldn't communicate very much, but Vassilis was relaxed and gorgeous and loving incarnate. In the mornings he'd dab water in his long wavy hair and blow me a kiss in the bathroom mirror. In a couple of months, I got fluent in Greek.

Instead of hiking and exploring, I got used to sitting around having coffee with friends. We would drive down the coast with company, *parea*, to eat lunch all together by the edge of the sea from a table heaped with calamari and salad and fried potatoes. I watched the way Greeks cut up all the shared food into fork-size pieces so they could eat with one hand and talk with the other.

I was in love with the beauty of Greece. I was in love with a sweet Greek biker, and I also loved the new me. Then Vassilis made an announcement one Saturday morning.

"Look, if we might have to split up at the end of the summer, better to split up now before you go traveling."

I collapsed with grief. Crying, shaky, I made my way across Athens to my friend Eva's place, suddenly afraid to be alone. She and her boyfriend were just about to leave for Santorini for a few days that afternoon, and invited me along.

I dashed back across town and threw the necessaries into a bag.

The Bible's Egyptian plagues and the parting of the Red Sea are all said to be connected with what happened in the eruption of Santorini's volcano in 1600 BC. People had been living comfortably and contentedly, it seems, from what remains, in houses with staircases to bright upstairs rooms painted with colorful scenes, and storerooms below stocked with decorated jars of flour and olives, wine and dried fish. Then the volcano erupted, and most of the island collapsed and sank four hundred meters below the sea. It all felt vaguely familiar. This was a good place to get your troubles in perspective.

Eva and Martin found us rooms in Oia, a whitewashed village that clung to spectacular clifftops streaked with black and red cinders, overlooking the deep blue sea and in the distance the burnt black rock of the volcanic islands. It was a violently beautiful landscape. When I said to a local fisherman in a café that these looked like good cliffs to jump off if you felt suicidal, he shrugged and replied you were unlikely to kill yourself; people had tried it and had to be rescued. My friends took me to their favorite café, a balcony hanging off the cliff suspended over the blue. I started to recover. You just couldn't help it when surrounded by such breathtaking loveliness. I decided if I could find work, I'd spend my summer here.

It was the start of the tourist season when I came back and went from hotel to hotel asking for work.

"*Kalimera*! Anyone there?"

At Caldera Villas, a large, red-faced man eventually emerged wearing a dainty pair of yellow rubber gloves; I wasn't sure if he was red from the cleaning work or from embarrassment, possibly a bit of both.

He wasn't looking to hire a foreigner, he said gruffly. "Do you speak Greek?"

My Greek was now good enough to convince him and I kept talking until he said yes. So Yorgos passed the yellow rubber gloves over to me, and from then on it was my job in the mornings to clean the rooms and to help him with other tasks around the place. He couldn't afford to pay me much, but he let me sleep in a camp bed in the cave behind the bar; like all traditional Oia houses, it was built into the cliff. In the mornings I slipped into my black swimsuit and trainers, walked out onto the terrace with the best view in the world, and started work. I found there was something satisfying about making these pretty rooms neat and tidy again. By lunchtime I'd be hanging up freshly laundered sheets on a line in the sun, and I learned how to fold them so they dried smoothly with no need for ironing. Then we'd close up and go down to the sea. Yorgos would drop me off on the little island in his fishing boat, and I'd dive straight into the deep, cool water, so clear you could see the fish without a mask.

We'd meet up again in the afternoon for our ritual ice cream, *to pagoto mas*, before going back to the evening's work—taking bookings, letting guests use the phone, making drinks and snacks for them. Yorgos often made me supper and bought mounds of fruit for us to eat.

"Eat!" he'd insist, piling my plate with food.

"I eat more than you do!" I protested truthfully.

"But I am fat and you are thin."

I wasn't sure I wanted to even out the difference.

Many a day, when the morning's work was done, I'd sit in the shade of the terrace and listen to donkeys scrambling up and down the steps, and look at that perfect view—the flat blue sea far below like a rippled lake, the boats with their faint chug and hum as they'd glide across the water. The terrace was whitewashed with blue tables, the same color as the sea, and lizards darted across my line of vision. Hard to believe one could ever tire of such a place. Sometimes I'd sit in little Selene Bar and made friends with the owner, Kyriakos, and occasionally we'd spend afternoons together. "Happiness is easy sometimes," he said. So I was learning.

One evening on the terrace, the singing of a priest drifted down from the church in the square. The wind was picking up dust off the quarries beyond Fira and a window banged. The water looked pale and cold, the dark islands lonely. I felt serene, content. I thought back to the sorrow that had led me here by chance. Thanks to some guiding force, the beauty of this place had brought me back to life again.

How long could a girl do this? I thought about staying

but there would be no work in the winter, and cleaning rooms wasn't an option forever. I needed to think about a proper career.

But years later, I would still think back to that great summer I'd had when I cleaned rooms in Santorini.

In the morning, I get up around six. I don't want to miss the only ferry of the day to Tilos.

The streets of Rhodes Old Town are magical at that hour, when you can still see the honey-colored stone before it is covered up by the souvenir shops hanging out their trinkets for sale. I stop at a corner store where the fruit outside looks temptingly ripe, and choose oranges and tomatoes for breakfast. The day is just starting: People are sweeping the streets, listening to romantic Greek songs on the radio, talking, having coffee, zipping about on scooters. Three girls totter on high heels down the cobbled street, arm in arm. I continue out through the magnificent city gate, past sponge- and shell-sellers to a marina where tiny wooden fishing boats painted prettily in blue and white sit in still water. The sun is already warm, the sky pale blue with a few clouds. The shiny orange Dodekanisos Express, which buzzes up and down this group of islands, is waiting to set out for the day. Tilos is the first stop, and for twenty-four euros I'll be there before lunchtime.

Last night in the bar, Nikos insisted on getting the time of the boat's departure by calling the port authority and putting their number into my mobile phone, but as I knew, all I needed to do was wander down here and find the boat, and as always the clock sign at the back would show what time it was leaving: eight thirty. I sit down to wait, and when the ferryman comes over to tell me I'm a bit early, I shrug happily to say that's fine, and feel compelled to tell him for no apparent reason that I am going to Tilos for a month, *ena meena*. I am enjoying the sound of those words.

Gradually other passengers arrive—a vegetable truck and then cars with parents dropping off kids with their teachers for a school trip. There's excitement in the air. I get on board and eat my tomatoes and oranges while sitting outside on the deck in the sun, savoring the way they taste in Greece, especially when I'm traveling somewhere. Eventually, the engines start up and we pull slowly away from Rhodes harbor, then faster as we hit open sea. The wind is too strong to sit outside so I go in to find a comfortable seat by a salt-obscured window and sleep a bit more.

As we approach the island I go back up on deck. It appears to be just a rough, uninhabited gray rock from that angle, steep cliffs plunging straight into the sea. Then we round a headland and the wide, familiar bay comes into view, with a scattering of dark green trees emerging halfway down the hillsides and thickening toward the shore; a few low, white houses along the water's edge; the dome of a church; and a cluster of buildings toward the north of the bay. The beautiful, happy children from Rhodes—all wearing red baseball caps, most of them taking pictures with digital cameras—jump up and down shouting, "Tilos! Tilos!"

In the huge semicircular blue bay, there is the view I photographed last year when I was leaving, which earlier this year I put on my computer as a desktop photo to remind myself every day I'd be back: the rugged brown hillsides, the immaculate, brilliantly whitewashed houses, lush green trees and pink flowers. As we close in on the quayside, I spy a terrace with a vine beyond the Mini Market and wonder if it will be mine. There's the deep clanking as the anchor's chain unravels and the anchor goes down, and adults tell children to wait (*Pereemeneh*!) as we all cram forward to exit.

Coaches await the schoolkids. And here I am, walking up the jetty, breathing in the clear, gentle air of Tilos. It is just as I remembered it: through the square and past the bakery and five minutes after I've disembarked, my landlords Rob and Annie are ready to show me around my new home.

The flat is just as wonderful as it appeared in the photos. The terrace is enormous, with a vine hanging from a trellis, and a line for drying washing, and a bench and table. The kitchen has a desk set up for working at one end; in the bedroom is a futon bed and rather too much storage space for my backpack of clothes. It takes me about ten minutes to unpack.

By lunchtime I am lying on an empty stretch of white pebble beach, looking out at the expanse of blue bay, listening to the waves calmly stroking the shore. The water is cold, but I plunge in for a quick swim and it feels amazing. I can't take my eyes off the view for long; life does not get much better than this. This is my gift to myself. And to think things looked so bleak back in January.

Eventually, I get up and walk. The main road has been diverted to the back of the village and a simple pedestrian walkway follows the curve of the bay, passing the church, restaurants, rooms for rent—and I love that there are still a few fields that come right down to the waterfront too. And at any point you can step off the path onto the beach and sit in the shade of a tamarisk tree. I follow it all the way around the bay, passing the last straggle of houses at the end of the village, and follow the road up the hill. It keeps winding up, amid the sound of goats and bees, toward a little chapel that looks out over empty mountains and deep blue sea. When I turn back and go for another swim in the late afternoon, sheep have been brought down into the fields behind the beach. Local children are playing a game, throwing stones into the sea.

Will Tilos bring me back to life and make me stronger? Can I find some sort of peace and happiness and figure out my way forward? I don't know—I'm just filled with excitement about having a whole month here.

CHAPTER FIVE

Sun, Sea, and Spanakopita

his might be the cleverest thing I have ever done, I think. I wake early to the noise of twittering songbirds, crows, and the odd cockerel. From my bed I can look up at the mountain. Brushing my teeth, I can watch the sun glinting on the sea. In my new home, I can glimpse sea or mountains from every room.

Heromeh. I am happy.

I decide not to worry my office by mentioning that the Internet connection in the flat is not yet up and running. Rob and Annie disconnected it over the winter while they were away, intending to restart it a few weeks ago, plenty of time before I arrived. But the technician has not yet come. This is not really a surprise to me. In any case, it's the perfect excuse to go and sit in the square and use the café's wireless Internet.

The square is the main hub of life, it seems. The bus that

loops around the island a few times a day departs from outside the *kafeneion*, whose chairs share the square with those of one other café. There are a couple of shops, a post office, and a tiny park for children. The art deco police station built during Italian rule in the early twentieth century, whitewashed and trimmed in Greek blue, stands just below, next to the marina used by visiting yachts and local fishing boats, and the jetty where the ferries unload goods and passengers once or twice a day. But now it's hot and still and quiet.

"*Ena frappeh sketo, parakalo*," I say. A plain frappé coffee, please.

Like the French, the Greeks can make a coffee last for hours. Older people tend to take a Greek coffee, espresso size or a little larger, with powdery grounds that sink to the bottom of the cup. The younger and trendier prefer, oddly enough, Nescafé ("Nes"), either hot or iced and frothy. The frappé is made in a blender so the creamy froth and ice take up much of the tall tumbler until it starts to settle, leaving brown bubbles stuck to the glass as you sip it through the straw. Café owners must spend their lives removing froth from glass. You can have it with milk, *me gala*, or sweet, *gliko*. If you like just a little sweetness, you order it *metrio*. I usually go for *sketo*, plain, especially when life feels sweet enough already.

I sit in the shade of the trees, working at my laptop. For the first two weeks of this month, I'll be working for my office as normal, except in Tilos, thanks to technology. Although it's Friday, my new freelance day for working for myself, I missed some work through traveling this week, and in a bid to show how perfectly I do my job from here, I log on to my office computer, say hello to my colleagues, and try to catch up.

Despite being the biggest settlement on the island, Livadia is a sleepy place, I think happily as I tap away at emails. But Tilos wasn't always so quiet and empty. Take, for example, the now-abandoned village of Mikro Horio, a mile or two away up in the hills. That "Little Village" once had a population of two and a half thousand.

In the days of the Crusades, up in the hills was the safest place to be protected against pirate raids. The Knights of St. John conquered the island in 1309 and built fortifications to defend the island, restoring Byzantine castles and building new ones. The hilltops of Tilos fairly bristled with castles in medieval days, and hillside terraces were farmed right up to the mountaintops.

After the Knights left, in 1522 the Ottoman Empire took over these islands and held on to them for four hundred years, giving them some freedom as long as they paid their taxes. Christian pirates raided under the pretext of attacking the Turks, so everyone stayed safely up in the hills.

Then in 1912 the Italians took over, fairly benevolent at first. The people of Tilos came into town, saw the flags had changed, and went back to their farms. Pirates were less of a threat, so some people settled in this area by the sea known as Livadia, or "Meadows."

The Italian occupiers gradually became fascist and repressive, and then World War II broke out and the German soldiers came. The German army imposed curfews, making it impossible for the islanders to look after their crops and animals, then ate through their livestock.

In 1948, Tilos and its neighbors became part of Greece again, but some local people had lost too much by then and started to leave to make a living in America or Australia. The remaining villagers of Mikro Horio moved down to the sea, bringing the roofs of their houses with them. But the Greek military junta created further food shortages and curfews, and people continued to emigrate.

Democracy was restored in the mid-seventies, and in the eighties, the first few foreign tourists started coming to the island. Livadia began to grow in a haphazard fashion. Many of those first people who came here twenty or twenty-five years ago are still coming back for a few weeks a year. There are medium-size hotels and rooms to rent along the seashore. Some newer buildings up the hillsides now stand out, ignoring regulations and the classic style of the islands, not exactly picture-perfect but not disastrous.

Being based here is perfect for my needs, as not only is there a backup supply of Internet in various cafés, all of them quiet enough for me to work in undisturbed, but I can also effortlessly spend my lunch break at the beach.

I close my virtual office, dropping the computer off at home to charge, and eat yogurt and honey and an orange on the sunny terrace, then walk down to the sea.

"*Yeia sou*, Jennifer," says Yorgos as I pass.

"*Yeia sou!*"

Yorgos works in a restaurant on the seafront; slim, almost studious-looking with his glasses, he always says a friendly hello and exchanges a few words in Greek, good practice for me. He seems to greet everyone and probably knows everything that happens on the island.

Then a little farther along, "*Yeia sou*," says the man who runs boat excursions for tourists to beaches around the island. In stark contrast to Rhodes, where excursion boats line the harbor and touts harangue you trying to sell you trips, it's all nice and low-key. He merely sits occasionally at his stand on the seafront with a few posters stuck on a tree and a notebook for leaving messages when he's not there. I'm not really here as a tourist, but we have a brief chat when I walk past.

The white pebbles give the sea a pale topaz color, becoming darker as it gets deeper. The waves lap the shore gently. Swimming every day is part of the happiness therapy for this month. The water is still quite cold in May, but plunging into blue sea whenever I want is pure luxury, and I can dry off in the sun. I could happily look at this bay for the rest of my life, this perfect semicircle of deep blue, with rugged hills curved all around.

At the end of the day, I walk down to the sea again and follow the path around the bay. Exercise and fresh air and far horizons make up for sitting at a computer all day, and I can pick some herbs to add to my dinner. I notice a lovely bar where a wooden boat on a small jetty has been turned into a nice place to sit looking out to sea. It's Friday evening, so I perch at a high table with the waves just below, order a beer, and open my book, though I'm distracted by the sun going down over the mountain to the left, casting a shadow that gradually creeps up over the honey-golden mountain to the right.

I'm idly reading and looking at the sunset when I notice a man in a black wetsuit and flippers emerging from the sea. Standing on the pebbles, he pulls a snorkel and mask off short black wet hair, removes his flippers, then uses one of them to help prise the wetsuit off over his shoulders. Half hiding behind the converted wooden fishing boat, he seems self-conscious to be undressing in front of me, and I can't help smiling mischievously. Maybe life in Tilos isn't that quiet after all.

"*Krio?*" I ask. Is it cold?

"Yes, a little," he says in Greek, but when he continues I look a bit baffled, so he switches to English. "Now is the season when it starts to get warmer."

"Ah! Did you see many fish?"

"Not many," he says, "and only small. There was an invasion of tropical fish last year."

Sounds dramatic, I think, and raise my eyebrows.

He continues to pull off his wetsuit and looks sideways at me with dark, shy eyes under dark eyebrows and the faintest hint of a smile in a rather serious face.

"Are you here for holidays? Where are you from?"

I do my "one month" routine in Greek, not holidays but working.

"I am Manolis," he says. It turns out he's a teacher at the high school; he looks about my age. As he's putting his fishing gear together, he says, "I hope to meet you again."

"Me too!"

"It is not difficult in Tilos." He strides away up the beach purposefully, looking a little flustered, like a man who's worried that his wife will hear he's been talking to strange foreign women on the beach.

The sky is turning pink and the mountains gray now the sun has disappeared. Walking home, I stop at a little shop to buy a bottle of Rhodes wine and some ripe tomatoes and feta cheese.

Back on my terrace I listen to music coming from various places as I sit with a glass of white wine and think how lucky I am. It feels so good to be alone, to be able to do exactly what I want, that I get off the chair and lie on the terrace instead to read my book, then just drink wine and look up at the mountains through the overhanging vine.

Across the road, I notice my neighbor is also sitting on his balcony. He's in his thirties with wavy chestnut hair down to his shoulders, and earlier in the day he was clearing an overgrown garden. Now he's flicking a string of worry beads around his fingers with attitude, and looking slightly dangerous. At one time it might have been alluring. Not now, and I'm glad. I go inside and make salad for dinner using delicious, juicy tomatoes and the pungent oregano picked at the roadside. Around ten thirty, there's a power cut and I hear groans downstairs in the bar—but, rather embarrassingly, I am already in bed, falling asleep.

⌒

I have the sea, the mountains, the sunshine. What could complete the perfection? Why, a bakery, of course. And the island bakery is just next door. The aromas waft straight up from their ovens to my terrace.

Spinach pie, *spanakopita*, and feta cheese pie, *tyropita*, would be very healthy if it weren't for the greasy, flaky filo pastry that makes them so tasty. The bakery next door sells all different kinds, and shortcrust versions too, but the spinach pies sell out fast so it pays to get there early. That's my excuse, anyway. I point and say, "*Ena tetio*," one of those, to the fair-haired woman behind the counter. Then I take my warm *spanakopita* up to the hot terrace.

My terrace has some old plant pots, but there are no shops to buy plants here, so yesterday I tried planting a couple of wildflowers. They're still alive for now, and it's nice to have a splash of color. Across the road to the right, the neighbors' garden is an amazing riot of leaves and color. A motorbike pulls up and someone shouts in Greek, "Is anyone in?" Who needs a doorbell? Just sitting outside, I learn bits of the language, Greeks being vocal types. Then there are the guys in trucks who drive around selling vegetables and fish, calling out, "*Tomates!*" "*Patates!*" "*Melitzanes!*" and "*Freska psaria!*" at the tops of their voices. The vegetable man stops just outside, so I rush out and buy some eggplants and tomatoes.

I have my own private steps up to the flat so I don't need to go through the bar downstairs, but it's nice to stop in and say hello to Rob, who today is dressed in a football shirt. On the way out to the beach, I learn his theory about the power cut: the cables come from Kos through Nisyros to Tilos, and last night was probably the night when all the nightclubs in Kos switched on their power for the start of the season.

After swimming and reading on the beach, I decide to put in a few hours' work, even though it's Saturday, to make up for the lost time this week. I shower and put on a flowery cotton dress and boots, and head down to the square to sit in the shade of the tree and work over a coffee. Everyone's in their usual spot—the old lady sitting on the wall under the tree, the old men on the bench, the young waiter chatting with his friends. The village square, or *plateia*, is a wonderful thing. At some point or several points in the day, you cross the paths of various people without having to make arrangements to see them. Of course, the important thing is to stay friends with them all, especially in such a small place. It's not escaped my notice that this could be a bit of a minefield.

One of the older men passed me on his *motosikleta* earlier, and when he stopped to chat, added he'd like to offer me a drink sometime. How do you know for sure what offering a drink means? I want to make friends, but I know that sweet older men are not always as sweet as they appear, having been propositioned and worse by Greek men old enough to be my grandfather. And yet somehow I don't know how to politely say no, or "yes, but only as friends," without giving offense. I can't say I don't drink, I'm married, or my schedule is extremely hectic, because clearly none of those things is true. And so I end up clumsily saying, "Er, maybe sometime, thanks!" It's probably the wrong answer, but I hate the idea of being rude or making wrong assumptions. This seems especially tricky in Greece, where hospitality is abundant and has different rules.

Back when I first went to Kos on a cheap package holiday, my friend Gav and I stayed in a hotel in the main town, using it as a base to explore the island. The neighborhood was a mixture of international three-star hotels and bland tourist bars among a pleasant local community. One night, walking back from dinner, I noticed a little place hidden behind trees. There was no sign, but I'd seen people going in and out and thought it might be a locals' café. We decided to take a look.

We opened the door and entered a small room with a bar, where we ordered a couple of beers. A man told the bartender he was buying them, and wouldn't listen to our protests. He introduced himself as Yorgos (Yorgos is, in case you hadn't noticed, a particularly popular name in Greece—if in doubt, call someone Yorgos and you have a fair chance of getting it right) and we got chatting. More people arrived, and the Greek music got louder, and when he went away to talk to someone else, we asked the bartender if we could buy a drink for him in return. The barman looked troubled. Yorgos would be very offended. We could return the favor the next time, but tonight was on him—it was the Greek custom. The evening turned into a long and convivial one; shots were placed on the bar, then the waitress was dancing on the bar and the barman was smashing bottles of champagne on the floor in appreciation—something I'd never seen before, though the old custom of smashing plates for a dancer, in expression of emotion, or "*kefi*," is so well known that it's become a cliché about Greece. It was a night to remember. I was invited up on the bar too, but thankfully declined. At the end of the night, seeing how much we'd enjoyed this evening, Yorgos said he to cook on my tiny electric hotplate designed for making Greek coffee. It's a *siga-siga* (slowly-slowly) sort of process. The white wine from Rhodes is just cheap table wine, but the grapes here are different from anything I know—Athiri, Mandilari—and it tastes just right. The herbs are oregano, sage, and dill, and I am sure the locals would say it's ridiculous to mix all those herbs with these vegetables, but I somehow want to fill myself with the fragrance of this island.

According to Greek mythology, Tilos was the son of Apollo, the sun god, who collected therapeutic herbs for his mother when she was seriously ill; she recovered, and he constructed a sanctuary in honor of Apollo and Poseidon. The island was named after him and for a long time was renowned for its rare healing plants and herbs, and I have no doubt that they'll do me some good. I cook the spaghetti until al dente and serve it with the sauce and feta sprinkled lightly on top to melt. On the balmy terrace, I devour a big bowl and name the dish "Happiness by Aubergines."

After, I stroll down to the *kafeneion* in the square. It's a place where men tend to gather and drink small coffees and brandies at any time of the day and watch the world, or in this case Livadia, go by. They swing their worry beads, or *komboloi*, strings of colorful beads like miniature rosaries that they clack back and forth to occupy their hands, relieve stress, and pass the time. I sit around the side at one of the high tables made of barrels painted in jaunty colors, and

CHAPTER SIX

My Big Fat Greek Sunday

The church bells are ringing, for it is Sunday, and although the church is within a few minutes' walk of my new home and probably a mainstay of the community, I decide life is too short to go to church today. This might sound like rather skewed logic. *Life is short—go to church!* But no.

I've been to church here before for the cultural experience. Last year, the four of us decided we'd go to the beautiful old church in Megalo Horio on Sunday morning. I put on the closest I had to Sunday best, remembering to cover my shoulders, wearing a dress rather than jeans as the Greek Orthodox church sometimes frowns on women wearing "men's clothes"; I remembered having to put a sarong on over my jeans at a monastery I visited once. I sidled with Kate into what we hoped was an inconspicuous position at the back, and listened to the priest chanting as various congregants drifted in and the incense was wafted around. Unable to understand any of the service, I admired the painted and silver icons that covered the altar, and watched the people. A tiny old lady with a faint mustache, ninety if she was a day, hobbled toward me. I gave her a small but reverent smile, thinking perhaps she was going to tell us how nice it was to see visitors in church. She fixed me with a stare, crossed herself, and then jabbed a bony finger at an offending length of flesh between my knee and the hem of my dress, crossed herself again, and hobbled away.

Chastened, I stretched my Lycra dress as far down over my legs as it would go. Kate and I tried not to look at one another to avoid bursting out into loud and unholy laughter. Tauntingly, the pebble mosaic courtyard outside the door was bathed in beautiful sunlight. I made a swift exit and Kate followed, though I didn't dare look back to see if the boys would come too. When it seemed they were staying inside, we made our way up the steps to the village café that overlooked the church, where the service from some other church in Greece was blaring out from the big TV over the bar, and a scattering of blokes with coffees and brandies and cigarettes were doing the next best thing and watching church on telly in a sort of halfheartedly holy way that suited me fine. Thus we neatly avoided the next part of the service that we heard about later from the boys: the part where they knelt on the cold stone floor for twenty minutes, possibly atoning for my bad behavior.

This Sunday, I decide to go for a long walk instead, a pilgrimage to Eristos beach, fortified with *spanakopita* from the bakery, which is open even on a Sunday—praise the Lord.

Living on a small island with many bays and inlets, you're never far from the sea. The wind today is blowing from the south into the bay at Livadia, so I hope perhaps it will be calmer on the other side in Eristos. I take the road that winds up from the square fairly steeply and then zigzags up the mountain. I'm wearing shorts and a T-shirt and, to keep the sun off my face, my gray baseball cap that actually has my name written on it. My dad had brought it back from a work trip for me as a present, I assumed as a joke, but then he said, "I never see you wearing your hat!" so now I wear it. It somehow seems appropriate during this month in which part of my mission is to remind myself of who I really am… and therefore what I want.

The road levels off, and near the turn-off up to the abandoned village of Mikro Horio I see the island's petrol station, where a big man sits comfortably on an old couch by the pumps waiting for customers. A few cars go by, but they're outnumbered hugely by the goats I pass among the oak trees and outcroppings of rock. Goats here are beautiful, noble-looking creatures, often with impressively curly horns, and with glossy long hair in shades of black and chestnut; they should advertise Pantene shampoo. They wander as if wild all over the hillsides, though some of them wear colored plastic tags like earrings.

"Want a lift?" A car stops and it's my landlord Rob, driving home for lunch.

"Thanks! If you can take me as far as the turn-off for Eristos, that would be great." I get in. "I was just admiring the old cars." Here and there around this island and many others is a car or tractor that is abandoned wherever it stopped working or fell down the hillside, but next door to the petrol station is what looks like a serene final resting place for them, a sunny car park of no return. Rob explains there's a man who fixes mechanical things and keeps them for parts. He fixed Rob and Annie's fridge.

As we drive, Rob gestures to the unassuming cave entrance fenced off by the Excavations Department of Athens University, where elephant bones were excavated a couple of decades ago.

"Have you been up there to Harkadio?"

"Yes—though not right to the entrance as the gate was locked."

"What gate? Probably just to keep the goats out."

"Oh… Have they made any progress on the new museum?"

"Are you kidding? There's no money left!"

Last year I visited the old museum, a single room near the church in Megalo Horio, where the bones, teeth, and tusks of a mother and baby elephant were on display, and a kind curator explained it all to me in English. Only four thousand years ago, back when people were living happily in their civilized homes in Santorini and the Minoans were frolicking in their palace at Knossos in Crete, there were elephants here in Tilos. They'd been here since prehistoric times, having probably wandered over from Africa, walking part of the way and swimming the rest when the continents weren't all that far apart. It's not that hard to imagine herds of elephants browsing for food in the valleys here and taking all the best spots on the beach. But big species get smaller when they live on a small island because of limited resources, and these had evolved to a mere 1.5 meters in height fully grown—still big enough to make a mess of the garden, but more like a pony than a hulking great African elephant. Then came those volcanic rumblings from Santorini (though others say it was the volcano on the nearby island of Nisyros). The last forty or so dwarf elephants in Tilos, and possibly in Europe, were sheltering in Harkadio cave when the volcano erupted, and they died, covered in ash.

When a professor from Athens unearthed the bones, most were sent to Vienna, and excavations halted until the Harkadio cave could be made safe enough to continue—but that was many years ago now. A new museum is being set up near the cave; when I went to take a look at the sleek glass-and-stone building last year, it seemed that goats were living there, from the evidence of their droppings all over the shiny marble floor. That's one of the relaxing things about Tilos, I think: in spite of its long and intriguing history, there isn't too much to go and see. But there's still the old one-room museum up there in Megalo Horio.

Rob turns off for the village and leaves me to walk the rest of the way.

The road through Eristos valley has farms on either side—orange trees, olive trees, fields filled with poppies and planted with rows of vegetables. Tilos is lucky to have spring water; when I lived in Oia on Santorini, fresh water was brought into the village by tanker. After half an hour I emerge through a line of shady trees onto the spectacular sweep of coarse sand embraced by wild mountains. The only other people are so far away I have to look carefully to make them out: it seems to be a man in a black wetsuit with a woman and young child, and I wonder if it's the teacher from the other day. I don aqua shoes, as the sand here gets blisteringly hot. The sea is indeed calmer, and I stretch out on what feels like my own private beach, passing the afternoon happily between sand and sea.

Eventually, gasping for a bit of shade and a cold drink, I pad up the road to Tropicana. The name makes it sound like a sleek bar with waiters making fancy cocktails, but is in fact a basic little family-run eatery on the edge of a farm, with a shakily handwritten sign, overhung with vines and overrun with cats. The family is out in the back doing some work, but an older lady in a flowery apron comes inside to help me to a can of lemonade from the fridge. I drink it sitting outside in the shade at a wooden table, and her husband shoos away one of the cats that creeps up to see if anything's on offer. Then I go back in for another can. "*Pagomeni*," ice cold, says the lady, smiling.

What more could a girl need?

Well, a bus home perhaps, but I know I've missed the last one. It takes an hour and a half to walk back in the early evening alongside lovely pink oleander; I watch the goats foraging about on the slopes or lounging on the roof of a chapel, and I listen to the cicadas. At one point I save a suicidal hedgehog, picking it up off the road and putting it back in the field. Normally it might quite easily make it across, but this evening the road seems strangely busy with cars heading to Livadia. I didn't realize there were so many cars on the whole island.

I find something very satisfying about being able to get to a place with my own two feet, and I love the fact that Tilos is so small you can pretty much explore the whole thing on foot. Because the island also has so many hills and headlands and inlets of various shapes, the view changes rapidly as you walk around it, and there's plenty of wildlife. I grew up in a village on the edge of Saddleworth Moor, with a bedroom window that looked out over hills, and as children my brother and I were always wandering around them; the bottom of our garden led out onto a wild hillside full of opportunities to play—picking blackberries, swimming in the reservoir, grass-sledging, climbing in the quarries. And every year we had a week's holiday in a remote cottage in the Scottish Highlands when we went to visit my dad's family. When we moved to the south of England, I was dismayed by the feebly rolling farmland.

I also find it incredibly therapeutic following a path and letting my mind wander as the simple movement takes over—as with swimming. For me it's good, easy exercise and I love the tremendous calm that comes when you finish. I enjoy feeling ravenous and looking forward to a big reward-ing meal. The final stretch of road with the view of Livadia bay is a welcome sight.

Exhausted but happy, I learn over a well-deserved ice-cold beer downstairs in the bar that there's been a christening up at the monastery, which explains all those cars, some of which might have come by boat. Annie says she also met a big group of Englishmen who came in on a yacht today, and they might be arriving shortly. On cue, in stroll a dozen jolly middle-aged men in bright pink T-shirts. Gay pride in Tilos? After all, this was the island that had the first two same-sex marriages in the whole of Greece in June 2008, which even made the *New York Times*. But no, a couple of the guys sit near me and explain it's just a beer-drinking jolly. One man is appointed "GOD" for the day—short for Growing Old Disgracefully—and makes the decisions to prevent disagreements. The "Finemaster" takes care of any bad behavior. After we chat for a while, they ask about a good place to eat, and I suggest the big taverna where the christening party is happening.

Having eaten nothing but oranges and *spanakopita* all day myself, I decide to treat myself to a meal out at the seafront restaurant where young Yorgos works. I like the way he never asks you to come in to his restaurant, in the way that touts do in some places; that's not the way in Tilos, thank goodness. You'll eat there if you want. In fact, in spite of being friendly, Yorgos's manner is somewhat detached, as if his mind is entirely on other things.

I sit down at one of the tables on the terrace looking straight out to sea, and he hands me a menu. In my experience of dining out with Greeks, they tend to ask what the restaurant has that's good that day—not everything on the menu is available all year round. One of my favorite foods, *horta*, spinach or any similar green leafy vegetable boiled and served with lemon and olive oil, is hardly ever available.

"What do you have?" I ask.

Yorgos appears to sigh, and starts to recite in a deadpan tone what seems to be the entire menu.

I laugh and interrupt. "No, I mean, what's fresh and good today?"

"Fish, meat, what do you want?"

"Um, do you have goat?"

"Yes."

"Is it local?"

"Yes. In lemon sauce." Yorgos looks as if he couldn't be less interested.

"Right then, um, OK, *endaxi*, I'll have that. And some *tzatziki*, please, and a quarter-carafe of wine."

"I bring you one ouzo free. Is for tourists."

Ah, Yorgos, you're really selling this. I laugh again. "No thanks. Just the wine." Been there, done that. I love Greek dancing, and unfortunately, during one night on the island of Kalymnos, ouzo convinced me that I'd miraculously learned how to do it. The locals must have found me highly entertaining as I blithely butchered their traditional moves with wobbly ouzo-inspired bravado. I have to retain some semblance of respectability on this little island.

Yorgos brings my plate of creamy *tzatziki*, made with thick yogurt and plenty of garlic. The wine comes in a tiny tin carafe, ice-cold, with a small tumbler.

"I make you laugh?" asks Yorgos.

"Yes, you make me laugh."

He shrugs and I still can't tell if the ironic detachment is an act or just his normal manner. Then we get talking.

"I work here in the lunchtime and evening, but I am also *nosokomos*. You know *nosokomos*?"

I think. It's related to the word for hospital. Something medical.

"I train three years for this. Now I go around the island to see the old people who live alone, check this"—he puts his fingers around his bicep to indicate taking blood pressure—"check they are OK."

He takes out a little digital camera from his pocket and starts showing me pictures of his elderly patients, and the sudden animation makes me realize that this is a bit more interesting to him than serving ouzo to tourists. He speaks quickly, talking me through the photos.

"Eh, Yorgo, slow down a bit, *siga-siga!*" shouts a chap with a tanned face and dark beard in the corner. "She can't understand if you speak like that!"

I am introduced to the man, a farmer who grows vegetables in Eristos where I walked today. With its fertile, volcanic soil and good supply of springs, the valley has the potential to produce plenty of food. Once, the residents of the island used to grow so much food that they exported it. But much of the land isn't farmed anymore; for most people, it is easier to build some rooms and rent them to tourists. As long as the tourists come.

"We live off solar power only, no electricity," he said. "No chemicals on the vegetables, only natural. It is a good life!" It's probably quite a hard life too. He murmurs something to the woman he's dining with, who also has the ruddy glow of a farmer, and she leaves, returning a few minutes later to hand me a plastic bag filled with lettuce and zucchini.

"For me? Can I buy them?"

"Nothing this time, just taste! The *kolokithia* only need water, nothing else. And the *marouli* nothing, just eat as salad."

My big chunk of goat cooked with fresh lemons arrives. I eat and listen to the bubbly, voluptuous waitress who has emerged from the kitchen and is laughing about the messed-up ferry service this month. Tilos raised funds from local entrepreneurs to buy its own boat, the *Sea Star*, to be assured of a regular connection to Rhodes and the airport; when ferries call in here less than once per day, it's difficult for businesses reliant on tourists. Unfortunately it's undergoing some sort of repairs, although its main problem seems to be a tendency to hemorrhage money. A new boat appeared yesterday, but no one yet knows its itinerary.

It's tricky; if Tilos had its own airport or hourly ferries from Rhodes, the island could be changed forever in a way that would probably drive away the kind of tourists who come here now—and destroy its character for everyone. Tilos's people want to make a living, but they are also proud to live on an island that is authentically Greek. Something in between, a dependable daily ferry service, would be ideal, which is what Tilos usually has in the summer season.

Paying the bill, I head toward the *kafeneion* for my arranged glass of wine with the other Yorgos, who I learn is uncle to Yorgos the waiter, not surprising given that Yorgos Senior has eight brothers and sisters. The café is filled with older men intently watching football on a large television behind the bar, silent except for when occasionally someone shouts a rude word.

Yorgos gets me a glass of wine and we all watch the football game. He's in a perfectly pressed Dolce & Gabbana long-sleeved white shirt, and designer jeans—rather dapper for a café owner, but then he always seems to be. His neatly trimmed white hair contrasts strikingly with his thick dark eyebrows. I look around the walls at old photographs and trinkets. Then one of the players gets a red card and soon the game is over amid disgruntled shouts, and the *kafeneion* empties quickly—*yeia sas, kali nichta*, bye, good night…

"Well, thanks very much! I'd better go home," I say, smiling.

"Why don't you come to my home?"

I laugh, thinking he must be joking, but he looks surprised. Oh dear. Am I really cutting some sort of Shirley Valentine figure, a lonely heart looking for love? Or is it just that there's a shortage of new females on the island, and a lot of red-blooded males? So much for tranquillity.

"Er, no, it's OK—good night!" Smiling, I beat a hasty retreat.

Walking the few minutes back home, feeling faintly shaken by the misunderstanding, I hear music and remember the christening party. Sure enough, there's a band still playing. The table of men in pink is hard to miss.

"Thanks for the recommendation! Come and join us!"

So even though it has already been a very long day, I sit with the crowd for a while to laugh and relax. Nearby is a table of guys in uniform and crew cuts from the submarine that appeared in the bay today on some sort of routine Greek navy maneuver. Tilos is so close to Turkey—its mountainous shore only a few miles away, looking like another large island. I've noticed sometimes when I'm on a walk, my phone buzzes and when I check, it's "Welcome to Turkey."

A little separate from the rest of the taverna is the private party for family and friends. A circle has been cleared, and people drift to and from the dance floor as the musicians play traditional Greek songs. A woman with jet-black hair and dark eyes is showing off her tall hourglass figure in a stunning dress. Arms raised, she twists elegantly as she circles the dance floor, her feet moving in tiny, delicate steps. I don't know how anyone can take their eyes off her. Then the music changes and some sit this one out, while others join in and hold hands again. Just like so many times before, I am mesmerized by the traditional Greek dances. For now, I am still very much an outsider here, but maybe one day I will learn.

CHAPTER SEVEN

Tangled Webs

I am sitting at a shady table in the square, sipping a frappé. I can just glimpse patches of sparkling sea beyond the blue-and-white police station. It's been the most enchanting Monday morning at the office.

Each day of my work tends to bring an unforeseeable ratio of headaches and triumphs—reading, negotiating, writing, discussing—and most of it is done by email, even interaction with my own colleagues, which makes it technically possible to do a large part of my job from anywhere with a good Internet connection. This should be in the flat but for now is the café. A good 20 percent of the job involves face-to-face contact—or meetings, a word that strikes dread into the heart of an office worker—but for two weeks we can get around that. I really want to make this work, partly to thank my boss for his faith in me—and partly, of course, to see if it's possible to combine work and island life. I make my way through the messages, gleeful that most people on the receiving end have no idea where I am. Eventually, as the laptop battery is running down, I download some files to work on later.

I pop in to the post office to try to pick up a Western Union transfer of funds I'm expecting. The man behind the desk completes the paperwork, asks for my passport, and tells me to come back for it in about half an hour. I'll come back tomorrow, I say. He seems surprised at how relaxed I am about not needing my passport. But why would I want to go anywhere?

As I sweep the leaves and mop the dust from my terrace, feeling at home, a flatbed truck is driving around the village with a loudspeaker advertising plastic tables and chairs—he must be taking a truckload from one little island to another. After a quick salad, I go down to the beach. The sea is irresistible, flat and clear with tiny rippling waves, and feels a little warmer than when I arrived a few days ago. I'm back at the desk mid-afternoon feeling completely rejuvenated and relaxed, and I hope it shows in my work.

In the evening, I take my evening *volta*, my walkabout. First stop as usual is Yorgos the Younger outside the restaurant, who asks how I enjoyed my glass of wine with his uncle. I raise my eyebrows a bit, prompting a laugh. A little farther along I pass the handful of restaurants on the seafront and recognize Vangelis, whom we met last year when he was serving drinks in a bar nearby. He's eating alone and acknowledges me with a wave and a *kalispera*, though it seems unlikely he would remember me. I walk the length of the beach, reaching the quieter end of the bay as a few tiny raindrops fall. The only sound is the engine of a fishing boat coming slowly into the harbor, and as I approach the mountain, the smell of herbs grows stronger and sheep are bleating. I walk as far as the headland, and then retrace my steps along the shore back to my place and a quiet night.

The following day, after my lunchtime swim, I'm taking the quiet back route through the village rather than the seafront where I have to chat with everyone along the way, when a familiar figure drives up on his *motosikleta* and stops. It's Vangelis, dressed for work in the fields, with a baseball cap to shield his eyes from the sun. He says he does remember me from last year (amazing—he must meet so many people), and if I feel like joining him for dinner, he'll be at the same restaurant tonight at eight o'clock. I'm delighted, as he's one of the people who made my first visit to the island so special, someone I hoped to get to know better, and this doesn't feel like a romantic overture. As we agree to meet later and he drives on, Yorgos from the *kafeneion* passes on his *motosikleta* in the other direction, shouting hello and waving but not stopping. It's all go here in Tilos.

I arrive that evening wearing my most demure cotton dress and flat leather boots, my modern take on traditional village dress. Vangelis is already there, and as I sit down he asks what I feel like eating. I say I'll leave it up to him. He discusses with the owner, Pantelis, what's good tonight, orders a few things, then over a little carafe of wine we start chatting comfortably in English. Wearing a plain shirt and trousers, Vangelis is a good-looking, slightly weathered man in his late fifties with dark brown hair and twinkling eyes; his charm, I feel, comes from a sense of being content in himself, but also his interest in listening to others. I ask about his work.

"Yes, I am still working with the animals, the goats and the sheep and the chickens. On an island like this, you must make the money where you can. And I make the charcoal in the winter, up there, when there are no tourists." He points to the headland.

"What, up by the church?" I realize he's talking about the mysterious arched mounds of intricately stacked gray wood I saw last night on the top of the headland.

"Yes, my father taught me how to do it. The people want too much, more than I can make. But my son, he doesn't want to learn this. Eh, it's OK to do this in the winter. It's very peaceful on the hillside. My girlfriend, she helps me. She is away now."

"And do you still run the *kantina* with your daughter?"

"Yes, on Eristos beach, you know, in the summer. I like to meet the tourists, to talk with them. I get to know many people who come here every year. In the old days, I have a restaurant, Zorba's. We had dancing—beautiful! The tourists, they know me as Zorba. I love to dance." The twinkle in his eye gets brighter. He carries himself well—I can see how he'd be a good dancer. "But this year I will not dance, even on my birthday, because… my brother died this year. He was only fifty years old."

"Do you have other family?"

Quickly, his face lights up. "My mother, she lives in Rhodes now. A beautiful woman, the best. She makes the best food. When my son goes to Rhodes, he brings back food from my mother that she cooks for me."

As we talk, we eat tomato and feta salad, *tzatziki* and fried calamari. I don't like to take the last piece of calamari but Pantelis, collecting the plates, instructs me to eat it, "*Fa to!*" Then a bream-like fish arrives lightly fried in oil and lemon juice, served with fried potatoes. It's delicious.

Vangelis, who was born in Mikro Horio just a few years before the village was abandoned around 1960, tells me he remembers the planting of the tamarisk trees along the waterfront here, when the land behind was all fields; they were originally planted as a windbreak to protect the crops in the fertile soil along the seafront from the dry north winds.

Migrating birds used to visit the wetlands in spectacular numbers. These days, although Tilos is a nature reserve for endangered birds, the encroaching development and the lack of crops to eat makes it harder for them. I mention that Kastro, the restaurant in Megalo Horio, served homegrown food last year.

"Ah yes! Dina, who has the restaurant, is my cousin. Maybe you like to go there sometime? Have you been to the museum in Megalo Horio?"

"Yes, it's very interesting—thanks to the nice lady who explains everything."

"Ah yes, she comes from Athens originally. Her husband is from Tilos; he is the barber. He goes around the island on his *motosikleta* to cut the hair."

"What about the new museum—when will it be finished?"

"Vicky will run the old museum for some time, I think. There is no more money to finish the new museum. What happen to the first money, nobody knows. It has been the same for five years."

"It's a shame, as it might bring more tourists to the island…?"

"Yes, and I would be happy to see more foreigners coming here. They bring the life back to Tilos. They are good people who come here."

I agree with his way of thinking: the right kind of visitors can help sustain the traditions and protect nature.

When it's time for the bill, Vangelis insists on paying. I thank him and say it's been great getting to know him better.

"You are welcome to come to my house any time for dinner, any evening. We are neighbors, you know. I eat every night at eight o'clock so you just come. You will come?"

I assure him I will.

⌒

This time in Tilos is also for reflection, and I mustn't fill it up too much with socializing. I want to relax my brain and mull over some things about my life: where I am and where I want to be. I decide to spend a tranquil couple of days alone, doing my work, swimming, walking.

The sea is completely smooth like a lake, or like oil, as they say in Greece, when I walk down to the harbor at six thirty, feeling rested after another great night's sleep. All is peaceful, and off the docks the water is still enough to see very deep. The mountains remain in gray shadow. At seven thirty I sit down at my desk, happy to be getting an early start on the day. It seems unnecessary to stick to a nine-to-five routine. I work for five hours then take a break, lying in the sun with the hot pebbles on my back, listening to the waves. Sometimes after sitting at the computer working hard for several hours, my brain is fuzzy and I just need to crash out. I take a long swim across the bay, watching businesses getting ready to open for the summer season, sprucing up their terraces and putting out signs. I'm drying off when I see Vangelis again: I happen to be in front of a little house where his goatherd friend lives.

"Where are you? Why you didn't come for dinner?"

I thought "any evening" was a loose arrangement, but apparently he cooked lamb especially for me and I didn't go. Oops.

"I have saved it—will you come tonight?"

"Of course—thank you!"

His house, as he explained last time we had dinner, is down an alleyway around the corner from mine—we are neighbors, it turns out, though I didn't realize it as I'd never walked down the alley before. When I arrive he is feeding the stray cats. Inside, the decor has a soft, sentimental quality that seems to suit him, with little cushions and embroideries on the walls which he says were made by his wife, from whom he's now separated. In the kitchen he pours the wine I've brought, and as he loads the table with food, he tells me how between 1968 and 1973, the dictatorship in Greece persecuted the communists, and Vangelis was a communist. The Scandinavian countries, unlike Britain, were willing to take them in, so along with a group of other men he went to Finland, where he spent four and a half years and met his Finnish wife, and where his children were born.

The table is filled to overflowing. There's the now

twice-cooked lamb, roasted with oil, a little vinegar, green peppers, garlic, salt and pepper, water, and potatoes. There's a salad of tomatoes with pickled gherkins, fat juicy olives, and feta. There are aubergines and peppers fried in oil and served with *skordalia*, garlic sauce. He piles food onto my plate so I can try everything.

He tells me he's started writing down his memories of growing up here; he writes notes while making charcoal in the winter. He says an Austrian friend has translated it into English and he's thinking some of the visitors who come here would be interested in reading it.

"I'd love to see it."

"I will find it and show you. An English friend of mine is looking after it at the moment. *Ela Jenni mou—yeia sou.*" We clink glasses. He feels like an old friend already, and we talk and eat and drink wine. Vangelis really seems like a Zorba character, from the Kazantzakis novel—a lover of freedom, of things that matter in life, a hater of rules and nonsense. He eats with his fingers, loves to dance and to swim. Maybe we'll do those things together one day, we joke. We raise a toast:

"Maybe one day!"

He reassures me that I can trust him, that we can just be friends, and I laugh and thank him, telling him how I gave the wrong idea to someone the other night.

"I like your company. You are welcome to come for dinner

any evening. You will work well if you eat well, if you have a good night before."

As I leave, he goes out to feed the leftovers to the stray cats, which wait patiently outside.

~

The weekend before I left for this month in Tilos, I stayed with my mum and was trying to show her on the computer where I would be for the next little while. Tilos does not have a major web presence, as you'd imagine. Greek island websites on the whole tend to make liberal use of unnecessary flashing things, scrolling screens, unreadable fonts, and plonking music, all of which can add up to something quite terrifying. But then I made a hilarious discovery, that the Tilos website run by Stefanakis Travel—a refreshingly understated site with a reliable ferry timetable—had a webcam page.

At least it claimed to, but when you downloaded it, it seemed to be frozen: just a still shot of the jetty, with a couple of fishing boats moored up. It must be broken. No, wait— what was that?! A seagull swooped across the screen. It wasn't frozen at all; Tilos just wasn't very busy.

Mum and I became obsessed, watching for five minutes at a time to see if anything moved. A man might potter around his fishing boat, retrieve something from on deck, then go back inside. Five minutes later, a boy or a cat might walk down the road. Stillness again, nothing, nothing—then the wind blew and the mast of a yacht tilted a bit. I was gleeful about going to a place where so little happened. And at least if my mum worried whether I was eating enough, I could just go and stand in front of the webcam and wave. She certainly needn't be concerned on that front anyway.

The view did look decidedly gray at that time, however, and the weather forecast showed Greece only a few degrees warmer than England, so I prepared for cool temperatures, bringing jumpers and a jacket. The jacket hasn't been out of the wardrobe since I arrived. Apparently there were a few days of rain in April, but it is palpably hotter by the day, unlike in England, where for a few hot days in April everyone pretends it's California, then you're back to icy winds and it's anyone's guess when the next sunny day will be. It's extremely relaxing to know that if you miss this bit of sunshine because you're busy, there'll be another one along in a minute.

Not only is it getting hotter by the day, but changes are happening—the Tilos Information Office next to the church is showing signs of life, a few more chairs have appeared outside one of the cafés on the seafront, and a couple more shops on the square have opened for business. I buy some intoxicatingly fragrant Tilos-made soap that makes the bathroom smell wonderful. Realizing my cash supply needs topping up, for the first time since arriving I try to use the bank machine, and it rejects my card, saying it's "unauthorized usage." I still have fifty euros and I'm hardly spending very much, but I'll have to figure it out when the bank opens on Monday.

The beach becomes even more beautiful toward late afternoon, the water calm and even clearer; the angle at which the sun hits the water means you can see the round white pebbles and the sand and the reed beds, and the layers of blue. I swim across the bay and back, going a little farther than the previous day, my reward and relaxation after a day at the desk. There's someone else doing the same, a man who arrives on a bike and reads a book; although he doesn't act like a local, it gives me confidence to swim out a bit farther. I dry off in the sun, reading a good book. Happiness is easy sometimes.

In the evening, I go downstairs to the bar and ensconce myself on one of the comfortable benches covered in rugs to read for a while. I'm just about to leave when Thanasis arrives and buys me a drink. When I first met Thanasis, who is deaf and mute, last year at this bar, I was amazed at how well Rob conversed with him, but I may be getting the hang of it. He sits down and we converse in his idiosyncratic sign language that's more like a kind of fast charades, and somehow he puts me in fits of giggles, telling me about the vegetable farm he keeps and how he taught himself to lay traditional pebble mosaic floors. He's built like a fighter, strong and wiry. He's happy staying single, he says, except he could do with a good shoulder massage after a long day's work. He came looking for me here the other day and was going to knock on my door upstairs, but Rob said it would freak me out. His mime of this freaking-me-out part is pretty funny. We agree to meet up for a drink the next night and he says he wants to cook me dinner. I wonder how to explain in mime "just as friends" but assume, perhaps wrongly, that it's obvious.

Friday night has rolled around again, so I wander down to a café by the sea, which is pleasantly busy. An English couple I've met before are sitting by the door and invite me to join them. They'd been coming to Tilos for years on holiday when he was made redundant; their kids had grown up and they decided to do something adventurous and moved to Tilos. For the first year they slept on camp beds in the shop they ran; gradually they built a house and a set of rental apartments. As we're talking, out through the door of the bar comes Manolis the teacher—not in a wetsuit this time.

They've not met so I introduce everyone. Before he leaves, Manolis offers to take me out swimming some day on a different beach to discover more of Tilos, and we arrange to walk to Gera together on Sunday, meeting at ten a.m. in the square. I guess he's not married after all, then. I hope to be able to practice my Greek, and it will be nice to discover another part of the island. Then the English couple invites me to a barbecue tomorrow lunchtime at their place. My social diary is filling up fast.

The next morning, I'm drying off from my swim when Vangelis goes by on his scooter and shouts, "OK for eight o'clock tonight?" I stupidly say yes, knowing I've got a barbecue to go to at lunch and forgetting I've sort of promised to have dinner with Thanasis. I do get myself into a tangled mess. The lunchtime barbecue is a lovely relaxed affair on a sunny terrace and I try not to eat too much.

In the evening, when I take my walk along the seashore, a man who was snorkeling across the bay earlier now stands at the edge of the water, slamming two dead octopus on the rocks repeatedly. The six-year-old son of Pantelis the restaurant owner watches, amazed. I stand to watch for a while too, and the fisherman gives me a big smile. I've seen this done before but I'm not quite sure why they do it. I'm thinking of asking, when Pantelis whistles to me, so I go up to his restaurant to say hello. He gives me a high five.

"How are you? Where is Vangelis?"

Pantelis may have gotten the wrong end of the stick, or maybe he's just fishing for gossip. "I don't know, but I'm meeting him later."

"OK, well, tell him to stop by!"

I promise I will. I have a quick drink with Thanasis and apologize that I can't come for dinner, which goes down like a lead balloon but is probably the safest option. I think about how quiet Tilos seemed through the webcam, and how busy my social life is here. What happened to the island of tranquillity?

CHAPTER EIGHT

A Walk to Gera

I wake up and, still lying in bed, pull the curtain back to see the craggy brown hillside and a deep blue sky. Bliss.

There's a screen on the window so I can keep it open all night without too much fear of mosquitoes, though occasionally I wake in the night to hear that high-pitched whine in my ears. There's a little thing I can plug into the wall that makes an odor they don't like, but mostly I don't need it. I've got used to the humming and rattling of the big old fridge in the kitchen, am getting accustomed to the futon mattress, and the cotton bedspread is all I need now—the duvet has been put away. When I get up to have a shower, I can see the sun glinting on the blue sea just above the rooftops.

It makes me happy thinking that I decided to do this and I pulled it off; I didn't wait; I made it happen. It is possible to take action to make life better. I remember how much I admired my friend Ali from university when she decided to move to the farthest reaches of Cornwall. She'd always wanted to live there but hoped to go with her partner. When the relationship fell apart, she decided to go anyway and take her chances alone in a remote village. Happily, she found someone to share it all with, and I went to their wedding near Land's End not long ago. Good for Ali.

Just before ten, I don comfy shorts and a clean white T-shirt and walking shoes, throw an orange into my back-pack, stop next door to pick up a *spanakopita,* and, full of the joy of a peaceful, sunny, Sunday morning, practically bounce down toward the café just off the square where I arranged to meet Manolis for our walk. He's not there, so I sit on the wall and wait. Five minutes later, I see him coming up the steps. He's wearing jeans, shirt tucked in, a man-bag on a belt, and what looks very much like a bad-tempered expression. His black eyebrows are scrunched down over his eyes and his full lips are set in a grim scowl.

"*Kalimera*! *Ti kaneis?*" "How are you?" I ask chirpily, trying to lighten the mood as he points down at his green car and starts to walk back toward it. This man does not look pleased to see me. There's a bit of silence. I follow him.

"Eh, OK," he finally replies as he opens the door. "Is different for us who live here than you visitors. We have things to do, wash the clothes, do things."

"Listen," I say, turning to him as we get into the car. "Don't worry—if you're busy, we don't need to do this. I'll be fine on my own! Thanks for offering but it's OK." Damned if you're going to bring me down on this lovely day, I think—I'll happily walk to the beach at Gera on my own.

"No, if I say I do something, I do it." He huffs, turns the key in the ignition, and off we go. I strap myself in as we turn around on the quayside. I smile. Hey, it's all experience. We drive pretty much in silence, past a couple of isolated tavernas and the new apartments on the headland and up to the little chapel where Vangelis makes his charcoal.

Manolis stops the car. "From here, we walk." He opens the trunk and gets out an enormous backpack that would be suitable for trekking for a week. What it's stuffed full of, I have no idea, but I secretly hope it's lunch. He also has a two-liter bottle of water in a thermal case with a shoulder strap, which looks very useful, especially as it hits me that I've forgotten to bring water to go for a walk to a deserted beach in the middle of the day. *Spanakopita* and an orange, but no water. I admit my mistake and grin in what I hope is an endearing way, and I can almost see him thinking, "Oh sweet Jesus, why did I agree to bring this silly woman on a walk?" I wonder if he can see my thought bubble too, which reads, "Oh, lighten up"?

We set off walking single file along the narrow path that hugs the side of the mountain, with a stunning view all the way down to a little bay. With my light bag, I am still bounding along, full of energy. Manolis, on the other hand, is soon very hot. Little drops of sweat build on his forehead. He's not smiling.

The slopes that fall steeply down to a rocky shoreline are covered with spiny brown scrub and yellow flowers. There's a clear view of Turkey across the unbroken deep blue sea. One of the things I love about Tilos is this close view of the shores of what was once called Asia Minor: the sense that we are on the very edge of Europe. The landscape here in the southeast Aegean, even some of the cultural idiosyncrasies of Greece, remind me sometimes more of the Middle East than Europe.

As we continue along the trail for half an hour, gradually the slopes become gentler and little coves are revealed, with a greener patch of land, a fenced pen for goats, and a couple of trees. Manolis says it's *Despoti Nero*, the Bishop's Water, where a natural spring feeds into the sea. We leave the main path to Gera and scramble down a goat track.

He leads the way, and every now and then he stops and turns around to check if I'm OK. I am managing to keep up fine, stepping off rocks and over small bushes.

"You have large legs. It is good for this," he comments gruffly.

Long legs, not *large*, ahem. Actually I'm pleased as they are already getting browner and more toned with all this walking.

"Eh, the plants on the path are sharp, pull up your socks,"

he adds, pointing to the scrub with its spiky, thorny branches adapted to surviving the long, dry summer.

Way ahead of you, mate, that's why I wore my nice knee-high gray organic cotton socks, in case you wondered, so I can pull them right up and not get scratches.

I am tripping down the path with an amused smile as we descend into a heavenly, deserted bay. On a beach with small gray pebbles I pull my bag off my warm back, strip down to my bikini, put on aqua shoes, and bound straight toward the cooling, perfect blue sea.

"Eh, be careful—it is not good the very cold straight after the very hot."

I look at Manolis the schoolteacher, who is still fully dressed and arranging his things carefully in the shade, and shake my head, smiling. "I'm sure I'll be fine, it's OK!" But then I decide to be careful, as I am the idiot who forgot to carry water, and it would be bad if he was right and something happened here, all the way down a steep mountainside with our phones most likely out of range. *Hello, Turkey? We have a problem...* I edge slowly into the water rather than plunging straight in, swim around the rocks briefly to cool off, then come back and flop onto my towel.

"If you like," says Manolis casually, "you can take the top off here. Many women don't like the white lines. Better to take off the clothes."

Dream on. I smilingly decline his invitation to disrobe

beyond the bikini and lie down on my towel. We've barely met, for goodness sake. The stones are rounded and very comfortable, and their heat through my towel feels better than any kind of spa treatment on my back. Then I notice Manolis moving his towel right next to mine.

Oh no, I hope he's not getting the wrong impression. Maybe he thinks this is what going for a walk together means? It's one of those difficult situations where I don't know if I'm overreacting to a situation.

Then his hand moves toward me and I jump.

Apart from the fact that it's all a bit sudden and came out of nowhere, and the fact that he's been grumpy with me ever since we met this morning, that is very much not why I wanted to walk to Gera with him. It's time to set the boundaries. So I thank him for his interest, but we're not going there. Not that I need to explain myself, but because I like him—and we are miles from another person right now—I do try not to hurt his feelings. I explain I've had a hard year when it comes to relationships with men, and that I'm numb and really don't want anything like that. I'm still in my six-month quarantine period, and this month especially is a time to stay away from anything romantic.

"Of course," says Manolis, partly amused and partly peeved. "As you like."

It's not exactly the understanding I was looking for, but I think the message has been received.

I jump up and say I'm going for a longer swim. He gets up too, and the contents of the enormous rucksack are revealed.

"You want coat?" He's actually brought a wetsuit along for me—what a sweetheart. "Is better, the water here is very cold because of the fresh water." I gratefully accept. I haven't worn a wetsuit since I tried surfing in Cornwall the day before Ali's wedding. These ones have short sleeves and legs, but they allow you to stay in the water longer than you would in just a swimsuit—good if you're out looking for fish in a place where natural spring water bubbles up from underground into the sea. And I feel self-conscious in my bikini all of a sudden anyway. I zip myself up and start swimming toward the other side of the bay. On one side the cliffs are gray, but on the other they're still very green; the dry season is only just starting. It's amazingly beautiful, the deep blue water and the green rugged hillsides.

Manolis swims slowly behind, wearing not only a wetsuit but also a kind of balaclava and a snorkel and mask, as he wore that first day I met him, and although he does look quite funny he gradually seems happier and friendlier; this is clearly his territory, his comfort zone. We get close to the cliffs at the other side of the bay and tread water to chat for a while. Then he says we should probably swim back close to the shore, not too deep, as there may be "big fishes that like to eat Jennifer."

"You must to drink the fresh water. The body loses water in the sea by, how do you say, *osmosis*?"

"Yes, osmosis. Same word."

Back on shore, he takes a couple of apples from his bag and starts to peel them with a knife. "You have the legs like antelope, good for climbing the mountain."

"Thank you. Why do you peel the apples? You lose some of the goodness that way." If he can be a schoolteacher, so can I.

"It is better not to eat the chemicals, they can stay in the body a long time."

It reminds me of my old boss Yorgos in Santorini, who was always instructing me to clean or peel (the same word in Greek, *katharizo*) every fruit we ate.

Passing me sections of apple, he says, "I am in Larissa for the Easter a few weeks ago. These apples are the last I bring back in the car. I keep them in the fridge."

"I'm honored. Thank you! It's very kind."

He's quiet for a moment and then says, "I think you have a warm heart."

He smiles, and I think I like him better than I did earlier. He says he didn't imagine when we met that we'd be spending the whole day together like this. I didn't think we'd be spending the whole day here either—I thought it was just a walk with a beach at the end of it—but now that we're getting on better I'm glad. He tells me he grew up in Larissa, north of Athens, went to university in Thessaloniki, did military service, spent a few months in Australia, then moved to Athens and taught there at several different schools in different areas before he moved here a few years ago. He says he feels like an outsider everywhere now, not truly at home anywhere.

"I know the feeling! I left England just after university and lived in Greece, Canada, France…"

"Yes, but is difficult in Greece."

"But you're a citizen of all of Greece then," I say, trying to make him see the bright side, but he's having none of it; maybe acceptance is more difficult here. He's getting a little morose again, so I go for another swim, and we stay on the beach until five o'clock, listening to the bees on the hillside and looking out across the water. As we walk back up the hill, he still orders me to stay on the right path in a rather bossy manner, but he also points out some wild herbs and, when I say I'd like to take some back with me for salads, carefully picks long stalks for me. When we reach the main path, he points out a big lizard soaking up the sunshine on a wall, and says people used to grow wheat in the fields around here. Gera was the place where families from Mikro Horio came to live in the summer, closer to the sea.

It being May, it's almost the end of the school year and he's preparing exams, but most afternoons he goes swimming or fishing, so he asks if I want to come along to a different beach another day this week, and we agree to meet.

"Two thirty exactly," he says. "I keep English time." Yessir.

CHAPTER NINE

Swimming with the Fishes

I'm thinking this morning—although I don't want to—about Ben, the guy I met in the Park Tavern two days before I left England. I wanted to come here unencumbered by thoughts of anyone. The stuff on the beach with Manolis must have started it.

I'd seen Ben around a few times but never for a moment thought he was interested in me until we got into conversation that night. In the exhilaration of knowing I was going away for a month, I let my guard down a bit and agreed to meet him again the next night. I told him all about why I was going away and how I wasn't getting involved with anyone. I shouldn't have given him my phone number; that's what the vow of celibacy was all about. There again, he seemed so lovely and so keen, and those long conversations we had were wonderful... I haven't heard from him yet, which is a little confusing as although I didn't want to be in constant contact, he did say he might call this weekend, around the midpoint of my month away. Perhaps he's not sure I want to be disturbed. After breakfast and getting down to work, I stop letting it concern me. I'm here to be healed of all that. It actually doesn't matter whether he calls or what he is thinking. Let it all fade. It's actually amazing how effective it is just thinking, *It doesn't matter, because I have this; I have a beautiful Greek island.*

I emailed Kate the other day to let her know I am in Tilos again; I knew she'd be amused. We've kept in touch intermittently, having fortunately stayed friends after my relationship with John broke up, and she's sent me pictures of her very new baby daughter Lucy, who possibly visited Tilos when she was just a few cells in Kate's body. It's so nice to have a girlfriend to chat to, even if it's only by email.

Hi Kate,

Fabulous photos of you and Lucy! Both of you appear to be rather happy and healthy. Shouldn't you have bags under your eyes and vomit on your shoulder?

Am indeed having a wonderful time. It is amazing going for a swim in the sea on my lunch break. I am enjoying my job much more from here and I think I have more energy to deal with things—I am trying to be the model employee so they will let me do this again perhaps.

Remember Vangelis from the bar in Livadia? Well, he is now a good pal and cooks me dinner at eight o'clock every night whenever I'm in the mood, and tells me story after story of life on the island. Manolis, a high school teacher, has been taking me to deserted beaches and lending me a wetsuit so we can go snorkeling together. He's a brainy geek... Still, otherwise I'd have to find myself a lonely geriatric goat farmer. It's all very inspiring, as is living next door to the bakery.

Jx

Jen,

That sounds absolutely wonderful. Personally I have often felt that working in an office five days a week is not always the right atmosphere to accomplish something. Often it is an excuse to make yourself feel you are doing something when instead you are constantly distracted and only half finish projects. Plus going for a swim in the sea at lunch—what more can you ask for? You are clearing your brain to take on the rest of the afternoon.

I am very surprised to hear you do not want a geriatric goat farmer. Just think, you could have goat every evening and what is even better is that you can get to know the goat before eating it.

Life here is good. My boss managed to burn the store into the ground within a few months of me being on maternity leave so I am trying to sort it out while still being on maternity leave.

Lucy did sleep through the night but the past month not so much. I was expecting to be very very tired but maybe years of tour management has hardened me because I am not finding it very exhausting. I think what also helps is that because she is so good natured I just take her everywhere. She has been to two concerts this week already.

Love—Kate

Mid-morning, I go to the smallest bank in the world, a tiny office just off the square, and after waiting a short while I find out that the problem is nothing to do with my card. The bank machine has been "upgraded" and now doesn't take foreign cards, so they must wait for the technician to come. It could be awhile. The woman in the bank is very sweet.

"We can still give you money here in the office, with the chip and pin, but unfortunately the commission is a little expensive." It's a nice apology, and really the extra commission pales next to the horrors of the exchange rate these days. Best not to think about it, and just take the money and run. She asks where I'm staying and we have a pleasant chat— she moved here six years ago from Rhodes and enjoys the slow pace of life. You've got to love a bank that's smaller than my kitchen.

Happy to be moneyed again, I go shopping for frivolities such as bleach—my bathroom drains are a little whiffy, which I suspect is a combination of heat and not having been used for a while before I moved in—and washing powder. I try every shop and they all have only powder for washing by hand, unless you want to buy industrial-size boxes. I discuss the problem with the chap in the Mini Market, and we agree with a shrug that the powders are probably all about the same. I am finally able to do some laundry while I get back to the computer. Then I hang my clean sheets to dry in the sun, which reminds me of all those years ago in Santorini.

Manolis picks me up, looking a little more relaxed in loose shorts and a T-shirt this time. We drive across the island toward Ayios Andonis. Along the way, they're making a ditch for some sort of pipe all along the roads, and some unfortunate man is spending entire days just sweeping away the dust left by the machines.

"What a job!" I remark.

"Ah, he is Albanian," responds Manolis, as if that explains everything. For many years now, Albanian immigrants have taken over the lower-paid jobs that Greeks would prefer not to do, making a better life for themselves here or sending money back home.

We turn left past the old windmill and continue uphill, stopping before the road winds up and around to the monastery to follow a track instead, and park outside the peacock garden. They're squawking, and Manolis observes how funny it is that such a beautiful bird has such an ugly cry. Apparently it's the mayor who brought the peacocks here. The mayor must be a very interesting person. He's the one who allowed the notorious same-sex marriages to take place here; the Greek TV stations who reported the scandalous event only wanted to film "outraged locals," Vangelis told me the other day—when he wasn't outraged, they didn't use his clip.

The tall, spiky plants, gray sand, and the squawks of peacocks make for an otherworldly scene. At the far end is a path onto the headland and then down again to a little stony cove with good snorkeling. Manolis has brought me his spare snorkel and mask as well as a wetsuit, which I put on over my bikini and T-shirt, and as we swim out together along the rocky shoreline, he points out the different types of fish. I get close to some long, thin *fikopsaria*, with long noses, swimming in formation like fighter jets; when straight, they look like short spears, with a delicate bow-shaped fin at the back like a poison barb. They spot us, turn swiftly and change color instantly, first to stripy camouflage and then to palest gray, heading out into the deeper water.

We then see black fish with spikes around them, known as *yermani* or Germans, tropical fish that came here just after the war. In a crevice in the rock we find the bright orange tendrils of anemones; they hardly look real, their waving orange hair emerging from white cylinders—until you go near them and the hair disappears inside. Everywhere there are the black spiky mounds of sea urchins, and the shore is folds of volcanic rock.

I swim quite far but start to feel cold and head back alone while Manolis continues. It's a rare cloudy day, quite cool, and the bay looks peaceful all gray, with mountains rising up all around. There's no sign of humanity, just a lonely cormorant bobbing up occasionally then diving back down again. I feel a chill when I get out, but the rocks still have the heat of the sun so I pull off the wetsuit and am just leaning against a big slab of rock to absorb its warmth when Manolis returns.

"Remove the shirt, is ridiculous to keep the wet clothes. On *Titanic*, many people die not from the water but from the cold."

I don't think this cold is quite of *Titanic* proportions. But I do as I'm told.

"It's so beautiful here," I say.

"Of course."

He tells me to put my towel on the beach mat next to his, but I insist on keeping them apart. He seems a little miffed but it's hard to tell; maybe that's just his demeanor. I'm not going to let it bother me. There's some black oil on the beach and I get some on me, but he shows me it's easily removed using sun oil. Walking back, Manolis points out various things along the way. "This type of flower stays for a long time when you take it in your house."

"I love the smell of these herbs," I comment.

"Eh, for us, is nothing special, this."

Back home, I make a salad to sustain me for the afternoon—juicy big tomatoes, lettuce, green pepper, feta and olive oil, oregano and thyme—and go back to my desk refreshed and happy.

That evening after work, I meet Manolis at his apartment so we can go for a beer together. I stand inside while he gets everything he needs. The first thing I notice is the smell—fish. It turns out he is drying a piece of eel skin from a particularly large one he caught recently. Right next to the door is an enormous stack of different fishing rods and harpoons. There are shelves absolutely stuffed to the gills with boxes and books, and a desk set up with two computers, and every available surface is covered with exam papers and textbooks.

At the café, we sit in the corner with a couple of small beers and a dish of peanuts and somehow get onto talking about England. Even though he's never been to England, Manolis seems to think he has the English perfectly summed up, because he met someone once who had an English girlfriend, and he sniggers telling the story of the guy going to her family's house for dinner and the only sound being the clinking of cutlery on plates.

"But, Manoli, I don't know anyone like that!" It's such a cliché, and sounds like a scene from *My Big Fat Greek Wedding*, which makes me wonder about the authenticity of the story. "It's amazing you know so much about the English when you've never actually been there."

"Thank you."

"I'm joking!" But he seems fairly convinced.

Afterward, as I head home, I stop in at the bar to chat with Rob for a while, feeling rather defensive about England and needing a bit of a laugh. Thanasis comes by and gives me a bit of a telling-off in his sign language for abandoning him and going out with other people when I could be eating with him. He's not really angry. I smile and offer an apology. Maybe we'll have dinner another time.

⁓

Tired in the morning, I sit down at the computer to do my work, stretch a bit in the sun on the terrace, and have a productive morning. Manolis sees me at the beach at lunchtime and comes over to join me. I was rather hoping to have some time to myself. Yawning, I tell him I stayed up too late.

"I am like grandmother," he says. "Except one night a year stay up late for *paniyiri* at Easter Saturday, I always have enough food and sleep. For this I will live to one hundred years."

I think I'd rather have a bit of fun from time to time, personally… I think I'm a bit more of a Vangelis type. I decide not to pursue the topic but to go for a long swim. Manolis follows, and I pull ahead, trying to hint that I'd rather swim alone for a while. After days of snorkeling it feels good to stretch out with long strokes across this big, open bay. I swim as far as Bozi, the nightclub right at the edge of the village that I've never yet seen open, then meet him in the water as we're swimming back.

"You are swimming like a dolphin," says Manolis. "And I swim like a duck." I giggle. He tends to do a kind of doggy paddle in the water until he finds something of interest on the sea bed, and then dives down—a bit like a duck, it's true. Because the bay here is mostly sandy, there's not so much to see, only tiny fish. He has to go to other places of course to catch big fish.

"So where do you find octopus?" I ask.

"Everywhere."

"But I mean, how do you find them?"

He pauses, thinks about how to explain. "You look for some little white rocks, is the nest, octopus hide inside."

Swimming back, he dives down and finds a big, beautiful shell half buried in the sand, which he puts in the net bag he wears around his waist while swimming. Maybe that's why he wears the other bag-on-a-belt on land. I swim on ahead again for the exercise, letting my eyes wander over all the details in the mountains around. By the time I get back to my towel, I've been in the water for forty minutes and am ready to rest.

Just as I've taken off my aqua shoes, he beckons me to come back into the water, pointing down to the sea bed. He must have found something interesting. I dash back in, putting on the snorkel and mask again, and try to see what he's pointing at—a rock with a little cave underneath, and something orangey-brown inside. Then suddenly he plunges down, kicking with his flippers, pulls up the rock, and in a flash he is back up with a small brown octopus in his hand, which he hands over to me.

I'm holding an octopus.

"Is not dangerous," he says.

It's small, and delicate, and the little suckers on its tentacles tickle my fingers as it writhes around gracefully. Manolis shows me how to stroke the octopus's head, which feels incredibly soft and smooth. It crawls around my hand, ever so lightly sticking to me, and seems to be trying to decide if my hands are a comfortable new home or not. I am so excited that as I try to keep my head underwater and hold onto the octopus without hurting it, I keep swallowing water through the snorkel and half choking. Manolis takes it back and the octopus decides it's had enough of this game, shoots purplish-black ink at us, and makes its escape down to the deep.

When I come up for air and can breathe normally again, I am still giggling and have a big grin on my face.

"Thank you!"

"Is only small one, half-kilo. It is illegal to take this out. But I want to show you. You look like a little child when you take the octopus."

Eventually, I have to go back to my desk, but having held an octopus takes away all semblance of stress for the rest of the day—I deal very well with anything that comes my way, even managing long-distance to smooth over a minor tiff between colleagues back in the office, emailing suggestions to one and then the other. Working from a tiny Greek island makes me better at my job, I am sure of it. And I'm entertaining my colleagues with tales of men on mopeds and now an octopus I held in my hands.

That evening, I shut down the computer at eight and walk beyond the lights of the village. There's a pink sunset, and I breathe in this heartbreakingly beautiful view of mountains and waves. As I walk back, some young guys at a bar are playing loud Greek music, and when they see me smile they beckon me in, but I'm too tired and just wave and keep walking. I see Vangelis at Pantelis's restaurant, and join him for a little while. They've been making arrangements to kill some goats in the morning; if it rains again, it will make this job harder as the animals won't need to come down from the mountain to drink water but will get moisture from the wet grass instead. Pantelis has given him half a chicken to eat, too much, so he's wrapped up the leftovers in foil to take home and feed to the cats.

I'm exactly halfway through my month in Greece. I think it will be very hard to leave.

CHAPTER TEN

The Sound of the Sea

The next night around nine o'clock there's a knock at the door. It's Rob from downstairs.

"Jen, I'm really sorry to bother you, and I'm sorry for the short notice, but um, we've suddenly got really busy—would you be interested in working for a couple of hours?"

"Sure! I'd love to. I'll be down in fifteen minutes."

Back when we were discussing the rental of the flat by email, I hadn't been entirely sure how long I'd be staying. If my office hadn't allowed me to take a month away in Greece, I had considered giving up my job entirely and maybe working in a hotel for the summer before deciding what to do next. Rob mentioned they'd just taken on someone to help out in the bar for the summer season, July to September, but he'd let me know if something came up before then. It had crossed my mind that it would be nice to have a break from the kind of work that you base your career reputation on and do some good old hard labor for a few months on a Greek island. In retrospect, I've always thought one of the best jobs I ever had was the one in Santorini, when dressing for work meant putting on my swimsuit, arriving at work meant stepping out onto that gorgeous terrace, and I could get some exercise cleaning rooms and then go swimming in the afternoon. Throughout my late teens I cleaned kitchens, served food, cleaned houses, served drinks to earn extra cash. I haven't done that sort of work since my early twenties, and maybe I've forgotten how hard it is, but I do worry sometimes that I spend too much time at a desk with a computer. So I'd said I'd be happy to help out if they needed me.

I have a shower and go downstairs to take on a big pile of dishes and pans that need washing. While she cooks, Annie tells me about how she used to sew theater costumes, then sold the business and started working on a doctorate—never imagining she'd be cooking in a restaurant in Greece for a living. It's funny where life and a love of a Greek island can take us. She leaves eventually to see her friend who just arrived from England, thanking me as otherwise she'd be washing dishes till midnight. I finish drying dishes and mop the floor clean and, oddly, it makes me feel young again. It's only a few hours, of course, a million miles from working a whole season. When he's not too busy in the bar, Rob comes back into the kitchen and we compare notes on our misspent teenage years drinking Blue Bols and lemonade in northern nightclubs.

⁓

The mornings smell sweet when you live next door to a bakery. Sitting on my terrace in a bikini, I think about the luxury of having two more weeks on this beautiful island. I love the wildness, the obscure paths to deserted coves, the freedom and emptiness and sheer space.

Manolis picks me up at lunchtime and is playing a compilation tape of eighties pop in the car. It feels weird listening to Abba while driving across the arid landscape of Tilos. He says it reminds him of being a teenager, and he wishes he could go back to that time. That sounds sad to me, that he would wipe away everything that is his life now to be a teenager again. I'm not sure I'd want to relive the extreme ups and downs of my teens and twenties—perhaps that sounds worse. I remember how happy I was the evening I turned thirty, single but surrounded by a group of friends, relaxed, enjoying dinner at a favorite restaurant.

He's been marking exams, which shouldn't be too arduous a task given that the whole secondary school has only about two dozen students. He slows down as we see a long black snake crossing the road. Apparently this is the season for them. We drive to Eristos, turning right to park at the end of the beach. He still has a habit of making sure the car is locked, even though there's not much scope for car theft around here, there being only one road and all. To get off the island, a visiting thief would have to wait for a ferry in full view of everyone, including the police, and register it on the boat.

We walk up a steep and shingly path, past a solitary house, over the headland, and then down a tricky goat track toward Ayios Petros. The half-hour walk is through empty hills covered with fragrant herbs, whose names seem lovelier in Greek: *thimari*, *rigani*, and *faskomilo*. The pink-flowered oleander, or *pikodafni*, grow in riverbeds, showing where the water flows from the mountain down to the sea after rain. Since I told Manolis I'm interested in learning more about the island, he's constantly pointing out plants and trees, and whether they're good for feeding to pigs or for curing diarrhea or constipation—people must have had a lot of stomach complaints in the old days. Walking to the beach, I receive a lecture on why Greece has so many more plants than England (apparently in the last ice age, the ice stopped in northern Greece).

There's a fair bit of plastic rubbish washed up on shore, sadly, and the print isn't all in Greek—some of it looks like Arabic. We keep going to find a sheltered spot, and I clear away the rubbish. We swim around to another beach, which has spectacular cliffs of purple bauxite and green copper, and pink boulders streaked with veins of white and crystal. When he gets out of the water, Manolis says, "I have surprise," and pulls out of his bag a lovely shell that he's found on the sea bed: like a conch, it can be turned into a horn, and is called *bourou*. We rest on the sand after the long swim, and he gets some Papadopoulos biscuits out of his rucksack, the cigar-shaped ones with dark chocolate filling.

I eat a couple and he offers more.

"Take it."

"No, I'll get fat!" Why is everyone always trying to feed me?

"You know the joke?" asks Manolis. "The man goes to the doctor and says, 'I think I'm dying.' The doctor says, 'Do you drink?' The man says no. 'Do you eat too much?' The man says no, just a little food and very healthy food only. 'Do you go with women?' asks the doctor. 'Oh no,' says the man. 'Well,' asks the doctor, 'why do you want to live?'"

I'm peeling oranges with my teeth and fingers, which he says is wrong, and he shows me how to do it properly— carefully and laboriously with a knife, making incisions down the sides and around the top. Apparently it's so you don't get the bitterness on your fingers. I've never noticed bitterness. I'm sure there's a parable there about our different ways of living. We stay until the sun is going down behind the mountain, around six, then walk back past goats that make me laugh by jumping up on the dry stone wall and walking along it. We disturb gray-brown birds that fly up out of the scrub to either side of the path. *Perdika*, says Manolis.

"*Perdika* must be partridge," I say, thinking back to that conversation in Rhodes.

"No, it is another name. The famous one is Scottish whisky. In Greece we say 'catch me a *perdika*' to mean pour me a Scotch whisky."

Ah, grouse then. I'm pretty sure *perdika* and partridge are related words, surely it must be the same family, but he says absolutely not. It's not worth pressing the point.

We pass the solitary house again, where a Greek man lives with his Ukrainian wife. The Dodecanese islands are actually closer to Odessa than to England. Manolis tells me about a Ukrainian woman who used to be a scientist at Chernobyl; when he met her here, she was washing dishes in a restaurant. He sees this as a bad thing. I look at the stunning view across Eristos and say it's not such a bad place to be washing dishes, especially after Chernobyl.

"It is very awful here, working only a few months in the summer," he says. He's probably right, but I'm sad that he seems to have no room for dreams of adventure. For me, after the stresses of university, it was wonderful cleaning rooms in Santorini for a summer. It's a different perspective. I would talk to him about this, but we don't seem to be doing very well at exchanging ideas; the discussion seems a little one way. The other day, he picked some delicious mulberries from a tree and told me about picking blackberries in his village when he was a kid. I told him it was the same when we were growing up, but he didn't seem interested. I wonder sometimes if the pleasures of spending so much time in a platonic arrangement are beginning to wear thin for him. And yet he seems to want to keep seeing me—so much so that I never get around to seeing anyone else. I really must make an effort to.

Later, I walk to the shop. There are several a few minutes' walk away from my flat, all stocking more or less the same things. The boxes of vegetables slowly deteriorate over the week until new supplies come in. But it's nice that they stay open late, so you don't ever have to rush to the shops before closing. I buy my usual few oranges and tomatoes, then back home I pour a glass of retsina and sit on the terrace again for a while. It's still hot but breezy, and sweet, tinkly jazz music plays downstairs.

~

So nice picture! Wow, do you swim in the sea? It looks quite deep and cold! And there lives octopus?? *_* That sounds brilliant. Do they eat octopus sushi? Just wondering ^^

Have a good weekend~*
Hanyoung

It's a message from a Korean girlfriend back in England, which I find when I go online to start doing some research about Tilos. I do miss having female friends around, which is why it's good to keep in touch this way. I don't think the Greeks would take to the idea of eating live octopus like the Koreans, and neither do I, though sometimes when I'm swimming I look at a particularly fat and meaty fish and feel hungry.

Because of its many islands, the coastline of Greece is one of the most extensive in the world in relation to land area, along with Japan and Indonesia. And yet in archaic Greece, around the time of Homer, fishing for food was regarded as a last resort. The people on this island supported themselves from the land, growing cereals, chickpeas, almonds, olives, citrus, grapes, and vegetables, and keeping livestock—evident in the ghostly traces of terracing that cover the slopes, and grain threshing circles that are marked out with large stones and found all around.

The main settlement in the eleventh to eighth centuries BC was on the slopes of the hill above what is now Megalo Horio. According to the ancient historian Herodotus, the golden age of Tilos was in the seventh century BC, when the island joined with Lindos in Rhodes to colonize Sicily. Over the next few centuries, Tilos society was still flourishing, as archaeological finds have shown—pottery and exquisite gold jewelry found in gravesites. In the days of classical Greece,

Tilos was famous for producing perfumes—the many ter-
ebinth trees were used for perfumery, medicine, and resin—
but gradually became subject to the influence of the far larger
island of Rhodes. Unfortunately, very few of the archaeological finds are on display yet in Tilos; very little excavation has
taken place, in fact.

One of the most famous inhabitants of Tilos in antiquity
was Irinna, a poet from 350 BC, often compared to Homer
and Sappho, although she lived a few hundred years later.
Her famous poem is "Ilakati," and only four whole verses
survive today: an elegy for her childhood friend Vafkida,
who died at nineteen after she was married and left Tilos. It
spoke of the rich and diverse natural beauty of the island, its
landscapes, and the surrounding Aegean Sea. I'd love to learn
more about the poem, but all I can find is this small amount
of information and a couple of lines translated into English.

I take my usual *volta* down the seafront, saying hello to
familiar faces. It's a hot but windy night, and beautiful. I
stop at one of the cafés to sit outside and read my book with
a beer and a dish of peanuts, vaguely listening to the chat of
the bartenders as they greet people passing by, women with
babies in pushchairs, tourists, the old and the young. On the
way home I see a chap who works with the ferries sitting at a
high table outside the *kafeneion* with a younger friend. They
invite me to join them. It turns out the friend is working in
the bank for a week, while the usual woman's on vacation.

"I think it must be the smallest bank in the world," I say.

"No," he says. "There's an even smaller one in Rhodes, in my village!" He resembles a football player, a tall, goofy-looking guy with a wide smile, while the ferry man is beetle-browed and always appears troubled. It turns out the reason he usually looks quite stressed is that he works practically every day and is often up at four, five, or six in the morning to meet the ferries coming in. In summer he's particularly busy and people from Athens can be especially troublesome, he says; one family changes their return tickets about six times every single year, deciding they're going to stay another day. I remember a story I heard, that one year he had a pretty blond Swedish assistant, and all the local men kept finding excuses to go check out the ferry times.

The two of them make great company, and we move on to another bar with a big upstairs terrace and good music. The drinks arrive with two bowls of nuts.

"Keep the *fistikia* away from me!" says the bank man and we all agree. One of the hazards of going out in Tilos is that every drink comes with a bowl of peanuts or some other salty concoction—Greeks prefer not to drink without eating something—and once you start eating them, they're too tempting to resist. The ferry man moves them all to the other end of the table, and his friend asks if he could just have one, so he passes him just one. Then he asks for another one.

"I can't eat anything without putting on weight," says the ferry man. "I looked at my mother's spaghetti yesterday and couldn't touch it—it goes straight here," he moans, holding his stomach.

It's hot, so we're drinking our red wine with ice, which feels wrong but necessary. The ferry man is trying to give up smoking so he has one of those fake cigarettes to puff on, but more often than not he lights up a real one.

I don't even try putting my hand in my pocket when it comes to paying the bill as I know it's futile. It's late, but the ferry man insists on driving us up to the small holiday villas he lets out to show us around. I have visions of goats crossing the road and us swerving off the road into the sea, but he knows the road better than anyone and there's no traffic, after all, given that no one else lives up here. It's been a fun evening. As I arrive home at two a.m., I notice the baker is already at work next door. We forget about all the hard work that goes on behind the scenes sometimes.

I have to make time to do some thinking, or rather, maybe, to clear my head of thoughts in order to remember what makes me happy. Back home, when I said to a friend that I was coming to the island to think things through, he said maybe I shouldn't think too much. And what I really need to do, perhaps, harks back to a Buddhist teaching: whatever you are looking for, you must start by letting go.

Still, there's something I really do have to address.

I've been banging on about the subject for a while, but now it would be irresponsible not to step back and reflect on possibly the most important issue of my life: do I want to see if I can still have children? For so long, I wasn't sure I wanted to be a mother; there are so many reasons not to, after all—the population is too big, the world is going to hell in a handbasket, and I didn't want to give up my freedom just to live near a good school. Funny how things changed as I got to my mid-thirties. What is becoming clear is that I don't want to look back and know I never tried. I may never have been able to have children—who knows? My plan was always to wait until I was with the right person. Now time is running away, and yet you don't know, until you've been with someone for a while, whether you would both want to stay together and have a family. It's not necessary to be part of a perfect couple, though, as Kate is now discovering, for my brave and brilliant friend is now a single mother and coping just fine. I have supportive parents, both of whom have made it clear they would love to be grandparents. Perhaps I could be a mother in a way that feels right to me; I don't coo over babies, can't sing, and don't like playing games—but surely there must be other ways of giving a child the love it needs.

So as my month passes here, I am coming around to the

idea that I'm not going to take contraceptive pills again. I'm not sure what will happen next, but I want my body to have a chance of being ready.

It's also becoming clear that I could probably live here in Tilos. The nice thing about being single is there's only me to think about. After the game of snakes and ladders of the last few years, the ups and downs of relationships, life feels so much simpler here hiding on the beach, finding my freedom.

I find there is something calming about being so close to the sea all the time. I sometimes go down to the seafront and sit on one of the benches. I understand how the older folks are quite content just watching the yachts and ferries and fishing boats come and go.

It's funny to look back and think that if I'd studied Greek at university as I'd originally wanted rather than being steered toward a "better" degree, or if I'd stayed on teaching English in Greece instead of chasing the career, I might have gotten to a place like this a lot sooner. Would it have been for better or worse? I can never know. I've learned so much along the way, have had wonderful adventures, and possess the where-withal to find new, challenging directions in my work. There are so many different ways a life can go. Yet here I am again, looking at the Aegean Sea.

Every day or so, Manolis and I still go for an afternoon swim, and I'm learning for myself about the trails to the beaches and the fish. I now know which sea urchins are ready to eat and which fish, patterned like a rock, shows the way to an octopus nest. I love swimming around the rocks underwater, watching how the sun plays on them and the sea floor drops away.

And then a real treat: Manolis finds starfish. The first is a fat red one, barely moving, though when I hold it in my hand it puts its feelers out ever so gently. I hold it carefully for a while and then drop it and watch it float slowly down to the sandy sea bed. The next one he finds is dark brown with long, thin legs, which it loops around my fingers, creeping and elegantly curling, until at last, unsure of this resting place, it propels itself away. I swim back to where I dropped the red one and see that it fell upside down and is still ever so slowly turning itself back the right way up. I wonder if that's what's happening to me.

CHAPTER ELEVEN

A Change of Season

anolis dishes out mounds of octopus, purple on the outside and snow-white inside. "Not like in a restaurant," he grins, "where you get three small pieces."

This isn't barbecued, as it was last time I ate it at a beachside taverna, but boiled, then chopped into small pieces and marinated in oil and vinegar. "Taste," he says. It's firm but tender, delicious. To go with it there are young shoots from *gramithia* trees, boiled and kept in brine with a bit of garlic, made by his mother when she came to stay before Easter, and fat juicy olives, a tomato salad, and hearty homemade bread.

He's also lit candles and got out some tall wineglasses, and it's all arranged precariously on a slightly shaky plastic table. I've brought a bottle of white wine from Rhodes, and as he's reaching to give me another helping of octopus and explaining how you must salt onions and rinse them to take away the sharpness before putting them in a salad, he manages to knock an entire glass of wine all over me. I assure him I'll be fine. He tries covering the pool of wine on the floor with newspaper, but I feel this bachelor-style method is not quite working, and wipe it up with a cloth instead. Then, to dry off, I ask if he wants to go out for a coffee.

"No, I don't like so much. People say 'Are you Greek?' because I don't drink coffee, I don't smoke..."

This plays into my favorite Greek joke about why Greek men have big noses: so they can smoke in the shower. But in other ways—his pride in the food he prepares, and his insistence on doing things in a particular way—Manolis seems to me about as Greek as it gets.

The wind picks up toward the end of May and the bay is a deep, vivid blue with white waves. The masts and trim are clanking on the yachts trapped by the weather. One day I watch a boat in the harbor unloading some kind of building material, perhaps dry cement, and the wind blows it all over the fancy yachts. The waves become big, and I wonder what it's like in winter when they're crashing into shore. If the sea is too rough, the ferries can't get to the island or stop to let people off. Across the water I can see details on the rocky mountains of Turkey and the neighboring island of Halki, which were obscured by heat haze a few days ago; today I could almost reach out and touch them. Everything is brilliantly clear but it's a restless time, no respite from the wind, and it feels like the weather is bringing a change of season. In the square are lush lemon trees and green shrubs with red flowers, but the mountains are now mostly gray and brown, the last bits of green on the terraces fading with the approach of the dry season, spring changing to summer. White bougainvillea flowers tumble across a stone terrace in the wind.

It's tempting to think the boats won't be running and I won't be able to leave, but it takes a lot to stop a big ferry.

I could have used another month here if I could have taken the time off. I concentrate on knowing now how good life can be here, and knowing that I can come back, whether it's for a month once or twice a year, or finding a way to work from here. Next August the mortgage on my flat at home should be reduced a little, and I could cover that by letting it out… I am thinking of this not as an end, but a beginning. I'm not sure what yet, but somehow it's a next step in my life.

In the morning, I'm awake at six when the sea is calm again, gleaming. The east hill is all soft contours as the sun hasn't hit it yet. I'm at my desk soon after, tinkering with a freelance project. I work until the lure of the bakery is too strong, then take a break and go to stretch on the terrace, ready to see what treats they have. I look down into red and yellow bushes shaped like fans. Another is smooth and empty, with just one little road going to the chapel. I'm trying not to stress about leaving here, but it's hard. I want to grasp every possible hour of sunshine, every view of the hills from every angle.

In the evening, I flick on the radio, have a shower, still loving that I can see the sea from my shower that smells of soap made from Tilos flowers, then change into fresh clothes and stand outside watching the last of the sun setting, a glass of retsina in hand. Later, after reading for a while, I walk down the seafront to the end to see the stars. Gathering around the streetlamps are thousands of May bugs.

I have waited until late to come out, hoping the livelier music bars will be open as this is my last Saturday, and the summer season should be beginning. There have been reports that Bozi, the nightclub at the far end of the village, is now open on Friday and Saturday nights. I'd love to dance.

My phone buzzes and it's a message from home that makes me laugh: "Oi, stop snogging that Greek waiter!" It's from Matt. Having met in the Park Tavern through John a year ago—they were mates—we would occasionally bump into one another early on a Friday or Saturday evening at the Dining Room, and chat about books and traveling. He's usually dressed in a suit and drinking a cocktail when I pass by the window of the bar, having been off traveling for his work during the week, but his real passion apparently is taking a tent up to the mountains in Scotland and just wandering on his own. It's funny and nice to hear from him out of the blue.

All across the square, people are watching basketball on television. I stop for a while at the edge of a fairly lively group of people outside one of the seafront bars, where they're playing some good music, but I don't go in; it doesn't feel like a place to sit on my own. When it's reasonably late I walk down toward the end of the village, swatting away the flies as I pass each streetlight. It turns out reports of Bozi opening have been greatly exaggerated. It is dark and quiet, no sign that it's opening tonight; maybe it's still much too early. I look in at the seafront cafés again as I walk back but end up with a glass of wine and a book at home instead. It's not exactly a Saturday night to write home about, but I'm happy.

❧

I have created the perfect indulgent breakfast: a huge bowl of organic muesli with milk, loads of thick full-fat yogurt and chunks of halva, a sweet cake made from crushed sesame seeds and honey, best consumed in the shade of a sunny, warm terrace on a quiet Sunday morning. I used to gorge on breakfasts like this long ago in Athens, followed by fresh, warm, crusty bread from the bakery.

I invite Manolis for tea on the terrace that is still mine for a day and he tells me that the trees I've been looking out at every day are eucalyptus and magnolia. Then we walk up to the monastery of Politissa, where I came alone on my first or second day here. It's so much hotter now, but peaceful in the hills, with the late afternoon sunlight on the fields and ravines, except for Manolis bossily pointing out the path. There's a festival up at Politissa in late August with dancing, music, and food. The island really comes to life in summer with the festivals, when the sea is warm enough for even Greek people to swim, and the fruit ripens.

I came here in the spring, the season when things were waking up, which seems somehow appropriate. Manolis tells me that in some ways I have brought him back to life. For several years he has led a very solitary existence, and kept to his routine of school and fishing. Just by being here and spending time with him during this period of bringing happiness back into my life, I've brought a little happiness back into his life too. There's no doubt our times together have meant a lot to him, and perhaps he wants something more to develop in the future. He says, "Whether I see you again in one week, or six months, or ten years, or never... Friend or acquaintance or whatever you want of me, I am here for you. You broke my shell, and for that I thank you."

This side of him appeals to me very much. I believe he really does care about me. I wish he had a more positive outlook on life, but he has been a good friend in a lot of ways and we like doing similar things. I sometimes wonder if that shouldn't be enough for me. And he does already live where I might like one day to live.

In the evening, he is meeting a friend of his who used to be a teacher here and has now moved away to the island of Kalymnos, a few hours away by ship. They meet at a trendy coffee and ice cream place on the seafront that's always full of young Greek men. It's hilarious how much Greek men love their sweet things. I join them as they're finishing off some crepes with ice cream and chocolate sauce. I order a beer— they only have large bottles so I offer Manolis half.

"What, alcohol with sweet? Ha!"

Uh, fine, you're welcome, mate. Just when I start warming toward him, he has a fine way of putting a stop to it. I shrug. Greek people do tend to have quite clear ideas on what can be consumed with what, and how; you can't drink orange juice with coffee, or say cheers with coffee, even a frothy iced coffee. I think in some ways I'm quite lucky to come from a culture that doesn't have such strict rules. I enjoy listening to the friends' conversation, though only understanding parts of it. They switch to English for my benefit for a while. Manolis once crewed on a boat for his friend and tells a story about taking a big fishing hook out of his finger himself using a camping gas bottle—something to do with freezing the finger. In case of emergency or global disaster, it's clear he would be able to help us all survive.

He's certainly helped me to get to know the island, to fall

in love with it, and therefore perhaps he's helped me to get strong again. For that I'm grateful.

~

It's my last morning, and I sit at my usual shady table in the middle of the square. There's a tortoiseshell cat with a glossy coat curled up on the chair opposite. It jumps up when I approach but can't be bothered to go far. Distracted for a while by my backpack, it finds the straps very amusing to play with, then leaps back onto the chair, slumps down half in the sun and half in the shade, and closes its eyes, extremely comfortable with its head curled into the edge of the seat showing its snowy white chin.

I passed the fish man with his curly black hair on my way into the square, with some big orange-red fish on ice in the back of his flatbed truck—*skorpio*, he said. A Chinese man who sells cheap toys is showing his wares to the old lady sitting with her walker in the shade of the tree. Oafish male tourists are walking around with bare chests; one has long reddish hair in a ponytail and a tattoo over one of his nipples. What makes them think it's OK to walk around like that? It's fun sitting in the square, though, watching people doing their shopping, women calling their husbands and children for lunch. *Ippocrati! Ela tho...* Hippocrates, come here!

My lunch is a huge salad using up all the vegetables in

the fridge, with lots of lemon squeezed into it and delicious tomatoes straight from the Eristos vegetable truck. What an extraordinary month it's been. I love this place, and I've found the happiness I was looking for in very simple things: yogurt and honey, tomatoes and thyme, and of course the sea and the mountains and the people.

I would love to be taking the ferry and then getting straight on my flight, but unfortunately because of the timing of the ferries I have to spend two days in Rhodes, a sort of decompression zone between my wild island life and going back to work. However, in the morning, getting on that ferry is made easier by the fact that half of Tilos is getting on it too: the baker, the lady from the shop, the young waiters from the café in the square, a couple of teachers. It's a popular boat as you can do your errands in Rhodes while the boat goes to Karpathos or Kastellorizo, then catch it back the same day.

I take lots of photos as the ferry pulls away. The time has gone so quickly, but it's filled me with hope for the future. And as Manolis says, "Hope dies the last."

After Tilos, Rhodes town is claustrophobic and overwhelming: the beaches are covered in sunbeds; there are so many people and shops and petrol stations and restaurants and pleasure boats. So much to buy, so much choice! At lunch, I already miss having my own Greek kitchen, just as I'm missing the emptiness and simplicity and wildness of Tilos. Here there is crazy traffic and harassed drivers, although of course there are still the stunning buildings of the old town. Everything is so much busier than a month ago, and Rhodes seems heaving with tourists compared to Tilos—but then so would most places.

I arrive at Eudoxia Pension looking windswept and scruffy and, in Greek, ask the landlady on the stairs if they have a room.

"You were here a month ago, weren't you?! Where did you go—Tilos… ?"

I am swept up in a huge welcome like a long-lost relative and made to sit down on the terrace with a Greek coffee and some nice brown bread and cheese and an orange while she gets my room ready. Her husband sits with me, tells me there's a celebration for somebody's birthday later and I'm invited to join them.

CHAPTER TWELVE

Meanwhile, on Another Part of the Planet

*I*t's surprisingly OK to be home after my month away. For a start, it's early summer. I already feel tanned and healthy. I've got the challenge of my new four-day working week. And I've made it back just in time for Joy's last party at the Park Tavern, a special occasion in itself and a chance to catch up with some friends.

I'm not sure what to expect of this party. Joy and Richard were running the Park Tavern together since before I moved to this town five years ago. The Park was my first haven here: a wood-paneled, elegant old pub with no music or television, it was a welcoming place to sit on my own in the corner, drink a pint and read a book, and never be given strange looks.

The place was full of characters, not least Richard himself, who was only interested in having the kind of customers he felt comfortable with—people who were polite, interesting, eccentric, respectful—and was fully prepared to ask you to leave otherwise. It was in that sense a kind of club; if Richard didn't like you, you didn't get served. I watched him once take to task a very correct Austrian tourist because he asked for his own drink before he asked for his wife's, but then they spent the next hour all laughing and chatting. Another time a group of rather boorish toffs came in and sneeringly asked for some sort of trendy drink; Richard just shooed them out the door. He enjoyed a glass of wine himself, which he'd hide from his wife, Joy, when she came out from the kitchen, a habit that turned into a bit of a charade. He didn't need the hassle of a busy pub; he'd worked in restaurants with some of the best chefs around, had seen the glory, and now was happy with a quiet life surrounded by people he liked. Then, last year, Richard was diagnosed with cancer.

For a long time now, Richard has been absent, living upstairs as he endures rounds of treatment. Joy has run the pub herself, and to all of us the bittersweet pleasure has been seeing Joy come out of the kitchen and out of her shell. Joy, from Thailand, is young and attractive but absolutely no-nonsense with the same wicked sense of fun as Richard, in spite of everything that she is going through. She also has an ineffable ability to look after people well. Since early this year, with energy that comes from goodness knows where, she has run the occasional party for regulars with music and themed fancy dress—gangsters and molls, vicars and tarts. It's been an inspired way to help everyone through a particularly grim winter; most Januarys she and Richard would close the pub for a month and go to Thailand, where they'd planned to retire in a few years, but this year he hasn't been well enough. If it seems strange sometimes that Richard is upstairs unable to join in, it is also a relief to see Joy having a brief respite from running the pub, looking after Richard—and watching him waste away. The treatment hasn't been able to stop the cancer, and after this weekend they will give up the pub, and the flat above it, and move to another house.

So it is a special party, a tribute to Richard. A group of us has become much closer during these last six months. No one can quite bear to imagine that Richard won't get better. I've made most of my friends in town—except for those I know from work or the gym—through the Park Tavern. The Park has always been a bolt-hole of civilization, a refuge from the dreariness of corporate chains. I miss Richard's sardonic laughter, his stories. He was always ready with a jibe—when I walked up to the bar all glowing and healthy after a holiday alone he asked loudly if I was back from "shagging my way across Ibiza"—but he also looked after me, asked after my mum and dad, sympathized when I was unlucky in love, and served me a half-measure of wine if I didn't want a full one late at night. It's hard to put your finger on anything in particular; I just miss him. Things simply aren't the same with him not around.

It's a big turnout, and people drift between the dance floor and the bar. It's great to see so many friends again. There's no fancy dress theme this time, but partway through the evening Joy circulates among the groups of people, chatting away and handing out paper bow ties to everyone. Richard was never seen without a nice shirt and a bow tie. Suddenly there is a flurry of excitement as everyone is asked to gather outside, and Richard is waving at us all from the open upstairs window, wearing an outrageous pink wig, while we all stand there raising our glasses to him and waving back in our bow ties.

~

Hi Kate,

Sorry, wasn't sure how much you knew about Richard. He poked his head out of the upstairs window during the party and chatted with us—his sense of humor is still there! But he is looking tired and apparently is very weak. Who knows what a change of scene might do, though? It is hard to believe. He was my wicked uncle from when I first moved here.

Current beau is barely worth naming, so unlikely to last given my recent form, so I have been referring to him as the

Man Who Will Be the Next Man to Break My Heart. He's lovely, likes hugs, lots of fun, way too young. It's doomed and beautiful. Am on my work-for-myself-Fridays now! Such a pleasure.

Hope all is well there.

Jx

Jen,

Oh I know all too well "The Man Who Will Be the Next Man to Break My Heart." I would love to meet one right now.

Kate

During those warm days of early summer, Ben, the young man I'd met a few days before my month in Tilos, is an unexpected sweet presence in my life. The six months I'd designated for celibacy back in the dark days of winter are nearing an end, and I feel the month away on a remote island has helped me to achieve distance from the previous despondency and vulnerability, to regain a sense of what I want and who I am. I'd tried to put this potential new love interest out of my mind while I was away, but we spoke a couple of times and he insisted on coming to the airport to meet me.

Ben seems rather special. He clearly wants to make a go of things, pick up where we left off, and he's not totally perturbed by the news that I came off the contraceptive pill while I was away. His dream is to live somewhere fairly wild, possibly abroad, where he can build a house and a family. But in the meantime he's busy with many different projects of his own. I like the way he's active and creative, though it doesn't leave us with much time to spend together—unless I want to follow and join him. I often do, but not always.

My phone has been acting up since I returned, and when it stops working one day and I have to buy a new one, I am frustrated trying to find my way through the maze of permutations of differing deals out there. I was, after all, probably one of the last people in England to get a mobile phone and I'm not interested in learning about them—I just want something simple that works.

"Why don't you get one of these?" Ben says of the snazzy bells-and-whistles affair he carries around, doing all sorts of things that I can't imagine wanting to do with a phone.

"Because it's more than I can afford—I've gone down to four days a week, remember? And I don't want to sign up for a twenty-four-month contract. I don't know where I'll be in twenty-four months!"

I don't realize I'm doing it at the time, but he points out I've been unwilling to sign long-term contracts for various things lately. I haven't yet decided what to do about Tilos and don't yet know if the new arrangement at work will be right; I want to give myself a bit of freedom. For him, it sounds like I'm off on the next plane.

That's not true, but I am still feeling like part of me is back in Tilos. Maybe in those months of staying away from a relationship, I got used to considering only myself. I try to be more sensitive. I think the time of enforced celibacy may also have given me clearer vision, removed my rose-tinted spectacles when it comes to a new potential partner. When I make arrangements for us to meet up with my friends, he tends to be too busy to make it. I think perhaps these signs are adding up to something, even if it's something he hasn't quite figured out for himself yet. I'm pragmatic about it and decide to see what happens.

Hi Jennifer!

Horrible drizzling weather goes and glittering sunshine comes to London. Nice to go out for a picnic. Should tidy up the office and leave for breathing the fresh air.

Yes, we should meet up before I go. Would you let me know how to get to your house from the station? We eat everything except rocks, metals, clothes, etc… ^^ Also, love to challenge a new world of food. So, never worries! :D

All the best,
Hanyoung

My friend Hanyoung is returning to Korea at the end of the month, having spent a couple of years working in

London. She and her boss invited me for home-cooked Korean food one evening before I went to Tilos, and now it's my turn to figure out a traditional English lunch for them. Eventually I settle on gin and tonics, roast lamb infused with garlic, roasted potatoes, and purple sprouting broccoli, followed by trifle. I buy local organic lamb from the farmers' market, and the vegetables come in my local organic Veg Out delivery—and there are secret ingredients, herbs from Tilos. Ben helps by making gravy, my friend Chris from work engages the Korean guests in conversation while Ben and I fall over one another in my tiny kitchen, and everything gets praised and eaten up. Afterward, we go for a walk into town. Hanyoung is wearing the highest high heels imaginable and funky clothes, looking very cool, and she is perfectly happy taking photographs of everything from the sixteenth-century market cross to a big bug she spots on the ground. She loves England but is terribly homesick for the way of life in Seoul and misses her family.

From living in so many places, I have friends all around the world. Thank goodness for email. Over the years I've sometimes felt homeless, not rooted anywhere, but I'm also lucky to have had homes in many places and to have a wealth of friends—many of whom have traveled and moved around too—who keep in touch over the years.

My Freelance Fridays make the weekends feel longer and the weeks more of a pleasure than before, although summers at work are always busy. The weather throughout June is great, and I spend as much time as I can in the garden I share with the other apartments. There's a day of panic when I realize they don't sell halva in Waitrose, as I'm currently addicted to my halva and yogurt with cereal. Manolis, who's keeping in touch by email and the occasional call, tells me you can make halva with tahini and honey and yogurt, and it works as a substitute until I finally find the other type at a health food shop.

My dad raises his eyebrows when, having arrived for a barbecue at his house with Ben, I get a call from Manolis. What can I say? Having decided I don't really need a man in my life right now, suddenly it seems they're—what's the phrase—like bees to honey?

One Saturday in early July, Ben and I arrange to meet up in the evening to go to a music event. In the afternoon he's going shopping with a female friend quite a way out of town, so we say we'll meet around four o'clock; he'll call when he's on his way back. When four comes and goes, I read in the garden for a bit longer and then walk into town. I run into someone I haven't seen for ages, so we sit outside somewhere and have coffee together. I go home, and when there's still no message, I decide I've had enough. I'll dress up for the evening and enjoy myself with friends anyway, as it's a warm Saturday night. I go to the Park Tavern where there's a small crowd outside enjoying the late sunshine, including Chris, who's been doing temporary work in our office and has become a Park Tavern fan.

He's leaving town tomorrow, so it's great to have chance for a quick farewell beer with him. I had set him up in digs with my friend Mike and they'll be heading out on the town tonight. And Matt is also there, my weekend cocktail friend who sent me the message while I was in Tilos to "stop snogging that Greek waiter!" We've meant to have a glass of wine together for ages, and it looks like I'm free tonight after all. Matt heads around the corner to the Dining Room to wait at the bar while I finish my beer and chat with Chris, then I follow him over there.

Matt will take my mind off things by telling me about some travels he's been doing or planning, often somewhere unusual. Sometimes he just says he's going away and we won't see him for a while. I call him the International Man of Mystery.

I find a bar stool next to him. The Dining Room is a lovely, intimate place, very expensive but worth a visit every now and then; it's where I held my celebration party last summer. As usual, Matt's in a black suit and white shirt, first two buttons undone; I suppose he's the kind of bloke you wouldn't really notice in the street, my age, slightly heavy build, thick dark hair. With a tan, you might even say he looks vaguely Mediterranean. We chat about mutual friends, and I tell him a bit about Tilos. He's never been to Greece, and I try to explain what it was like, then tell him about my new Freelance Fridays.

I confess I'm feeling weird and emotional because of Ben and his strangely unreliable behavior. Matt and I don't often talk about this sort of thing. He has said many times, "I don't do relationships," and although I know he has children somewhere, he really doesn't seem interested in romantic liaisons in the slightest so I normally wouldn't bore him with details. He listens sympathetically, however, as I tell him why I've decided things have to be over with Ben. It's part of my new resolve to take charge and look after myself.

"Can I confide in you?" I ask.

"Course you can, Jen," he says.

I talk about how I did a lot of thinking while I was in Tilos about what my priorities are right now. I tell him a whole lot of mixed-up things, that I'm feeling it might be too late for me to have a family but I want to see if it's still possible. I'm not interested in messing around in a relationship with a person who isn't dependable—I know what I am looking for now. I'm a little upset but I'm also pleased that I can take control of the situation like this. When eventually the source of all this worry answers his phone, having been AWOL for five or six hours, instead of apologizing for going missing and not answering my many calls, he complains about what a bad day he's had because the car broke down. It's just not good enough. I am upset, there's no doubt about it, but better to get the pain over with now. I've decided it's over, and I'll talk to him about it when he has time to see me.

Matt and I decide to go out and sit in a garden some- where, and we find ourselves in a nearby pub, enjoying the last breezes of the evening, sharing a bottle of red. Since I've been opening up to him about all sorts of things, he's talking to me too about himself, things he's never revealed to me or any of our friends about his work and his family. The man I had previously dubbed the International Man of Mystery spends an hour or two spilling all his secrets. He's normally so private, so guarded; we've known one another for a couple of years but I'm suddenly seeing him in a different light.

It's more than a little surreal, which perhaps explains why, before the end of this strange evening, with all that heart-to-heart going on, and perhaps the euphoria that I am control-ling my own destiny by resolving not to let that young man break my heart, it seems like a good idea for Matt and me to kiss. It's quite an innocent sort of kiss but it is undoubtedly a kiss. Oops. Perhaps that last glass of wine wasn't such a good idea, although it took my mind off the pain of finishing with Ben, and at least I feel safe knowing that this is the guy who Doesn't Do Relationships and I'm not going to get embroiled in another doomed fling. He makes sure I get home in one piece and I fall into a dreamless, untroubled sleep.

The next morning, Sunday morning, I cycle down to the beach six miles away. I'm feeling slightly the worse for wear after the drinks last night, but also happy that I'm not moping over bad behavior by a man in my life and talked a lot of stuff through with someone. A good bike ride and then lying on the beach in the sunshine is the perfect pick-me-up, even if it's a little breezy and I need a jumper.

So, there are a couple of things I need to sort out.

Thinking about the end of last night, I smile and cringe at the same time. Let's hope it's not going to be really awkward. Since John and I split up, Matt's sent me the occasional late-night affectionate text after a few martinis while he's waiting for a pizza—hilariously, Matt slurs the words in his texts when he's drunk—but I always ignore them and it's never changed anything between us, which is why it's so easy being friends with him. He sent me a picture of roses on Valentine's Day but then stiffly apologized in case I read too much into it because it was just for fun. This is just an extension of that harmless flirting between friends. I think I'd better call him to reassure him that nothing's changed, but there's no answer when I ring, so I send him a quick text.

He responds, saying he's sent me an email and would I get back to him when I've read it? I know exactly what it'll say. I don't mind, as I really want to stay friends with him. I won't get my email until next day at work as I don't have Internet at home, so I'll deal with it then. In the meantime, the main item of business is that the man who was to be the next man to break my heart is being relieved of his duties, and I need to let him know. There's no word from him all day, and there are still confused emotions inside me, but I tell myself that there are some things you just can't fathom and I have to go with my instincts. I try to snooze on the beach.

After I've cycled back to town, I pass by Ben's house, where he's outside building or repairing something as usual, and he says he's busy but will call me or come over later to talk. But when later comes, there's no word; he gets carried away doing whatever he's doing and forgets. I remember when I was in Greece and he said he'd call and then didn't. At the time I didn't let it bother me because I had Tilos, and the same is still true. I know where to find happiness, and there's still a piece of that island inside me, keeping me strong.

I get to work next morning and open my email from Matt. It's not what I expected.

"I love you," it says.

CHAPTER THIRTEEN

Out of the Blue

He wants to get to know me better, says Matt, if I want to. I've never been so surprised by an email in my life.

Matt is not just some guy I met in a bar one night; we've known one another over a year and have mutual friends. But suddenly everything has changed. He's out of town as usual during the week, so emails fly back and forth between my computer and his phone, up north somewhere apparently. He sends me a poem he wrote for me—about me. I'm bowled over by this new Matt.

We're also incredibly nervous about all this. But next Saturday we catch the train to Portsmouth, where he takes me to giggle at the guinea pigs in Victoria Park, then because we like that so much, we walk to the ferry and take it across to the Isle of Wight to visit Amazon World. The ticket lady at the entrance thinks we've just come from the pub because we're acting so silly, and refuses to believe we're completely sober. Matt makes me laugh so much my stomach hurts, and we spend so long watching the animals that we almost get locked in, only found by chance by one of the staff before they lock the doors. It's pouring rain as we wait for the ferry back in the dark. We're still just friends, keeping our distance, but we're getting used to looking at one another differently.

No one's ever told me they love me out of the blue like that. I can't remember anyone making me laugh so much either. But we also decide that we'll only start seeing one another if we're going to make a proper go of it, try to make it work; there's no point in ruining a good friendship just for a fling.

While he's away on business during the week, we exchange messages again that make my stomach jump when they land in my inbox; it's weird getting used to romantic messages from the guy who used to send me jokey pictures of animals in hats.

It's very odd, I must contact the Internet service provider. You have the same email address as an old friend who used to send me only silly photos of animals dressed up as nuns—very confusing to be receiving gallant offers of dinners instead.

I know that guy. He always wanted to be more than a friend. The comedy cows still exist so if you decide the enigma is not for you, just invite the clown back.

I've always found him interesting, and now I'm realizing he's just so much *fun* too. Yes, a little mad, but funny and interested in everything, and easy to be around. He already loves the Jen he knows, so I just have to be myself.

When he gets back at the weekend, we move from our usual bar stools in the Dining Room and sit outside under an umbrella in the light summer rain, the whole garden to ourselves, and we eat an extraordinary dinner and talk more about everything. He says that if we want to take this any further, he can extract himself from the work abroad so he can be around more.

"It might get a little crazy, but I can assure you we will have a good time," he says. I can imagine. No one's ever bought me a hundred-pound dinner at the Dining Room before, but Matt can afford it. He made John extremely jealous last year by showing him a picture of the Audi R8 he was driving for a while, and he has an apartment in an amazing location overlooking the sea, which he'd even offered to let to me at a very cheap price last winter when I was thinking of making some changes in my life, although I never went round to see it as I wasn't sure if he really meant it. He has another house in town, which he also lets out, and is part-owner of a place in Paris and another in Dubai.

I just find all of this bizarre and funny because Matt is so down to earth. The following night, he orders a taxi to take us to another expensive restaurant in a village close by, and we laugh and talk all evening again. He says he's had feelings for me since the first time he saw me, but I was with someone else. I cycle down to the sea on Sunday afternoon and meet him there and we just sit on the beach together.

I'll never forget being on that beach with you for as long as I live. Like I told you, friend or lover, I'll always be here for you. Lining up some local work so I don't have to go away again.

Meanwhile, I take care of business with the young man who I thought would be the next man to break my heart. He doesn't want it to be over; he says he loves me too. *Now you tell me.* But I know it's the right thing to do.

When my mum comes to visit the next weekend along with my stepdad Peter and Sam the dog, I decide they're meeting Matt; part of my new program of self-protection is that the new potential boyfriend needs to be approved by friends and family. We meet up in the middle of town and he hands me a gift: a silver necklace with a tiny diamond in it. Oh goodness… While we're waiting for Mum to arrive, we look around a craft fair in the park even though it's raining, and again he has me in stitches with laughter—he sees the bizarre in everything. He's very patient while we all sit around talking and then he comes along with Mum and me to walk the dog on the beach. Although they only met briefly before at my party last year, it feels like the most natural thing in the world. And everyone gets along well; I get the sense they find him very easy to chat with.

Matt has kept away from love and emotion for a long time, so this is all as terrifying and simultaneously joyful and exciting for him as it is for me; deep down, although it's been buried for a few years, he's still a dreamer who believes it's worth taking a chance. I want a calm relationship so I can enjoy my work, my family and friends, and all that's good in my life without too many ups and downs. There are lots of things you can't know about when you enter into a relationship, but Matt is almost the same age as me, he's English, lives locally, knows a lot of the same people, loves kids, has his own business and some security, and he already loves me. If I can't make this one work, I'll give up and be single, frankly. It feels like we're going about things a good, old-fashioned way, thinking things through carefully before taking that kissing stuff any further.

Finally he asks me one more time if I'm really sure; when I say yes, he says he is going to take the plunge and buy back his old factory close by, so that he doesn't have to be traveling all the time. It's an ailing business but maybe by managing it again, he can build it back up to be a success and give us a nice income (yes, "us"). He manages to raise the funds, and just like that, he makes it happen.

The commitment is appealing. I'm tired of looking. Life suddenly seems a lot less complicated, and yet it also seems like a wild adventure too.

People seem happy to see us happy together. We make a striking couple; we both like dressing up in slightly outlandish outfits sometimes when we go out, skimpy dresses for me and colorful shirts for him. And because we're having fun, some of that good feeling rubs off on everyone around us. He likes taking me out in the evening to nice places. Hey, I deserve it. The people in the Dining Room breathe a sigh of relief as if wondering what took us so long.

He's been living in a temporary flat as he was traveling so much, and the place overlooking the sea was let out, so we decide he should come and live with me until the tenant's lease is up in a couple of months. He goes shopping and comes home with the ingredients for a good fish soup and a bouquet of red roses.

We go camping on the Isle of Wight, and wear silly hats in Brighton, and go camping again up north in Saddleworth, where I grew up, for a late-summer festival. Every weekend, we are doing something different. Sometimes he buys endless frivolous mementoes of the day; I tend not to buy myself things I don't really need, but with Matt around, if there's an item of clothing I like, he just buys it for me. Other days we just walk for hours on a beach or through the countryside. "If I ever ask you to marry me," he says, "it will be on a beach, I think."

When I was married before, the year after I left Greece for Canada, it went wrong very quickly. It started beautifully but ended messily, nastily, and I haven't been in a rush to do it again. But maybe one day?

Matt and I are constantly having good times. I remember once being accused of being a "good-time girl" by someone who was bitter about me leaving him. It was supposed to be derogatory. But I don't see wanting to have good times as a bad thing.

⁓

At first, going down to four days a week, there was a dizzying feeling that I suddenly had lots more time to myself and significantly less money. I'm not a materialistic person, have never gone in much for "things," but I really don't like being poor and was ultra-cautious at first. Within a couple of months of my Freelance Fridays, however, a wonderful new opportunity offers itself out of nowhere: would I like to set up a blog about travel in South Korea, supported for a few hours a week by the Korea Tourism Organization? I've been reporting on Korean events in the UK unpaid for a couple of years, and this is a chance to develop it further for a fee. I readily accept. The contract includes a press trip to Korea, and since I know the country well, they ask where I'd like to go. I come up with a dream itinerary, and they set everything up. I even ask them if it's OK to bring Matt along, as long as we pay for his flight, and they agree and make the arrangements. I'm thrilled.

But the week before, he tells me he can't go. The business is having a lot of problems he hadn't wanted to talk about, and it really won't survive him being away for ten days. I'm disappointed, and we meet at the beach that evening to talk it all over.

He risked a lot by buying back that company during a recession, and now he tells me he's gone into debt, taking out an overdraft to keep it going. The bank wouldn't have allowed him the overdraft without some security, so it turns out he's given them his lovely flat by the sea, which we were hoping to move into as he knows how much I would enjoy working from home there, and which is where all his things are stored. I'm shocked and sad that he's kept all this from me until the last minute.

He cares so much about that business, which belonged to his father. He is proud of keeping the guys there in work, and goes to the bank to check their pay has gone through every weekend. If his business goes under, he loses everything, he says, the factory and the flat. He didn't want to tell me because he wanted to take care of it without me knowing about the problems.

"I could lose everything. Everything I promised you. I've let you down, Jen."

"No, you haven't. It's only the dishonesty that upsets and bothers me. I thought we were telling one another everything. If I'd just known what was happening…"

It makes me realize, however, how important he is to me. He's made me very happy over the last couple of months. I know as we look out to sea that night that I want him in my life whatever happens—even if he does lose everything. Some of the best times we've had have cost nothing.

"I don't deserve you, Jen."

"Don't say that. Of course you do. Just please, never lie to me."

"I won't. I won't let you down again."

We sit watching the waves for a while in the cold evening air.

~

I'm barely back from Korea—a fantastic trip, but absolutely exhausting, full days of traveling and interviewing and making notes, followed by downloading photos and blogging into the early hours, sleeping a few hours until jet lag kicks in, then starting again—when I have to go to Frankfurt for work, another full week of days packed with meetings, late nights, and meeting old friends. It's hard being away again for a week so soon, but Matt and I talk every day. One night I leave my phone in my bag and forget to call him, and he leaves a ridiculous number of messages on it, and then we spend an hour on the phone apologizing to one another. I know he finds it extremely tough when I go away, and doesn't know what to do when I'm not around.

He's hinted a few times about wanting to ask me to marry him. I've had plenty of time to think about it and decide if I'm ready to try marriage again. The morning after I get back from Germany, somehow I get the feeling he's going to say it when he goes quiet and looks at me deeply and nervously. I pretend to be oblivious and start nattering away about other things until finally giving in and laughing, and letting him speak. He asks, "Jen, will you marry me?" And I say yes. He dashes out to buy a ring that day, and in the evening we put it on my finger, and we're both so clueless that I wear it on the wrong hand for a couple of days until his secretary sets us straight.

I keep the wonderful secret for a couple of days before telling anyone, just in case he changes his mind, though I tell my mum. She and my stepdad Peter send flowers and a note: "What a difference a year makes."

Hello Jennifer

I am very glad you answer me. I have thought something wrong was happened to you or you have fallen in the "honey" with Matt and you forgot the other people.

When you will be crossing the half earth, I will be in a small island somewhere in the Aegean sea. I am jealous of you about the traveling around the world.

Of course I am every day at least for a couple of hours into the sea swimming and fishing (I have work to do also but the daily date with the sea is fix).

All best Manolis

The last few months have been such a whirlwind that I haven't had a chance to write to Manolis, although he's been following my travels through Facebook. When I tell him the news of our engagement, he offers congratulations and grumbles something about other people having all the luck. But he wants to stay friends, which I'm pleased about.

Back when Matt and I were just friends and used to meet up for a drink, he'd often talk about his idea of one day just taking off with a tarp tent and walking around Britain, living off a pound a day. He used to go hiking in the highlands of Scotland, and the one photo album he has at my flat shows him alone in the snow on Ben Nevis. One day he comes up with the idea that we could indulge our love of walking by tackling the South Downs Way over the course of the winter, one section every couple of weekends. At least it might keep us out of the shops—my flat is getting filled up with all manner of quirky things we've found and liked—though he does find me some good walking boots; I complain they are too big and hard to walk in at first, but soon wonder how I ever did without them.

On Saturday mornings we get up when it's still dark and the moon is bright in the sky, and we walk down to the train station in our boots and fleeces, and go off to a new place for a spectacular day's walking up hills and through forests, arriving somewhere different every time. We get cold and soaked some days, but other days are bright and sunny with breathtaking views, and invariably there are things to discover along the way: churches with interesting histories, wildlife, and warm pubs. It's a perfect way to get outdoors in the darker winter months.

Toward the end of the year, Kate visits from Vancouver with her gorgeous little girl Lucy. John is working in New Zealand now, but their mum is here and we all have great fun catching up. Kate looks amazing in her funky clothes, spike heels, glossy black hair, and red lips, and is just as flirtatious as ever; there is no sign that this woman is a stressed young mum. When we go out in the evening, pretty little Lucy behaves impeccably, never doing anything but smiling and laughing. We invite them round to our place another night so Lucy can crawl around the floor and even stand holding onto the coffee table. She's utterly sweet and charming. Matt is especially good with children: they love him and he will spend hours playing peek-a-boo games.

Kate comes into the kitchen to help me with some food and, when we're alone, asks the obvious question that's hanging in the air.

"So, are you thinking about trying for one of your own?"

I grin. "We've been trying since we decided to get together, more or less. It's one of the things we discussed from the very start."

She flashes me a wide-eyed smile and wishes me luck.

It's very weird not having a clue whether you might become pregnant that very month... or never. It's strange having absolutely no way of knowing. We're hopeful that once my body rights itself, it will happen.

Only time can tell if you're with the right person—but time is something I don't have if I'm going to have a chance of conceiving now. I've given up trying to judge for myself if someone is right, and figure that all I can do is introduce a guy to everyone I know, friends and family, in the hope that they will spot any obvious problems for me. You can never really know anyone for sure—we're all so full of surprises. Kate has shown me how you can manage to be a good mother alone, so I didn't worry about the possibility of getting pregnant even in the early months of this relationship.

The truth is, after what happened with John last year, and after toughening myself up and taking control of my own happiness a bit more, I have become more pragmatic. I don't expect a relationship to make me happy, if I ever did before. And yet this relationship is more than I ever expected. I'm expecting less and getting more. Interesting how that works.

Matt does have two young daughters from his last

long-term relationship—the one that turned him into a Man Who Didn't Do Relationships. He had discovered his partner was having an affair, and he was so shocked and hurt that he dealt with it by walking out and leaving her, having a breakdown, and going abroad. But that meant he left his daughters too, which was wrong, because it wasn't their fault. He sends money every month and carries around their photo in his wallet, and cries about them from time to time, but for years he hasn't been able to bring himself to get in touch even though he is legally entitled to. We talk about it a lot, and he has promised me he will try to make contact with their mother, who is now remarried, and see if we can find a way to bring the girls back into his life in some way.

In January, I'm called for jury duty, and at the same time I end up with four different writing deadlines. The pitches I sent out before and after my press trip to South Korea paid off, and of course everything comes in at once. It's not ideal that I still don't have Internet at home; I was going to sign a twelve-month contract finally, but then we've been waiting for Matt to get his flat back so we can move. It's a little frustrating. It crosses my mind that the house he owns in town doesn't bring him very much rental income and we could live there, but he likes the tenants, and it's probably best to leave things as they are until the business problems are sorted. It doesn't really matter, and anyway he is contributing to my mortgage while he's living with me, which leaves me better off.

So somehow I manage to write and research at the Internet café in between court sessions, in one of the snowiest weeks England has seen in years. It's an exhilarating time; my Gift to Self of Freelance Fridays has certainly brought rewards. The months fly by in a blur of happy activity. We go to France and to Spain with my mum for long weekends, but of course it goes without saying that we'll be spending a week in early summer in Tilos. Perhaps it should feel weird going back there with someone, but as it's Matt, it just feels perfectly natural.

In the meantime, however, Manolis is coming to visit.

CHAPTER FOURTEEN

Dolphins and Dolmades

When Manolis had emailed during the winter saying how lucky I was to be traveling all over the world, and how he never gets to go anywhere, I said, "Why don't you come and visit us?" The next day, he told me he'd discovered the easyJet website and had booked for ten days over Easter. I had hoped by the time he arrived, we'd have moved into Matt's apartment by the sea and he could stay in mine, but it's not to be. Rather than risk the awkwardness of all living at such close quarters in my flat, I book Manolis a bed-and-breakfast at a good rate for a week and pay for it in advance.

It's a bit nerve-wracking wondering how Matt and Manolis will get on. I'm actually rather excited about seeing my old friend from Tilos when I take the train to meet him at the airport. I'm proud that he's coming to England to visit.

On the first night, we take him out for a pub dinner at the Park Tavern, where he announces he can't eat meat because it's the days before Easter. I had no idea, but we find him a vegetarian lasagna on the menu. As we're ordering drinks at the bar, the friendly new landlord asks him if he'd like a beer.

"Ha ha! No. I cannot drink beer. One Coke," he says in his deep and imperious voice.

"A Coke, *please*," I add, plus "thank you" for good measure. I'd forgotten that the Greeks don't really use please and thank you like that. Manolis lived in Australia for a while, but I guess he's forgotten. Matt insists on paying for everything.

The next night, we've invited some friends along to meet him after work, and they are a little perplexed by his apparent lack of enthusiasm after his first day in England.

"I have discovered all of London," he claims, as if nobody had noticed it before. We were working so he took the train to the city, an hour and a half away. He's also been extremely cold; unfortunately the weather is living up to his expectations of wind and rain. Anyway, we make plenty of noise, which must put paid to his stereotyping of the English being polite and quiet. For a few days, Manolis continues to discover London and we take him out for drinks and dinners at night. He and Matt get along well, although Manolis has this idea that in order to bond with another bloke—and perhaps to show that even though Matt has the girl, he is the more manly—he must regale Matt with stories of nubile Eastern

European seductresses he has encountered. Hello! Female at the table over here!

On the weekend we're all able to spend some time together during the days and take him to Arundel. Matt and I always have fun on days out like this, and even though we've had breakfast I can't resist buying some goodies at the delicatessen for us to munch on while we explore. At the castle, we are lucky to find a reenactment day, with archery contests and blacksmiths forging shields. A man dressed as a Crusader talks about what life was like back then in the time of the Knights—which should have some resonance as they built all those castles in Tilos. Manolis surveys the scene with indifference, but Matt and I are having a great time. Maybe Manolis is nonplussed because the sun is shining, so he can't make any wisecracks about English weather. Afterward, we take a walk along the River Arun to a popular pub, and Matt tries to make conversation with him along the way. When we get there, we ask what he'd like. He harrumphs.

"What, eating and drinking again? No, I am not hungry."

So Matt and I order ourselves some *tzatziki* and hummus and pita and olives. When they arrive, we are speechless as Manolis tucks in with gusto, but I'm glad he likes the English version of the Greek *meze*. We walk back past a pond with beautiful swans and geese; Manolis talks on his mobile phone throughout. We get back to town and there's half an hour to kill before the train, so we pop into a cozy pub, which of course prompts a guffaw from Manolis about drinking again.

"I take it you don't want anything then?" I say as I order ours. Matt tells me to behave.

It's the long Easter weekend, so we go on a country walk on Sunday, then on Monday take him to Brighton and wander through the lively, artsy shopping streets, which fail to raise a smile from Manolis (disappointingly—I thought this would be interesting for him as something completely different to Tilos) until I buy him a painted wooden fish as a souvenir. Down at the seafront we have lunch at our favorite fish café, and finally find something that Manolis can get excited about: good, home-smoked salmon. We buy a big piece and assume it will do for dinner later—until we see Manolis polishing it off.

The trip seems to have worked out fine, although I wish he'd had more fun. But then, that's Manolis. Something he says also makes me wonder if he's been more uncomfortable than he lets on about being around me and Matt. On the last night, he completely surprises me when he says he much prefers our town to London, and how he could live here. Maybe he enjoyed himself after all, in his own way.

And when we go to Tilos, he is ready to return the hospitality.

"What's a Greek urn?"

"Erm…"

"About seven euros an hour."

This is Matt's favorite Greek joke, which ranks right up there with my dad's awful "feta compli" joke.

Matt's seen a lot of the world while traveling for work, but he's never been to Greece before and isn't sure what to expect. He's been trying to learn a few words of the language. I suppose knowing how much I love Greece puts pressure on him to like it, and it makes me nervous in case he doesn't. Disappointingly, the flight to Rhodes is late in the evening so we don't get the magnificent view of the islands suspended in the Aegean, but Matt's excited even by the lights before we touch down and he's taking everything in as the taxi drives us into town.

That's one of the great things about Matt: he's completely unjaded. He sees everything with a childlike wonder.

Back when I booked the flights, there was a ferry leaving the next day for Tilos, but since then the ferry schedule has changed so we'll be here for two nights. When I started idly looking around at nicer hotels online, I found a gorgeous boutique hotel called Spirit of the Knights in a restored Ottoman house in the old town, with a Jacuzzi in the garden. It was an exclusive place and not surprisingly beyond my budget, but I remembered that I was now a published travel journalist and they might be interested in me writing a story for a magazine. They were and offered us the Grand Masters Suite. It sounds too good to be true—but I'm forgetting how much I've achieved this year.

The taxi drops us at one of the gates of the old town, and we're escorted back to a garden lit by candlelight and given large glasses of cold white wine. The owners are an English family, who had been coming to Greece for years and decided to set up a business to work on together, buying an abandoned but historic house and rebuilding it over several years. At our leisure, they show us upstairs through the library and into a room with dark beams (original Ottoman) and antique furniture, white gauzy curtains, and plush dark crimson covers on a palatial bed. Not a bad start. The room is warm though, and Matt says we must put the air conditioning on.

I get a horrible sinking feeling. Air conditioning is too cold for me and I hate the sound of it. It's actually not that hot. Can't we just open the windows and get a breeze? But there are no mosquito screens on the windows, and although there's a rather fetching mosquito net draped over the bed, Matt does look extremely uncomfortable. I hope he's going to be OK. He's spent enough time in jungles and hot countries, but it turns out recently he's gotten used to air conditioning. I do hope the man I've agreed to marry is going to like Greece. I think he'll like the nightlife, anyway. Back at home, we're sociable creatures in the evenings.

We freshen up in our sleek marble bathroom, change,

and head out on the town. We wander down the cobbled alleyways and find ourselves a lively bar in Arionos Square, opposite the old Turkish baths. It's in an old stone building, with good music and no British tourists anywhere. Matt asks me how to say "two beers" in Greek, and the guys at the bar are friendly. He asks them about the name of the bar, I Rogmi tou Chronou, and they explain it's named after a famous Greek song. Matt clearly likes the atmosphere, and I feel relieved.

After a slightly weird night's sleep amid air conditioning and mosquito scares, we have a luxurious breakfast in our almost private garden and spend a relaxed morning wandering around the old town. Matt buys himself a leather satchel, and the seller waves the fifty-euro note over our heads and then down to below Matt's belt, "for luck." I introduce Matt to the delights of the frappé coffee in a quiet rooftop café, then we wander down to Elli Beach, where we sit for a while, Matt in the shade while I relax in the sun, so happy to feel that warmth on my bare skin. We have a late lunch at Indigo, where I lingered over a delicious salad last year when I was leaving. We take a walk around the walls of the Old Town and finally return to lounge in the peaceful enclosed garden of the hotel. Matt makes use of the Jacuzzi while I work at my computer with the gentle sounds of a fountain enhancing the sense of calm. It's not hard to feel right at home.

Around six o'clock in the evening, sounds of distant traffic beyond the massive old walls indicate that the day is revving up again after a long siesta. We head out and lose ourselves in the empty alleyways until we find an old *kafeneion* with groups of men sitting around outside and in. I'm not sure how welcome we'll be, but I'm proved happily wrong as the old guys point the way inside with genuine smiles. We order *mezethes*, or *meze*, with the beers, and for a few euros are presented with a plate of feta, cucumber, olives, and *dolmades*, vine leaves stuffed with rice.

From there we move on to a rooftop bar/restaurant; we're just leaving when we notice that right downstairs is a sleek dance bar and we stay a while dancing to Greek rap. When we leave and head back up the same little side streets as before, it's completely disorienting as everything has changed. The old *kafeneion* is shuttered up while across the way are strobe lights and a funky red plastic bar. Alleys we strolled down listlessly earlier are now so heaving with chatting crowds of men and women they're almost impossible to pass through. Videos are beamed onto walls, and dance music and talk fills the night air. There's not an English voice to be heard. Weaving through all this buzz, and across squares where ruins lurk in the darkness, we eventually come back to the square where we were last night and spend the early hours of the morning in a tiny open courtyard filled with stylish people, listening to music and celebrating an excellent first day.

It's the same early-morning start for the ferry to Tilos,

but this time it's a little noisier, as Matt is trundling his big wheelie suitcase across the cobbles of the old town. My preference is still for the backpack, which may not be to everyone's taste, but at least people can't hear you coming half a mile away. For weeks he's been buying himself T-shirts and shorts and flip-flops and linen trousers, worried that he needs to have the right clothes for the trip. He is a funny old thing, completely eccentric it has to be said, but I like most of his quirks—and he can afford to buy the stuff, after all. He's in a bit of a mood, perhaps because we overindulged last night (thankfully I drank only water for a while), so I leave him to relax at the ferry dock while I hunt down something to eat and drink for us both. My Greek is a little rusty, but I manage to get directions to a shop with flaky cheese pies.

The sky starts to cloud over, and it's decidedly gray when the ferry stops in at Halki en route. There's even some rain, plus dark clouds in the direction of Tilos. It all feels a bit worrying, especially as we left some lovely weather back in England. Then suddenly there's a buzz of excitement and everyone is looking out to sea—*delphini*! It's a group of dolphins leaping out of the sea as they follow the boat. I've hardly ever seen them, and it's thrilling as the arcs of their backs broach the water. It lasts just a few minutes, but what a good omen, coming to Tilos with dolphins. And as we approach the island, the dark clouds are passing over, leaving blue skies and sunshine.

"Welcome!" Manolis meets us off the boat. He embraces us both and bundles the luggage into his car. "Where you want to go?"

Rob and Annie have given up the flat above the bar, so I found us a place to stay on a website, a traditional-sounding place run by a Greek family, and made a tentative reservation. I hope to take a quiet look at it before we decide for sure, but Manolis takes us straight there before I can think properly and the owner comes to the gate, smiling, and I see all too clearly that I have somehow found the one charmless place in Tilos, right next to a semi-abandoned building site. I flail around for the right words and then chicken out and ask Manolis to do the dirty work, to say that it's very nice but we want to find somewhere overlooking the sea. I feel awful letting her down and insulting her rooms, but there again, the alternative is staying here.

Optimistic that we'll find something else, I suggest we simply walk down the seafront and take a look. At once, we spot a little house by the bridge, which I always thought looked pretty. The terrace was recently done up with stone, and the owner has decorated it simply with shells. It's perfect: a little bedroom with a window looking straight out to sea, a tiny kitchen in the corner, and a small private bathroom, plus a balcony with just enough space for two chairs and a table. And, most importantly, there's a ceiling fan. We move our stuff in at once.

Matt's a little taken aback by the twin beds. It's funny seeing Greece afresh through his eyes. There are of course little quirks that you just get used to. I explain that you simply move the twin beds together to make a double—OK, it has a rather large gap between the mattresses, but it makes for a big double. Then he goes to the bathroom and comes out confused, as he'd assumed the shower was behind the door but now he can't find it. I explain: the shower is the bathroom, no doors, open concept, just a shower cord and a drain in the floor. It means it's a large shower and you're not cramped into a small cubicle, but it does mean the whole bathroom gets soaked and you have to remember to move the loo paper if you don't want to make papier mâché.

Oh, and talking of loo paper… Matt's already been introduced to, and is trying his best to cope with, the new concept of not putting it down the toilet but in a bin. Greek drains aren't equipped to cope with paper. I've been coming to Greece for so long that I never even think about these things until I come back. Matt travels to different countries regularly for work, so I guess it's not the first time he's had to adjust to a different kind of bathroom.

But the tiny window in the bathroom looks out to the mountainside, and the kitchen and bedroom look straight out to sea. It's disarmingly lovely. We shower and get into Tilos mode: Matt in linens, sunglasses, and the leather satchel he bought in Rhodes, me in bikini and shorts again. It's good to be back.

~

Manolis is ready to introduce Matt to all of Tilos. We take the road across the island toward Megalo Horio, turn toward Ayios Andonis, then past Plaka; from there, the road winds upward along the edge of the tallest mountain, Profitis Ilias, with sheer drops off the cliffs hundreds of meters to deep blue sea below. Goats wander around the side of the road, but there is no other sign of life, no buildings on this steep mountainside, which is nothing more than vertical rock in places. The road keeps winding up and up until we reach the monastery. Thankfully, Manolis is a careful driver.

Panteleimonas is the patron saint of the island, and the monastery has been here since 1430. But long before that, the site was an ancient place of worship, once a temple to Poseidon, god of the sea. It's no longer working, mostly used for weddings and festivals. As we walk around, we're followed by a friendly gray-and-white cat, which Matt the cat lover instantly befriends. It curls around his legs, and this place is so silent you can hear its purring. I think it must be a good sign that animals and children instinctually love this man.

Manolis drives us back down to Eristos beach, and we follow a trail over the headland to the cove of crimson cliffs

and red sand, swirls of red volcanic rock, wrinkled and lay-
ered, with bright green capers clinging to fissures indicating
spring water. The waves are sweeping in to shore, and I'm
mesmerized by its glorious emptiness again, happy that it
really is as beautiful as I remembered. I wonder how Manolis
feels; when he first brought me here a year ago, I don't think
he expected this situation. I know it could have worked out
differently. But he seems happy to have both Matt and me as
friends. We're all grown-ups.

Back in Livadia, we walk around the town and I spot
people from last year—Yorgos in the *kafeneion*, younger
Yorgos in the seafront restaurant. It takes people a few minutes to remember, but just as I'm explaining in Greek that I
was here last year they recognize me and greet me like a long-
lost friend. And I introduce them to my *arravonyiastikos*, the
unwieldy word for fiancé, which we learned before we came.
We find Pantelis in his restaurant and I get kisses on both
cheeks before Matt gets a firm handshake. There's no sign of
Vangelis, but I'm sure I'll see him around soon.

We walk around the bay and up the hill onto the headland,
stopping at the little chapel of Ayios Ioannis, whitewashed
with pale blue trim and red panels in the doorway. Inside are
gold-painted icons of saints. Wearing a hat to keep the sun off,
Matt sits on the stone bench by the chapel to sketch the view
of the bay while I go on a bit farther past Vangelis's charcoal
mounds. Then I come back, sit and look at the views, sketch

a bit too. As we walk back, I gather herbs for the kitchen. We stop to buy some breakfast things in the shop—I choose yogurt, honey, and oranges, and Matt buys bananas.

It's been a long day by the time we meet Manolis for dinner. We choose the gyros grill place near the bakery, which is already busy. Matt gets a mound of pork and I am craving *tzatziki* and tomatoes, so everyone's very happy: it's cheap and tasty.

"Do we start smashing plates now?" says Matt, winding me up, and I grin.

"Yes, they expect it, of course! They'd think you hadn't enjoyed your food otherwise."

There are plenty of cats milling around looking for scraps, as usual. When we ask for the bill, I overhear Manolis telling the waiter in Greek to put it straight into his hand, *sto heri mou*. I let Matt know. There's a bit of friendly wrangling over who should pay, but we let Manolis win this one.

"I do not forget what you do in England! I am a camel," he says enigmatically. We think he probably means an elephant, but maybe camels have long memories in Greece too.

CHAPTER FIFTEEN

First Catch Your Octopus

Manolis carries two enormous bags as we all make our way across the beach at Plaka. I'm excited about seeing the peacocks in the park as we head around the edge of the bay to the smaller beach. Matt's excited about going fishing.

It's calm and peaceful, the only sound the occasional cry of the peacocks. They make a strange squawk, something between a crow and a yowling cat. As we get closer, we glimpse them through the trees, showing off their magnificent plumage.

I go for a swim, and when I return Manolis has set up several rods for each of them on stands with various paraphernalia. Within a very short space of time, there's a triumphant shout and Matt has caught his first fish. He holds it up proudly, grinning. Not very big, but half a decent supper I imagine, so it goes into the net for keeping.

I sketch the view of the bay while they fish. I haven't done much drawing for years, but seeing Matt do it has encouraged me. It's been so long that I'm completely out of practice, though I like to sketch when I find something beautiful in a museum, as it means I look at it carefully. I watch a cormorant, a "sea raven" or *thalassokorakos* in Greek, diving and coming back up again; actually, technically it's a Mediterranean Shag, but I think we'll keep that for a bad joke later.

When I occasionally wander over to see how the fishermen are getting on, Matt seems to have brought in quite a few. Manolis is very carefully explaining which fish to be careful with because of poisonous spines, introducing him to the different types. They've caught a pinkish-yellow fish called *skaros*, which the Ancient Romans liked so much they carried them in nets between their ships back to Rome so they could have them fresh.

Manolis goes off spear-fishing for a while and catches an octopus. Once it's dead he slams it down hard on the rocks and rubs it around on the uneven surface. Mostly it's to tenderize the meat, he explains. If you're going to marinate it for a while, it's not necessary, only if you're going to eat it soon—and he plans to cook it for us this week.

In the evening, Matt agrees with me that the bar on the beach where you can sit in a fishing boat is a perfect place to watch the water flattening out with the sunset, the encroaching dusk, the lights beginning to come on here and there.

We wander down the seashore and I look around again for Vangelis but there's no sign of him. I start getting a feeling he's not on the island; maybe he's in Rhodes visiting his mother. I find out the little shop opposite Rob and Annie's bar that used to be an Internet café, gift shop, and used bookshop has closed down, a new Internet café has opened in the square where the butcher used to be, and the butcher has moved to the back road. Otherwise, not much has changed in a year, not that I can see.

It's clear that Matt is loving Tilos and island life, which makes me happy. Already people are saying hello and welcoming him. And he sees how much I love it here. He sees how at home I am, how the warmth wakes me up, how I stretch out and relax with swimming in the sea, happy to take off the layers of winter and feel the sunshine on my skin. We are settling into our little home at Maria's very comfortably; already a few things we found on the beach today have made their way onto the table. The sound of the waves in the evening, the cool breeze, the freedom and simplicity—it's all so relaxing and conducive to love.

On the morning of day three, I go for a swim and come back to find a note in the room saying "Gone to the square for a frappé." This is definitely a good sign that Matt's feeling at home. I meet him at the café under the tree, where he's also sampled their "special omelette" with peppers and onion and sausage, and we talk about hiring a bike to go to Megalo Horio. An office by the marina has scooters to rent, according to a sign, so we go up the steps to inquire.

While Matt is talking to the English man behind the desk, I snoop around their secondhand bookshelf and property notice board. Funnily enough, there's a house for sale in Megalo Horio, near where I stayed when I first came here. Matt comes over to see what I'm looking at.

"Just curious. I know that house!" I've never looked at property prices on Tilos; I would rent again if I wanted to stay here longer.

"I'd be happy to arrange a visit if you're interested," says the man. "The owners are there at the moment so they could show you around. It's really worth seeing."

"Oh, I know!" I say. "I've been up there and it's an amazing location. We're not here to buy a house, though…"

"Ah, famous last words! Well, if you change your mind, let me know. Right then, let's see, have you driven scooters before? It's just that it's pretty windy today and I wouldn't really advise going out on them unless you know what you're doing."

I rode a scooter on Santorini during that summer after university, but never since. There really isn't any traffic to be concerned about, but the road that winds up out of Livadia is steep: there are sheer drops and, of course, wandering goats beyond, and as he says, a strong gust of wind can steer a scooter off course unless you're used to driving one. I remember a common summer accessory among tourists on some Greek islands was the bandage on the lower leg from bad handling of a scooter on an unforeseen pothole. My brother looked away from the road for a second on the island of Paros and the next moment was at the bottom of a gully and spent the rest of his holiday recovering.

"Er, no, we'd better not then." And when I look at the pushbike option, Matt says cycling up that hill out of town is out of the question. So we thank the chap and go off to catch the bus the four miles to Megalo Horio instead.

Once there, we walk up through the pretty, whitewashed old village to the top church, with its views over the valleys and mountains. As usual we spend ages poking around, looking, reading signs, and taking photographs. From there we decide to try to find our way up to the castle. There's a handwritten sign, but it's extremely vague, as were the directions we got earlier from the ladies in the shop, where we bought a bottle of water and apples and a small loaf of bread. We pick our way in what we think must be the right direction but end up in overgrown dead ends at the back of people's houses. There's nobody around to ask, as everyone's inside having a siesta, which would be the sensible thing to do in the heat of the day.

We take a scenic route through the back of the village that clings to the hillside, and eventually pick up the right path. It's a fairly steep hike. No one of sane mind would be tackling such a climb in the middle of the day in June, and when we reach the top, puffing and panting, we have the whole place to ourselves.

It's hard to imagine that anywhere on this small island could be quite so spectacular. The castle may have been built on an ancient acropolis around the fourth century BC; this gateway and steps once led to a temple to Zeus and Athena. The ruins here now are mostly from when the Knights of St. John took control of the island from 1309. There are imposing stretches of tall stone walls of the medieval citadel, part of a church with the faint vestiges of frescoes, and the ruined walls of countless buildings, odd stones from different periods. Although there are no signs to help us interpret the remains, we are free to wander at will and imagine. Once again, it's only the goats that come here regularly now. The views take in the bay of Ayios Andonis and the island of Nisyros. From this stronghold people would have seen any trouble coming a long way off, plenty of time to prepare and get everyone and the livestock within the walls.

We scramble over the stones taking it all in, and Matt hunts around in the rubble, in his element, dying to unearth some ancient artifact. After an hour or so, we wander back down, stopping to pick up and examine shards of pottery.

Matt wants to take them home to add to the collection of weird stuff in our flat, and I have to break it to him gently that it's not allowed. The path meets the village near the house we saw advertised for sale earlier, so although we're hot and dusty from the afternoon's adventure, we walk up to take a look.

The driveway is redolent with the smell of the wild herbs and a fig tree. The house is on the edge of the village overlooking a quiet valley of beehives and goats, and beneath the ruins of the castle. Someone comes out and waves hello.

"Can I help you?" she asks.

"Sorry, we don't mean to be rude! We just saw the place for sale today and were curious."

A man comes out too, and he seems very friendly. He invites us in. We're not exactly dressed for it, but it would be great to look around. He takes us first up to the terrace with its panoramic views, and then the bedroom that looks down toward Eristos Bay. The living room leads out to another terrace where vines are just maturing so it will be overhung with grapes in a year or two. There's a garden filled with blossoming flowers and even a resident cat, Matt notes with interest. We chat with the owners for a while then thank them for showing us around, and they say we're welcome to come back and take another look any time. They thought we were bonkers for walking up to the castle in the middle of the day, so we don't tell them we're walking back to Livadia. It's a good hour's walk, but it's so pretty, just open countryside with goats grazing at either side. I bet Matt's glad now he's not carrying a satchel full of old pottery.

"What did you think?" asks Matt once we've hit our stride.

"It's gorgeous," I say. "Can you imagine living there? You could convert that garage into an office and just look out over the valley…"

"I know, that's what I was thinking."

"It's nice that there's a real fire."

As we walk back, we talk about the things we liked, dreaming of living in that house. The crazy thing is, though, it's a possibility.

It's been a difficult year for Matt since he bought back the company, a year of struggles. There were signs of improvement as he reestablished good relations with old customers and found new ones, but every month he worried that the work wouldn't come in and he'd be in too much debt to continue. Then a few months ago, a couple of guys came along who had a small group of similar companies and wanted to expand into his area—by buying the company. He was torn, but in the end things were still too risky and it was a decent offer; he couldn't refuse. He's still in the process of working out the final stages of the deal, which will involve him staying on to run it, but he won't have to worry so much anymore, I hope, and he's been wondering what to do next. I'm so pleased for him.

I couldn't do all of my current job from here, but I could certainly do many aspects of it as I did last year; I noticed they had wireless Internet in the house. Matt and I have talked many times of places we'd like to live, adventures we'd like to have. We're always going somewhere and wondering about living there.

I love the idea of working from home in a house in the countryside. I remember that wonderful studio my friend Yiannis had on the island of Aegina back when I lived in Athens. I also recall a trip I took to a small town called Kalambaka up north, where the people were so welcoming, where everyone said hello, and there was a smell of woodsmoke in the air. Back when I lived in the south of France before I moved back to the UK, I started looking at property in the villages and found a wonderful old village house for a bargain price surrounded by mountains, with its own allotment for growing vegetables, but it needed a lot of work, and I wasn't making quite enough money. I moved to England and built up my career again. Since that month last year, the notion of living in Tilos has been always in my mind.

But it's only Matt's third day on the island, only his first week in Greece. *Siga-siga*. Slowly does it.

We get back to Livadia in the early evening, and Matt jokingly vows never to do that walk again. Even though he's always talking about how he'd love to walk around Britain, and even though the South Downs Way was often much more strenuous than this four-mile road walk, the difference is the heat, especially after our jaunt up to the castle.

We are extremely tired, but it's been an exciting day, and as we walk down the seafront after showering and changing, we stop in at the Silversmith. It's a tiny shop selling hand-made jewelry inspired by the Aegean Sea. I buy Matt a ring that he likes, and he buys me a bracelet. It's leather with a flat silver ring like the face of a watch, but empty. I nickname it my Tilos watch: always time to do nothing.

That night, Manolis has invited us around for dinner to eat octopus. He's prepared mounds of the stuff, plus there are *gramithia* leaves and salad and fried slices of eel. The apartment is sweltering from all the cooking, and Matt seems a little uncomfortable. Not nearly as uncomfortable as he appears when Manolis piles heaps of glistening purple octopus tentacle on his plate. He enjoys the thick white pieces but soon looks squeamish at the twisty bits with lots of suckers. I surreptitiously help him out.

***

"I'm pretty sure it's this way," I say to Matt as we head out of the village. It is late morning when we decide to walk to Ammohosti, as I've now discovered it's called, and already hot as we follow the track along the hillside. Matt said he wanted to see a new beach, and I asked him if he was sure he wanted to try this one. I do have a slightly higher tolerance for long, unplanned walks than most people, and I had a feeling he would rather be sitting in the shade of a café with a frappé and an omelette. But he insisted he wanted to have a go. I know it's worthwhile and that people walk to this beach and beyond all the time, many of them much more senior than us—and Manolis, when he took me to this beach first, was of course carrying two wetsuits and the usual paraphernalia. It's only half an hour along a good track. But Matt looks overheated and decidedly unhappy. I hope he can appreciate the spectacular views of the blue bay and little beaches far below and the emptiness of the landscape.

"I don't think it's much farther. Ah, yes, I think I remember this now."

We reach the turn-off and descend through scrubland with thorn bushes, slipping occasionally on small stones, zigzagging down toward the cove, scrambling as the delicious blue seems tantalizingly close. Once I'm in the water, I look around.

The whole beach is varying shades of pink—the rusty crimson and brick-reds of the coarse sand, purple and pink rocks streaked with the white of salt crystal. Out to sea the view is shades of aquamarine and royal blue and bare brown mountains, not a single man-made structure visible. Our only company is a few black goats, which keep to themselves in the next cove.

The water here is very clear, with jagged pale rocks to investigate under the surface, perfect for snorkeling, and I soon spot a pointed nose and thin snake-like shape—a small eel. It draws itself farther under the rock as it notices me.

My spare snorkel broke so Matt bought a cheap one from a little shop this morning, the only option on the island, and ends up swallowing lots of seawater, but he loves exploring and fish-spotting and barely emerges from the sea for a couple of hours. When he gets out and puts on a white shirt, I take his photo and he points out that he is the same rich pink color as the beach. But he is pleased that we ventured over here.

On the walk home, clouds provide a little welcome relief and Matt finds a snakeskin, almost intact. When he was growing up, he spent a lot of time out hunting with ferrets, and he's fascinated by animals—something that surprises most people who only knew the Matt who sat drinking cocktails in a suit on the weekends. As we reach the first few houses of the village, we see someone has set up a makeshift stall of pickled capers and we buy a jar. We try them later on the balcony and for our evening meal I cook *kolokithakia tiganita*—giving Matt his induction into the Tilos favorite of fried zucchini. They're not terribly exciting but with the capers and a few other snacks from the shop it's a decent picnic dinner.

Later, we go to a café-bar on the water's edge where there's a lively Greek crowd. It's a tiny stone building with wooden bar and windows, and most people sit outside on the terrace looking out into the dark night, where a few yachts are moored. The sea laps at the stones just below, and the music is great so we dance a little. We meet some people at the bar, and free drinks come around at some point. It's so easy and relaxing. And when we want to go home, it's just a few minutes away.

It's another sleepy, quiet morning in Livadia. Swimming lazily in the bay, I see a *fikopsari* and follow it, hovering, for ages. This is my absolute favorite kind of fish. It's extremely long and thin—hence its name, seaweed-fish or reedfish—and shoots along like an arrow but has almost cartoonish googly eyes, and even better, it changes color if it spots you and wants to hide. The water is amazingly clear, as always; the beds of posidonia, like long underwater grasses, harbor a variety of wildlife. Monk seals and sea turtles are spotted in the bay sometimes.

When I meet Matt in the square, we talk about renting scooters again, but this time when we go to the rental office we find out we need a driving license, which of course makes sense, and neither of us thought to bring one. I've been thinking again how odd it is that I haven't seen Vangelis once, so I ask the people in the office, David and Lynda, if they know him, and find out what I'd begun to fear: he's not well. He was diagnosed with cancer late last year and has been undergoing treatment. He seems to be getting better, but he's over in Rhodes having more tests. Even though it had crossed my mind that he might not be well, this news makes me feel sick and sad. He may be back on the ferry this weekend, when we're leaving.

We have a gentle walk, then Matt reads in the shade on the balcony while I pad down to the shore in my aqua shoes. I love feeling the heat and the texture of pebbles under my feet. I find the shade of a tree and spend some time trying to compose a note to Vangelis in Greek, which I can leave at his house if we don't see him before we leave. I read for a while and go for the last swim of the day.

That evening, we pick a restaurant on the seafront that I've never tried before, mostly because I've never seen anyone but tourists there. But their menu sounds interesting and includes local dishes so we give it a try. It's a pretty terrace, which is obviously why it's so popular with visitors, and the setting sun casts a honey-colored light over the hillside. A gaggle of cats play in front of us, and we're very relaxed.

As I'm looking at the many colors of the bay, Matt is typing something on his phone—most likely, in spite of the look of concentration, he's just sending a photo of a cat to someone back home with a silly message. Or posting something on

Facebook: he did desperately want to post a picture of himself, naked and sunburnt (posterior view), and finally gave in to my suggestion that he wait, so he's sent it to his mate back home instead. I drink my retsina and look out to sea. He continues with his phone, a determined look on his face, and I hope it's nothing work-related that's stressing him out. They did ring him even when we were in the airport, panicked about something they didn't know how to do.

Matt finishes what he's doing and looks up. He holds up the phone and reads:

"I am writing to let you know that I am interested in the house…"

I smile and raise my eyebrows, surprised.

"And I would like to put down a deposit, with the full price to be paid when the sale of my business goes through next year."

"What?!"

"You do like the house, don't you?"

"Yes! But…" I'm grinning. I can't believe it. I refill our glasses.

CHAPTER SIXTEEN

Dreams of a Greek Island

Matt knows how much I would love to live in Tilos and that I've felt ready to move for a while now. The idea of buying that house and coming back to stay here together—well, it would be amazing. Still, his decision to make an offer on the house so quickly did take me utterly by surprise. He actually warns me he won't be happy leaving Tilos, and if the sale of his business had gone through, he'd probably have stayed while I went back on my own to work out my notice. He's even more impulsive than I am.

Whenever I express an interest in something, he does tend to buy it for me: a painting we both like, or another night in a B&B if we're having a lot of fun on the Isle of Wight and don't want to leave. I try telling him not to, but it seems to give him pleasure. He did take the leap to buy a business and change his work in order for us to get together, he proposed to me after only a few months—he's the guy who makes things happen. If he can buy that house, then why not?

I know that although he still cares for his business, he's more than ready to give up the day-to-day responsibility and do something new. It's been amazing to watch him transform from the man in the suit having cocktails at the bar to someone who would be happier playing with kids and animals in the shade of a tree, and catching a fish for supper. It's the simple life he really wants. Sometimes he talks about selling everything he has and just living the rest of his life on as little as possible, not having to work again.

I enjoy my work and would like to keep doing a version of it. If Matt bought a house for us, I could afford to scale back my job a bit, something I'd be nervous about doing otherwise. And if we're lucky enough to start a family together at our grand old age, something we would both love to happen, what better place to do it?

We go back to see the house again one afternoon, passing a pig casually walking along the driveway, which seems like a good sign. We take in all the space and the views. The owners seem conflicted about leaving the place that has been home for ten years; they seem happy for the selling process to take a while to allow them to stay a bit longer. The vines and pink bougainvillea they planted are just maturing. On the roof terrace, we end up in a surreal discussion about water rates, builders, banks. All I can do is look up the mountain to the castle in wonder, not really believing this is happening.

The sale of Matt's business would have to go through to free up enough money for a deposit, and then completion would depend either on sale of the flat that he still needs to get back from the bank, or waiting until next year for the final payment from the business. For now, we're still on holiday and don't want to be talking about lawyers and documents. Matt has someone back home to deal with that side of things. It's a bit of a shock how quickly Matt has decided he'd like to live in Tilos, but he's bought property with less discussion before as he often tells me. Why shouldn't we—what are we waiting for?

During the winter, Richard from the Park Tavern finally succumbed to cancer. There was a big service with hundreds of people who've known him over the years, though not so formal that they couldn't play "My Way," and I realized how apt it was for him. At the reception, there were photos all around the walls and what struck me most were the pictures of him completely happy and relaxed on a beach in Thailand. That was where they'd hoped to retire in a few years. How sad that he never got to do that. Why wait if you don't have to? Matt's parents both died relatively young, and it probably accounts in part for the way he makes things happen right away rather than waiting.

For now, though, we still have a day of relaxing on Tilos. I love waking up in this little rented room, the stillness of the bay in the early morning right outside the window, the occasional boats coming in and out. Maria, whose home is downstairs, often goes to meet the ferry in case there are tourists looking for rooms, but other times she just watches with binoculars. When she's not working, she sits outside and friends come to visit.

Matt takes the bus to Megalo Horio to get a feel for it by himself. He tries out his Greek at the *kafeneion*, and the lady explains that she's closing but she leaves him on the terrace to finish his coffee, where he has some sort of conversation with a builder who shows up. I'm impressed by the way he's picking up some words of the language after only a few days. He enjoys the walk from there to Eristos, goes to the taverna and has a chat with the owner, does some sketching. Meanwhile, I walk to Lethra, drinking in the views, knowing this is my last chance for a few months and happy to have a little Tilos time to myself.

We're both looking brown and relaxed on our last evening, and at the bar on the beach we see a woman with a lively little dog who came over on the same ferry as us. She lives in Rhodes with her husband, but they spend the weekends here and he goes out fishing.

"*Kalispera!*" I say.

"Ah, *kalispera!* How are you?"

"Very well, but we must go home tomorrow, sadly…"

"Oh, such a short time here! But you will come back?"

"Of course! We're coming back in September."

"Ah, September is the best time!"

Later we have a fabulous dinner—Greek salad, *tzatziki*, goat in lemon sauce, the little local shrimp or *garidakia* that you eat with their shells on, and an enormous swordfish steak with potatoes. We wind up the evening with drinks at the café-bar by the sea, of course, standing outside until almost three in the morning, talking with Manolis and Yota from the bakery, who used to sell me my *spanakopita* and other treats every day when I lived next door for a month.

Our last morning before the boat arrives is a Sunday and very quiet. When I go down to the sea, there's only a mother teaching her little boy to swim; I admit I probably do watch with a little envy and hope. Tilos looks as spectacular and magical as ever as I swim across the bay. I'll leave my note for Vangelis at his house after breakfast. I meet Matt in the square and we walk up the hill to drop off any books we're not taking back at the "Cat Bookshop," a secondhand book exchange run by an English couple from a bookshelf on their front terrace: you leave old books in the basket, and if you choose another from the shelf, you leave some money, which is used to buy food for the stray cats.

We decide to have breakfast at a traditional-looking café under the shade of some trees just off the square. We turn the corner and, lo and behold, there's Vangelis. It's wonderful to see him again, even though I'm not sure he immediately recognizes me—understandable, after everything he's been through this year. He looks a little tired. Then he seems to remember me, greets us, and invites us to sit down.

"I arrive back on the *Sea Star* just last night, but I didn't go out—I was too tired."

"I was looking for you all week since we arrived… And then somebody told me. How are you now?"

"Eh, now, I feel OK. I eat my mother's cooking and get a bit fat. But even last year, I feel OK. When my girlfriend first find this thing on my neck here, I think is nothing, a bite from an insect, when I look after the animals. But my girlfriend, she tell my daughter, and they say to go to the hospital. Then I have to go to Athens for an operation. I go fast, because we pay. So now, after the tests in Rodos, we wait and see. Life is life!" he says with a wry smile. "If I finish down here, maybe we go upstairs—maybe it's better upstairs!"

He's in good spirits. Gradually, he remembers my interest in the book he was writing and goes off to fetch it. When he returns, he brings his five-year-old grandson, who is shy at first but gradually emerges into quite the talker, just like his grandfather.

"Where do they speak English?" he asks.

"In England," says granddad.

"Where is England?"

"Far! You take the plane."

"You must take the plane at night."

Vangelis explains: the family visited him in Athens when he came out of the hospital, and they had to take the plane at night. I'm so happy to have seen him. I flick through the printed pages of his manuscript about Tilos in the days when he grew up. Apparently his English friend, who runs the Cat Bookshop, has it on a computer and could email it to me. Maybe I can help to get it printed.

"Send it to me, I'd love to read it," I say. "And I hope we'll see you properly when we come back in September."

Summer in England starts off with a heat wave, but then turns rainy, damp, windy, and gray. I cheer myself up by looking at the webcam of Tilos. There it's sunny, and nothing is happening, just the boats shifting slightly on the blue water.

Matt and I are both rushing about with work, weeks passing by in a blur. Summer is always a busy time in my job, and Matt is dealing with all the legal headaches of selling the business. Take me back to Tilos.

But to Matt, weekends are sacrosanct. One of the best things about trying to get pregnant is that it gives you a great excuse to spend all Saturday morning in bed. We have a late breakfast at our favorite place by the train station, lingering over a newspaper and crossword until we've decided where to go and wander for the day.

One of the worst things about trying to get pregnant is the way I try to interpret the signs of how my body feels, count the hours when my period hasn't come yet and hope this might be the month, and feel sad when my period does come, even though I've told myself not to. And as if that isn't bad enough, then I have to break it to my hopeful partner too. Sometimes it's a week or so late and it's hard not to get your hopes up. It doesn't get any easier. I feel doubly cursed to have had childbearing hips since I was a teenager.

With a year gone by, I decide I need to do something rather than merely wait and hope. So I go to see my doctor.

My doctor is an extremely scary woman. On the rare occasion I visit her, I get the sense I am wasting her very valuable time, even if I have an injury that needs stitches. She is, indeed, very busy. But I manage to book an appointment and write down the few questions I need to get into our brief conversation. Unfortunately since the surgery moved out of town, it's hard to pop in on a lunch break, so one evening I cycle the few miles to her late surgery session.

The cleaner is hoovering around the almost-empty waiting room as I sit reading. The receptionist says the doctor has had a very long session and is running late; could I come back another time? I say no, I'll wait. Eventually, I'm called in. She barely looks up from her paperwork as I somehow manage to stammer out the reason I've come. Then she looks up to the computer screen and starts tapping away at the keyboard and firing questions at me. It all sounds so pathetic when I start telling her, very far from being a medical crisis or indeed your conventional attempt at family planning. I'm pretty old to be suddenly trying to get pregnant. And then I started trying barely weeks after getting together with my partner…

Dr. Chatham doesn't bat an eyelid.

"Well, when you reach a certain age and know what you want, you don't need to wait, do you?"

Suddenly I relax. I notice a photo of children on Dr. Chatham's desk. This is going to be OK.

She even begins to warm to my case, I think. She finishes her questions, sorts me out with a slew of tests at the hospital, and agrees to do my first examination right away rather than make me cycle back out here. I leave happy, knowing I'm on my way at least to learning more about what's going on inside me.

I also try looking into the possibility of adoption, knowing that it wouldn't matter to either of us if the baby wasn't biologically ours—we just want to be parents. A few years ago I met a little boy and girl whom my aunt was fostering; their mum and dad were addicted to serious drugs and in prison for serious crimes, but the kids were wonderful and it made me think. I'd even spoken to my dad about it. However, it's surprisingly hard to get information and find my way through the maze of different agencies, and then when I do manage to have an initial interview on the phone, the discussion leaves me feeling discouraged.

I had naively thought that adoption agencies would want to hear from people like me wanting to take institutionalized children and give them a happy home, but talking to this man, for whom empathy for potential adopters is evidently not a priority, the impression is the agency would rather feed the children to wolves than let me be responsible for them. It's so humiliating; I'm not sure I could go through two years of that. Anyway, the man on the phone concludes, if I still have any notion that I might want to have my own child, they won't even consider my application. So that idea gets firmly shelved for now.

Matt still hasn't made contact with his daughters. I know the adoption people wouldn't like that much either. It's an emotional topic but I mention this to him, and he again resolves to get in touch with the family and make the first steps. I'd love to meet the girls, who are now six and eight; they live a few counties away, but if he reestablished a connection, it would be easy to visit. I think of them whenever we meet up with friends who have young kids, as Matt always captivates children.

As so often happens, the contract negotiations for the sale of Matt's business take longer than expected. Back and forth it goes with the lawyers. The ups and downs of the business continue, as I hear in great detail. His flat by the sea, which we thought we'd have back to enjoy for the summer, remains in the hands of the bank. These delays make it impossible to progress with buying the house; I wish I could do something about it but his financial advisor Don is handling it. We keep our finances separate; the way he spends money would drive me crazy if I had to worry about it. I do mention at one point that I could look into selling my flat and somehow raise some capital to contribute toward the house. But he insists I'm not to put any of my money into this. It's his deal, so I stay out of it.

It's not only frustrating to us that things are taking so long—to make matters worse, it leads to increasingly stressed emails from the owners of the house in Tilos, who don't understand that our hands are tied. It's hard to find the time to deal with it when we're so busy with our jobs. With everything so uncertain, I decide to hold off on making any changes to my work, but I continue training my colleagues in the hope that when the time comes, it will be easier.

The other problem with us not being able to use his flat by the sea, though, is that it's where he has personal belongings stored—things like photograph albums of his parents, who both died a decade ago, or of his daughters. I'm longing to see them and hear more stories of his past. It feels like that part of him is missing. Even though he's taken me to his office at the factory where I met a couple of the guys, and I hear all about the business constantly, I've never seen a home he has made. He says I'm not missing much—his place was a real bachelor pad with a large TV and some outdoors equipment and not much else. Still, one night as we are walking home from our Friday night out and a few drinks, it comes into my head and I decide to share my thoughts.

"It's strange not knowing anything about your past. I can't meet your family, most of our friends are mine—I know it's not your fault, there's nothing you can do, but can you see how sometimes it feels... I don't know, like I don't really know the complete you?"

He's quiet for a while. "What can I do, Jen? I promise I'll work harder on sorting things out. I just want to make you happy. I want us to have nice times together. And I hate dealing with all that stuff, you know I do, which is why I have Don take care of it. I think he's lost interest now he thinks I'm selling up and moving to Greece. And I've been trying to get ahold of that woman at the bank. But now I've made you unhappy, which I never wanted to do..."

He's clearly upset. I feel guilty for bringing it up, and I don't want him to get me wrong and think this is about me wanting a nicer house. I'm not interested in what he owns—if I was, we'd have talked about all that long ago. But at the same time I don't think I'm wrong for telling him, being open about my feelings. I offer to help with some phone calls but he interprets it as suggesting he's incompetent. It spoils the end of our evening, and he decides to sleep on the couch.

home. But right now I don't see a need to keep searching. Tilos and I get along very well. When people ask me why, I talk about hills and space, but for Matt it's all about the people—the warm welcome.

With the technology so easily available now, working from home anywhere is seen as perfectly normal. There's a risk I won't get as much work as I'd like, but I'll never know unless I try. I have a tendency to take on too much anyway, and it's only when you free yourself up that you have a chance to discover new directions, as happened when I started my Freelance Fridays. Will I miss friends? Well, the funny thing is that with all the friends I have back in England, we're all so busy that we rarely find time to get together. "We must catch up sometime!"—how often do we say that? In Tilos, the friends you have there, you see regularly because you cross paths naturally. I'll still have my international friends on email. And as I found before when I lived in the south of France, when you live in a beautiful place, friends and family come to visit and you get to spend quality time together.

Funnily enough, a few months ago, I got an email from someone I never expected to hear from again: Lisa, my friend from when we were six, growing up in a village north of Manchester. She and her family moved away to Gibraltar when we were eleven, and we lost touch as teenagers. Now, she's found me on Facebook and, as she moved back to England years ago, we are coincidentally living and working a few miles from one another near the south coast. We spend a happy afternoon catching up over a walk. Home is certainly a moveable feast.

In London for the weekend, Matt and I look for Greek language books. As summer progresses and the stack of books by my bed grows higher, the Greek language books slip lower down the pile; but at least the disk belonging to the vocabulary book makes it onto my iPod, so I can repeat Greek words aloud as I'm cycling or walking to work, ignoring the strange looks from passersby.

Now we are thinking of moving to Tilos, we have fun thinking about how we'll do it and what we'll take with us. Books, of course: maybe I will finally get through that stack by my bed. Clothes. Computers. Not much else. Most things we can buy there and take over gradually, when we come back to England for work and to see family and friends. And if we run out of Marmite, it's a good excuse for my mum to come out for an emergency visit.

CHAPTER SEVENTEEN

A Bumpy Beginning

W hat, you're going back to the same island *again?*" asks a friend.

I understand why. I used to be baffled by people who went back to the same place. I always loved exploring new places, and I still do, without a doubt. But now I want both. I want to go back to places I love too.

"What's it called again?" people ask. People feel more comfortable with a name they recognize, and they don't understand how it can be any good if they've not heard of it. But I tend to prefer the lesser-known places; for some reason I always have, and can be quite obsessive about finding my own places, unguided. That's not to say I didn't love beautiful but famous Santorini, of course. But with direct flights and "must-see" status, it's busy, like everywhere else. Tilos, harder to get to, is the hidden gem, and the few who know it return year after year.

There are a few reasons for going back in early September. Firstly, it's Matt's birthday, and what better place to spend it? As everyone says, September is the best time. When I first started coming back to Greece, it was always in September if possible, when the intense heat and the crowds of summer are over, and there's no problem finding a place to stay. Secondly, after a frantic summer, work always eases up at that time of year for me. Thirdly, Manolis told us the last festival of the summer happens in the first week of September at a little church just outside Livadia, and there's a feast where they eat baby goat. Matt rather enjoyed his *katsikaki* on the last trip, and he's focused: even though they serve baby goat at every festival in the calendar, he's got it in his head that we're going to Tilos for the Baby Goat Festival.

Before then, he wants to get a real snorkel and mask that works properly, not a pretend one from a souvenir shop. He's researched online and spoken to the man in the shop, and we take the train to Portsmouth on a sunny Saturday morning. I'd been hoping to get this shopping out of the way early and go to the beach, but the walk takes forever down endless roads of run-down houses and shops; how can Portsmouth be so big? The weather is now clouding over and chilly: ah, August in England. Among all the Chinese takeaways and charity shops, finally we spot the place. It seems to be the real thing: all they sell is snorkels and masks and other diving equipment. And the man isn't giving us a hard sell.

"I could sell you this one up here, but you don't need it. This one down here for a third of the price will do everything you need, and it's what I recommend to all the diving students." It sounds great to me, but I saw the look in Matt's eye. "Why can't I have the expensive one up there?" he's thinking. It's got to be better if it's expensive. Sure enough, he buys the most expensive mask. I suppose we might as well buy good ones, if we're going to be spending a lot of time in the sea. And he buys me a good one too. Well, I like a man who wants only the best.

We pop in to the Park Tavern from time to time to see old friends, even though it's changed with the new owners, who are making a success of it.

"How was Ithaca?" asks our friend James.

"You mean the Greek island we go to? It's not Ithaca, it's Tilos…"

"I know, but to me all Greek islands are Ithaca. Did you find that poem yet? It's a wonderful poem."

"No, not yet." I must remember to look it up. James is a sweetheart, one of the best. In the meantime, he tells us we're invited by Joy to a celebration of Richard's life.

James drives us down to a quiet spot by the sea a few miles away one gloriously sunny evening, and we find a couple of dozen people gathered around a picnic on the beach. There's no one else around except for a fisherman in the distance, and behind us there are marshes and woods and an old church. Richard used to like coming down here to walk his dog, Pimms, apparently—which comes as a surprise to some of us, as Richard's usual dog-walking sessions of an evening saw him and Pimms doing the rounds of favorite hostelries. Joy has decided that this is where Richard would like to be. As usual, she's arranged things beautifully. We all walk down to the shore together, and there's a bowl of rose petals, and we're all invited to take a handful and throw them out to sea as she scatters the ashes. There are some tears shed, then some laughter when we gather back up on the beach and have a drink together.

⌒

"When do we get to eat baby goat?" Matt keeps asking. We arrived in Rhodes late last night and took a taxi to the back of the old town.

The first hotel we found—even though the woman at the desk offered a good discount—was still a little expensive, genteel, and antique-strewn for our purposes, so we asked in a shop if they knew of any others nearby, and around a corner was Stathis Hotel, where I stayed years ago. I am surprised to happen upon the exact same place. Hotel is decidedly an overstatement, but I'm sure the guy who finally answered the doorbell, scratching his chest as if we'd woken him up, was the same guy from last time. The comfy little room felt the same, worn but clean with a strong fan and mosquito netting on the window, and a double bed with a firm mattress. For thirty-five euros, it was a bargain.

Within half an hour we were ensconced at the bar of the same *kafeneion* with our first ice-cold Mythos beer and a dish of peanuts, while the blokes played cards at the tables below black-and-white photographs. I was happy to see Matt so at home. We found the beautiful bar from last time and had glasses of wine, which came with a plate of grapes and peach slices. We wandered farther and found ourselves dancing until the early hours at a place with flashing chandeliers and artsy design and a good DJ.

In the morning, we leave our luggage in a storage room at the hotel and walk through town to Elli Beach with the new masks and snorkels, and we take turns swimming while the other person looks after the valuables. I immediately see vast numbers of fish around the rocks. The beach bar has squishy sofas in the shade and lovely sunloungers, some in the shape of four-poster beds. But I am looking forward to Tilos, where you can actually see the beach itself and not just endless beds. The water here feels a little murky, which surely it must be with so many people and so many ships in the port nearby.

I know Matt will stubbornly stay out in the sun for hours and be burnt to a crisp tomorrow unless I move, so I say I'm going into the shade to get away from the English man smoking a pipe near me, and he comes too. We eventually retreat for lunch at the taverna on the beach. From up on the terrace you can't see all the foreign tourists and furniture, only the deep blue sea and the mountains of Turkey, with a backdrop of music. We linger until it's time to pick up the bags, then wander back past the sweet-corn sellers and stands of freshly squeezed orange juice, and the guys fishing off the dock. When we get back to the hotel and ask the old lady dressed in black if we can retrieve our bags from the storage room, she doesn't come down from her balcony but gestures to us to help ourselves—it turns out the padlock was purely decorative and not locked at all. But mother and son are sitting there upstairs, and they wish us a good trip, *kalo taxithi*, to Tilos—"a very beautiful island!"

It's an evening ferry, Tilos's own *Sea Star*. I go to stand outside on the deck to enjoy the perfectly sunny evening, but annoyingly, one of the crew tells me to go back inside. When the ferry gets going, it's soon abundantly clear why. Once we get out of the harbor, the waves are huge and I have to strap myself into my seat. I try to concentrate on the old Greek film on the TV screen to stop thinking about my stomach. Matt seems fine. Stupidly, I chose seats right at the front of the ferry, which are the worst in weather like this, but moving is now unthinkable. When I say I love taking ferries, I'm talking about idyllic summer days lying on deck and reading or playing backgammon. Just as I think it's calming down, we ride up a massive wave and thwack back down again. Thank goodness it's only an hour and a half.

I was wearing sunglasses when I got on the ferry, but when we arrive it's dark and my other glasses—which I need for seeing distance—are buried somewhere in my bag. I'd hoped to retrieve them during the journey but there was no chance of making it to the luggage racks. So it's all a little confusing arriving and not being able to see very well. Still, I immediately spot a few people we know on the quayside, including Maria.

All summer, I kept seeing Maria's card on my desk and thinking I must call to book a room for the first week of September, but dreaded the call because the longer I left it, the more impossible I knew it would be to communicate in Greek on the phone. The room would probably be free anyway, I thought. Finally, a week before, I dialed the number and trotted out the phrase I'd rehearsed about wanting to book the room upstairs that overlooked the sea. Her friendly response seemed a mixture of yes and no. I asked her to repeat it a few times, but to no avail: finally I said I couldn't really understand but we'd see her when we arrived.

Face to face, it's easier to understand what she means: she doesn't have the same room overlooking the sea; it was booked back in June by someone else. We go to see the alternative, but to say it overlooks the sea would be generous. We've set our hearts on a place looking straight out into the bay. I awkwardly but apologetically explain that it's not quite the same, while she graciously apologizes for not being able to give us the room we want.

Thanking Maria, we start walking down the seafront, and Matt leaves it to me to ask in Greek at various other places. The man at Nautilos greets us, smiling as always, but when I ask about his rooms he says he's fully booked; next door, there's an apartment available but it's too big and looking away from the sea. I notice all the restaurants are full; I've never seen them like this. It gradually dawns on me that September must be a busy time in Tilos. One of the things I always enjoy about Tilos is arriving and relaxing immediately. I think if I were alone, I'd probably just take any place to stay for one night and sort it out in the morning, or sit somewhere with a drink first and at least find my glasses in my bag so I can see; I'm not good at arriving places at night anyway, and I do feel like a bit of an idiot having misunderstood the situation at Maria's. But I know Matt is hungry and would rather settle in somewhere properly so I'm happy to persevere for a while. Better if we're both happy.

Eventually, we see a building with little blue-painted balconies and shutters overlooking the sea—but there's no one about. I try calling the number on the sign but there's no answer. An English woman emerges from her room on the ground floor, having overheard us talking, and explains the owner lives at the back. I walk round and see people inside sitting watching TV, and have to knock and shout a few times before a smiling woman comes out in her slippers. She shuffles around looking for the right keys, and eventually takes us up to a room. It's simple and uncluttered, with the perfect view straight out across the bay. We're home.

Yorgos—the younger one from the seafront restaurant—shouted *yeia sas*, hello, when he saw us walking past earlier, and so before long we're back there drinking cold retsina and ordering lamb stew and swordfish steak. I ask for *tzatziki* too, craving that creamy, garlicky taste.

"*Then echi*," says Yorgos. There isn't any.

I'm taken aback. How can they not have *tzatziki*? It's like saying there's no salt. But they've actually run out. It's yet another sign that September is popular. I'll survive a day, I'm sure. As we're eating, Manolis walks by, does a doubletake as he spots us, and comes over. I'd only vaguely mentioned when we might be arriving in an email. It's always a bit chaotic in the days leading up to a holiday, and we've been going out an awful lot. Plus, I sneakily wanted to surprise him.

"Welcome! You arrived. I think maybe you are not coming."

"Sorry! I wasn't sure which boat we'd be taking."

"Tomorrow, for Matt's birthday, we go to dance at Mikro Horio!" he says.

"What? It's still open?"

"Yes, eh, only a few days a week, but it's still open for September."

I've always been here in the wrong season for the open-air bar in the abandoned village. I'm excited.

"Great! And what about the festival at the church? The one you said was the first week of September." When I tried looking up information online in the last couple of weeks, I couldn't find anything about it.

"Of course," he replies enigmatically.

In the night, the wind dies down, the temperature seems to rise, and we're awakened by a mosquito. We hadn't noticed the lack of mosquito netting or a fan when we took the room, so relieved we were to find it. Lying awake, trying to cool down and keep the mosquito off, I am plagued by doubts about moving here. It feels somehow strange this time. I can sense Matt finding the heat and mosquito difficult too. Maybe we rushed into this whole moving-to-Greece thing.

But the open windows also bring a spectacular dawn over the sea.

I realize I'm just achy and uncomfortable with the start of my period, and too little sleep for several nights because Matt insisted on going out. My period was almost two weeks late and I had really been hoping it wouldn't come at all, but no, it arrived last night. So I'm stuck with my period just in time for my week's holiday, and I think back with envy to the days when I could control it with pills. I'm also disappointed and angry. What the hell does it take to get pregnant? Lord knows, I'm trying; maybe it's just not possible anymore. Maybe it never was. Even eighteen months after coming off the pill, my body is still having trouble adjusting to natural rhythms, it seems, so maybe it's not ready yet. I try not to worry; at least I've been doing the long series of blood tests, cycling up to the hospital to have a syringe stuck in my arm before work for months now, so Dr. C can start analyzing those soon.

I go for a long swim in the early morning and then fall asleep on a sunbed. When I wake up, rested, Matt says I look a whole lot more relaxed and happy. Maybe Tilos is working its usual magic after all. We spend a quiet day easing into Tilos holiday mode, in and out of the sea, in and out of the shade, with no need to make plans as everything is right here. I feel bad that I haven't had the chance to buy Matt much for his birthday, though I bought him a leather birthday hat yesterday in Rhodes. He had said bringing him to Tilos was gift enough, but I should have gotten him a few surprises.

A lazy day reaches a lazy evening on the rooftop of the seafront café with a beautiful view of the lights of the bay in front and the hills in silhouette behind. We talk about things Matt might do when we move here; as he reminds me, he could just exist fairly frugally on the rent he receives from the new owners of the business, as he owns the land, but it would be good for him to do something.

At the restaurant off the square, with its tables spread out under the trees, Matt gets his local baby goat in lemon, and I also order us some little Tilos shrimp, and an enormous beef *stifado* (stew with onions) for me, a salad, and a bottle of retsina. It's a nicely old-fashioned place, with tall windows and wooden shutters, and a few locals sitting talking at a table. The owner has a dry sense of humor and corrects my Greek smilingly. Then it's time to meet Manolis and drive up to the bar in the abandoned village, Mikro Horio, which opens at midnight. So he's not in bed by ten every night as he once told me—either that or this is a special occasion.

The rough track turns off the main road and it's a scramble up a dark and rocky hillside, twisting and turning past little pens for animals, until we see the lights and park the car. From there it's more stony pathway, and I realize wearing high-heeled sandals was rather ambitious. They're not exactly practical for a rural Greek island at all, but I bought these beautiful wood-and-leather strappy creations two years ago and it's only been warm enough to wear them twice in England.

The village is pitch-black, and the bar is built in one of the old stone houses, with stone terraces and discreet lights hidden in doorways. In the houses around the church, open windows are lit up as if by candlelight.

From this high you can see the lights of Turkey and Rhodes, but the most spectacular sight in the darkness is directly above: millions of stars and the Milky Way, like a light wash of white paint arching across the sky. There's a DJ in the open-air bar playing mostly Greek pop, dance, and reggae, and people are sitting quietly at tables. Gradually more people arrive, and we move to the dance floor, a terrace completely open to the stars. From time to time as the music gets lively, the lights on the hillside flash—which must confuse the Turkish military no end. We dance for hours, abandoning the laziness of the day. When I go to the back of the building to find the bathroom, treading carefully in my heels on the rocky path, I startle some baby goats who are probably trying to get some sleep.

Watch out, baby goats. Matt's about.

After all the dancing, Matt said he wouldn't be walking anywhere today. So how is it that midday finds us hiking up from Livadia toward the ruined castle of Agriosykia? Since it was a bit too windy to sit on the beach, it seemed good weather for a walk and I thought I'd go up the hill to see the amazing views on the other side of the island; I asked Matt if he wanted to come and he said yes—though I suppose I had forgotten exactly how far it is, or in fact exactly how to get there. We lose the way for a while and have to scramble through a thorny ravine, then continue on another long stretch of the tarmac road—which unfortunately leads toward the island's dump.

I wish we could solve the problem of what to do with rubbish, all the plastic bags and drinks containers, old mattresses and washing machines, on little Greek islands. At least now they tend to be taken to the dump, rather than simply abandoned at the roadside; Greek people do have a tendency to leave stuff lying around when it's not useful anymore. In Rhodes, I noticed nice big recycling bins, so maybe it's just a matter of time before Tilos has them too. The ferries could easily transport them.

Although it seemed breezy when we set out, it's far too hot and farther than I thought and I ask Matt a couple of times if he wants to turn back but he says no. He stops being his usual talkative, playful self, though when I ask what's wrong he insists he's fine. Perhaps because he is generally the most fun and happy person to be around, when his mood drops it is difficult. I think perhaps I'm the only one who notices it; he tries to keep up an appearance of normality, but to me it is painfully obvious that he's not himself.

I'm now used to these darker moods, though I don't like them. I have to remind myself they have nothing to do with me. I have to remember the scars on his arms from where he hurt himself with a razor many years ago. Sometimes, for no good reason, he simply becomes detached and there's nothing I can do to bring him back, except leave him alone and wait. None of us is perfect.

When we finally reach the end of the headland and look down into the fjord-like inlets, the bays far below are calm and idyllic, the cliffs at Tholos a striking mineral blue, the aquamarine water so clear you can see the rocks underneath. If you had a boat, you'd want to tie up in one of those bays for a while—like a year or so. We pause to look, although Matt keeps his distance, silent, and then we start back again. I try to switch off from his mood and respond to the nature around me instead. Even the stretches of hillside covered in rough dry scrub are thrilling to me in their rugged emptiness.

Matt walks back separately while I take my time enjoying the views and taking photographs. It's good that I'm used to spending time on my own. Later, while Matt rests in the room, I sit on the beach and read. A rather lively Greek family has moved in to the rooms next door and I keep looking up from my book to watch the kids playing in the sea. Listening to them is a good refresher course in simple bits of the language. Papa joins them in the water. "Get up on my shoulders. Stand up, carefully. OK. Let go of one hand, then the other hand, then…" They each dive into the sea from Papa's shoulders with varying degrees of success. When I go for a swim with my mask and snorkel, I see eight different species of fish just a few yards from shore, including one with a bright blue face.

I go back to the room, hoping Matt is feeling better, but it turns out it's been too warm for him to close the windows and the kids playing outside are driving him slightly bonkers. He goes out, and I talk to our landlady about the air conditioning unit that doesn't seem to be working. She can't get it working either, so she makes a phone call and within twenty minutes a man arrives and opens it up, figuring out pretty soon that it's just the filters that are blocked and need cleaning. It's all sorted easily enough, and I'm pleased to report the news to Matt, who I find relaxing in a seafront café with a coffee, examining a map of the island. We think longingly of that comfortable house up in Megalo Horio where we could be living—perhaps on our next visit to Tilos. Note to self: we'll need mosquito screens on the windows and plenty of fans.

Next morning I wake up freezing cold in the air conditioning, but at least we've both slept, and I can thaw out in the sun.

CHAPTER EIGHTEEN

An Octopus in My Ouzo

Vangelis is outside his house down the alley off the square, sitting with a Danish friend who's drinking ouzo and lemonade. They bring out chairs for us and offer drinks, but midmorning feels a little early for ouzo.

"Are you OK? How are you?" I ask.

"Eh, OK! I can't work. I am not strong enough to work, so no money, but I feel OK." He's looking fine—a baseball cap covers any signs of the recent treatment.

"How is your son Nikos?" I ask. "Is he still working at the bar?"

"He has a new plan, to open a bar above the mini market below the square, where Balthazar used to be. He wants to open an *ouzeri* there. But he still must get the permission. I will give him some money to help him."

His friend grins and makes a joke about the troubles of having family. But Vangelis shrugs.

"Me, I never have any problem with my children." I know, from his stories, how much he thinks about his own parents.

"So, I have something to show you," I say, and I take out a file of paper from my bag.

Over the summer, Vangelis got his friend to email me his book. Titled *Tilos in the Past*, it contained Vangelis's memories of growing up in Tilos in the fifties and sixties, a fascinating account of a way of life that's all but disappeared. It wasn't long enough to be a book, but I imagined it would be easy enough to print as a booklet, the kind of booklet that you find in churches and places of historic interest in England, and that visitors to the island would love to buy to read while on holiday and take home as a souvenir. I started working on a rough layout, keeping it simple. It wouldn't be difficult to sell it in the shops here, especially as there's so little other literature available.

I show him the printout of the pages, not yet bound into booklet form. I know he can't quite picture it, but I've brought a couple of sample booklets to show him so he can choose the style. Although he's typically reserved, I think he's rightfully proud that the book he's worked on for so long may finally be printed. Apparently the Austrian friend who translated it for him is also staying on the island this week. When he explains where, I laugh. Soon after we moved into our room, we noticed a German-speaking couple in the room beside us, who would play something that sounded like Wagner through the open shutters, and politely said good morning every day when they were enjoying a civilized breakfast on their balcony, delicately ignoring the increasingly filthy and smelly towels and walking shoes and shells we left outside on ours. It turns out we've been neighbors with the translator of Vangelis's book and her German friend.

With Vangelis's approval of the pages, I can go ahead—I've consulted with a printer back home and got a very reasonable price.

"Well, see you around this week, I hope! Will you go to the festival at the church?"

"Eh, not this time. I have been to plenty of festivals…"

I'm excited about going as I've been to very few. In Crete years ago, I followed the Easter celebrations and was invited to join the feast. And I have a vague memory of arriving on a tiny island at the time of a festival in late August, when the flowers in the church were said to come to life, and joining in sensuous, intricate dances around the square and out through the dark streets long into the night. The music was still playing and people still dancing at dawn.

Leaving Vangelis and his pal to enjoy the morning, we take the bus to Eristos, and consider trying the hotel at the end of the beach for a late breakfast; it's set back among the trees so you barely know it's there. We follow the path and find rather a smart place with a swimming pool amid lush gardens. There's a pretty terrace, and Matt orders his usual "special omelette."

This one must be fairly special as it takes a longish while— though, to be fair, it is long past breakfast time and long before lunch so it's good of them to serve us at all. We are entertained by a couple of cute young cats that find our bags of snorkels and masks endlessly fascinating. While one hides unsuspecting underneath a tent of flippers, the other plots how to attack him like Cato to Inspector Clouseau, creeping over the top and then leaping down to put the other's head in a death lock. Then he'll walk away looking innocent, and the other will suddenly leap in the air and retaliate.

It's a very pleasant way to while away an hour or so. Then we set up our hammock between a couple of tamarisk trees, and I go to swim with the fishes.

⌒

The next day, as if to make up for being a bit of a wimp on that walk when we first arrived, Matt proposes an afternoon of "adventure swimming": a long swim along the north- ern headland of Livadia Bay. With masks and flippers, we steadily make our way from just near the port, swimming a few meters from shore, stopping here and there to watch fish or three cormorants perched on a rock, or to rest for a while on a tiny beach at the foot of steep cliffs and look across the huge blue bay to the hills on the other side. We swim for about an hour before turning back. It's exhausting but amazing, and Matt seems to enjoy every moment of it, though he does admit later that the only thing keeping him going was the idea of eating a huge pizza afterward.

I've been concerned since we arrived that Matt is feeling forced into going through with moving here and is having doubts. Maybe the more I worry about his feelings, the more he feels like every emotion is under scrutiny. I just don't want him to regret it later, partly for his sake and partly mine. We're having a meeting with the owners of the house. I ask him if he's sure it's still the right thing.

"No," he says. Then he adds quickly, "I'm only kidding. I'm absolutely sure. I'd still rather stay and not go back to England." Ah, that's what's bothering him. I always worried that Tilos would be too quiet for Matt, but he seems to have found plenty here.

In the meeting, the vendors are clearly concerned about the delays, anxious to show us everything we need to know about the house, and get all their belongings packed up. They've worked out numbers and drafted documents. We would love to be this far along but the sad truth is that they're asking the impossible. The main problem has been the protracted negotiations for the sale of Matt's business. We say we'll do all we can to keep to the timeline agreed upon.

Manolis had said he wanted to have a celebratory drink with us in the evening, so after our pizza, which takes a while since there's a power cut as soon as we arrive, we go to meet him at the seafront café. The good news from the school is that he is being promoted, and it's a promotion that comes with an increased salary. Finally, his work has been recognized, and we greet him warmly, expecting to hear all about it. But that wouldn't be Manolis. He shrugs and sighs heavily. There is much work, and it is very difficult. It's only September, and it will probably take him the entire academic year to learn the demands of the new job. Already he has to deal with mountains of paperwork.

"Eh, celebrate in June."

Now the air conditioner is working, but because I wake up frozen, Matt refuses to put it on, and instead scratches his mosquito bites raw in the sleepless heat of the night. I use a little trick I invented on hot summer nights in Canada, when I lived in the top floor of an old house: dampening the top sheet with cold water to cool my body down until I can get to sleep. I know it's an odd thing to do but I explain it to Matt in case he would find it useful; he says he's fine.

We go up to Megalo Horio, imagining how it would be living there: the rural views, the castle, the utter peace and calm, the flowers. Then we walk to Eristos, past the olive and orange trees and the skittering little lizards, what would be our regular walk to the beach. And we decide, on a whim, to stay at the hotel for the night if they have a room with a fan and mosquito netting. We arrive at the check-in desk and the man disappears for a while. We wonder what he's doing. Then he arrives with a couple of cold drinks. I love it here already. He gives us a quiet, clean, huge room with a view of the mountain, surrounded by greenery and flowers.

Matt goes to read his book in the hotel pool, and I go to the beach. I take my snorkel and mask, and have just started to swim out from shore when I spot a lovely fish with vertical chocolate-brown stripes and a billowing yellowish fanlike tail ducking in and out of the rocks. Then I see it's following an octopus. Its body is brown, with blue webbing revealed when it spreads its tentacles around a rock. It stretches its legs out like the brown headlands of Tilos stretching into the sea. It shows no sign of being scared but moves quickly around the rocks, followed and circled by three different fish, the stripy one, the blue-faced, and a *melanouri* with a black spot between body and tail. The octopus lets me dive down close to it in the shallow water and even stroke a tentacle. It's small, not much bigger than the fish. I feel the little pull of its suckers, but it doesn't hide or dash away. At one point there's an altercation between the fish. I spend about twenty minutes just hovering above watching them. Eventually I leave them to it and flop down on the empty beach in the late afternoon sun.

There's someone doing yoga, a few people on the hotel sunbeds, a few snorkelers, others in the shade of the trees with a tent, but in between there's acres of beach to spare. There's a sun-haze on the mountain of Profitis Ilias, and the huge emptiness of the mountains.

In the evening, the terrace restaurant is packed with blond Europeans over the age of sixty, and dominated by a large table of Swedish people who start standing up and singing together. They are friendly and having a good time, but to us it's quite bizarre in a Greek taverna, and hard to ignore as they are right next to us. We finish our food and beat a hasty retreat to the room, but before retiring for an early night, we walk down to the sea to look at the stars and the pale arc of the Milky Way. In the distance, the castle at Megalo Horio is lit up and looks magical, like a Disney castle with yellow lights curling up around the hillside.

We wake up after a good night's sleep and watch the sun coming up over the mountain. It's tempting to stay another night, but the owner tells us the hotel is full with the yoga group and many Scandinavian guests who return year after year. In a way, I'm already craving getting back to Livadia with its choice of places to go at night, the bakery and the square. Before we leave, though, we decide to walk to Skafi beach, so Matt can see what would be our closest beach to the house. Thankfully there are a few clouds and a gentle wind.

Almost as soon as I go in the water, I spot a small eel. It's a beautiful thing, yellowish with green and brown patterns, a flat body, and a pointed nose, snaking around from one rock to another accompanied by what I call a zebra fish and, because of its colors, a mint-choc-chip fish (I really must get a proper book on Greek fish). The eel stays in view for a while as I hover over watching it, but eventually is unsure and hides. If I'd been having any doubts about Tilos, these brushes with its wild side are reminding me why I love it. It also feels good that I can now find them for myself.

We race back for the bus. It's good to return to Livadia, shower, and settle back in, full of a day's exercise, with an evening ahead of us and plenty of people around who won't start singing hymns in Swedish. We go for a cold beer and are greeted by Keith, a Scot who rents a flat and lives here most of the year, wears cowboy boots, and always carries three pipes. I met him briefly on my very first trip to Tilos, and even then he gave me tips on the best way to travel here during the winter.

So far, whenever I've mentioned I might want to live here year-round, it's a cue for the resident expats to start telling horror stories. Everything's closed in winter! It gets cold! Of course you know about the scorpions… It's as if they think you've never left England for more than a two-week package holiday. Thankfully, Keith is a breath of fresh air, and very encouraging when he hears our plans. Plenty of things stay open in the winter, he says, and there's no problem getting fresh vegetables and meat from the butcher.

He's sitting with a very big man in a Harley Davidson T-shirt. He says he's a friend of Vangelis and he's heard I'm helping him to get his book printed. It's amazing how word gets around. He says it's really important and he hopes I'll get it done soon.

The night ends up, as usual, at the café-bar by the sea with some dancing and merriment. Matt disappears for a while, saying he's just going to the bathroom, and when he's gone awhile I'm sure he's stroking a cat somewhere, but in fact he returns with something in his hands for me—a bracelet from Silversmith, like a spider's web made from silver. It's great that he's back on form after our mini-holiday within a holiday and a good night's sleep. And I have another beautiful thing to add to my jewelry mountain.

In the old days, there were not many opportunities for farming families on a little island to go out and enjoy themselves, which is why throughout the summer in Greece various religious festivals were celebrated with dancing and feasting. And the festivals are still a big part of the social calendar in the villages. All the foreign residents and visitors are welcome too. Tonight is the last festival of the summer at the church of Our Lady just outside Livadia.

Manolis's mother is staying with him; she's had a cataracts operation and can't go outside in bright light, but the festival won't start until dusk anyway, so we all meet and drive up together. It's a small church just back from the road, and when we arrive, the service is still being sung by the priest, resounding across the courtyard. About sixty or more people are sitting outside in silence at tables and benches, so we join them. Manolis conveniently remembers something he's got to do, and abandons us, so we sit saying absolutely nothing for three quarters of an hour, exchanging the occasional smile with his mum, listening to the haunting voice, and feeling slightly awkward since we can't understand a word.

It's a good moment to pause and reflect on this society we are hoping to be part of. A new life awaits. There's so much I don't know about what will come. Will we be welcomed when the locals realize we're here to stay, to add to the foreign population of the island, not just to spend money as tourists? Though we will be contributing to the economy by bringing our own work with us, and be part of the local community. Will we get bored of this small island when it's familiar, routine? Of course there are risks involved, but that is life, and this is the best chance I've ever had to spend more time in a place I love. It's an adventure, but let's hope it's a gentle one, a homecoming of sorts.

When the service ends, a basket of brown seeded bread is handed around, and then it's every man for himself as people grab the best seats in the house. We have no idea what to do, and Manolis's mum is an outsider to the island too, so we find a few chairs outside the gates and watch. Making small talk is a good opportunity to test my Greek. "Have you been to this festival before?" I ask.

No, she usually comes here in the winter. I ask her about the part of Greece she's from, a village near Larissa, and she says I must come and visit, I'd be very welcome. I tell her how much I like the *gramithia* leaves she prepares for Manolis. Little pork souvlaki are now being cooked on a barbecue and handed out to the tables; the smell is tantalizing. Matt's getting hungry and anxious that we don't know what we should be doing. I'm pretty sure there's a system and the locals, possibly actual churchgoers, at the tables should be served before anyone else. Eventually I go up and buy some souvlaki for the three of us and he relaxes a bit.

The musicians arrive and start to set up, and then Manolis appears too. It turns out he'd not just been avoiding the churchy bit of the evening, but he'd gone to pick something up for the school from the late-arriving *Sea Star* ferry. That's why the musicians were late—they were also on the ferry. If the weather had been too bad for the *Sea Star*, I guess we'd

242

have had no music. The courtyard starts to look festive, the smoke from the grill rising up toward the banners and lights above, and more people arriving. In the corner, huge vats of goat stew and enormous pans of roast potatoes and shovels of glowing coals are hefted over fires. The night air is just warm enough to be comfortable, and because we're out in the middle of nowhere, the stars up above are brilliant in the sky.

At last, the dance music begins. Some people, especially the older locals, have been waiting for this moment and they are at once in a long line, holding hands, a man at either end of the line holding a white handkerchief up in the air. Many of these are slow dances but the footwork is deceptively tricky. It continues for song after song with minor variations, sometimes a long circle winding inside itself.

We wait in line for our plates of baby goat in tomato sauce with potatoes and bread, and from the bar we buy a bottle of retsina. We watch the dancing and the people gradually arriving to fill up every empty space in and around the courtyard. The owners of the restaurant off the square seem delighted to see us here, and there's the man who sells fish from his truck, and Yorgos, and Rob and Annie… It seems that folk simply come as they shut up shop or finish work for the night.

The dancing is a great leveler of society. The fish man in his hot pink T-shirt and jeans turns out to be a very good dancer, as is a little wiry man who seems to have just stepped off a building site in his dusty baseball cap, paint-splattered shorts, and work boots; they dance alongside pretty young women in skintight jeans and vertiginous heels, and little girls in Sunday best who have learned all the moves in school, and the old ladies and old men who barely sit out a single dance.

We participate in a couple of dances, first observing the steps carefully and then finding people who'll let us in the line, and it's exhilarating trying to get it right and keep up. The second time, there's some confusion about how to hold our hands and we almost disrupt the dance. We decide two dances are enough for our first time. Manolis congratulates us:

"Now you are natural Tilian citizens!"

He actually looks happy. It's very much thanks to him that we came to this festival. I am lucky to have him as a friend. And finally, I am beginning to join in the dancing.

⁓

For the last afternoon, we go off on our own separate adventures for a while. I walk to the end of the bay and am mesmerized watching a kind of small brown heron that stands so still at the water's edge, looking for fish, that I wonder if it's real for a while until it moves its head ever so slightly. I gather some herbs to take home. I swim in a light rain with gray clouds overhead—very calm and beautiful. When I stop to chat for a while with another woman in the water, I have a sudden flashback to watching the old ladies in Kalymnos harbor, who would gather every day for their dip in the water, and wonder if I'll be doing the same one day.

CHAPTER NINETEEN

Living the Dream

On the first day back in England, in spite of having been up half the night with a delayed flight at Rhodes airport, I have the urge to say *kalimera* to everyone I see as I walk into work. Where are the old ladies on their terraces? The sun is shining and the town looks nice with a blue sky above. I still have music in my head from the last few nights we spent in Greece. Where is the music here? Everyone's plugged into their iPods, listening to their own. I miss seeing fish every day.

I think about the community of Tilos, how it's a bit like a club or a Park Tavern as it was in Richard's days. I'm sure the people who run the bakery will be sitting outside in the shade, Yota's brother working on his laptop computer checking for bookings for the rooms. At the big taverna, a waiter will be sweeping up leaves and pods from the overhanging trees. Opposite, the old man in the bungalow is most likely digging his garden, planting vegetables. Across from the church, maybe the workmen are still applying cement to the new building. Maria will be sitting on her terrace with a couple of friends. From time to time, I look at the webcam and see what's happening on the ferry dock. Though I'm attracted to the wild empty spaces of Tilos, the solitary aspects, it's also a small and social community where you do see people every day and exchange a few words at least.

My mum and I meet up in London one evening and I tell her all about the latest trip to Tilos.

"So," she asks afterward, "have you decided anything about when you're going to get married?"

Mum's not hassling me. She'd probably just like to be around this time.

When I got married the first time in Canada, my intended and I planned it to be a very small affair, but then gradually he started inviting all his family and friends, and mine didn't get told until it was too late. I know, perhaps that should have been a warning sign… ? He was a lot older than me and I trusted he knew what he was doing at the time. Thanks to him, I ended up missing my mum's wedding to my stepdad too; not that we're particularly sentimental about weddings in my family, but I feel I really should make a bit more of an effort. I think that if I ever got married again, I'd want to do it properly—nothing lavish, but I want my nearest and dearest to be present. And that's still the plan, technically.

"Well, I'm not in a rush. I mean, how well do I really know Matt?"

"What do you mean?" asks Mum, surprised.

"All his personal belongings are still in storage in the flat so I've never seen pictures of his family or of his life before he met me. I know it sounds paranoid but I've never seen anything except for a few photographs and bits of camping equipment. The bank still has possession of the flat, though apparently it's just a technicality that Matt needs to get around to sorting out. Everything I know about him—except from times we've run into old school friends of his—is what he's told me... Which is fair enough, it just feels a little... intangible."

"But you've been to his office, haven't you?"

"Yes, but it was at the end of the day. He could just be the janitor for all I know! Well, obviously he isn't—we've run into his secretary in town and that—but you know what I mean?!"

Mum laughs. Maybe I'm being a little over-sensitive. I mean, Matt looks after me better than anyone ever has, and he was genuinely upset that one time I mentioned to him that it was weird not having anything from his past. If he could do anything about it, he would. But I am still hyper-protective of my feelings and don't want to get hurt again. So I'm not hurrying along any wedding plans, that's all. If people ask, I'm just enjoying being engaged for a while. And that's the truth, anyway. The last year and a bit we've shared books and walks, travel and food, dancing and laughter.

One Saturday afternoon in late October over coffees at the Dining Room, the negotiations for the house come to an end— but not in the way we'd originally hoped. It's been turning into a huge headache, with increasingly harassed emails arriving, and we dread having months of this ahead—buying a dream house shouldn't be like this. Unforeseen complications at Matt's end have intervened, and he now can't meet the deadlines the owners want in order to leave for the winter. The deal is off. We walk away feeling some relief in a way that the pressure is over.

We have already decided to move to Tilos anyway by late spring. If the house is still available then, great, but otherwise we'll find a place to rent.

It's over Christmas that the plans start to assume a reality, when we see my family and friends and tell them that we're moving. Everyone takes the news well. And we don't want to cut ties with England—we'll be back every few months. But we have to go. I don't need another Richard or Vangelis to get sick and remind me to seize the day.

The Dining Room is closing down—New Year's Eve is its last night. The owner has decided to sell, and the space will be turned into something else. It seems very symbolic since it's where Matt and I met—as if it's saying good-bye to us. My mum jokes that they knew they'd never survive without us. Matt's wearing the shirt I bought him for Christmas, and he looks great in it. I never thought I'd spend over a hundred pounds on a shirt, but he loves this designer; only someone as dramatic as Matt can pull off wearing something so flowery. To mark the last night of the Dining Room, Matt buys us the last bottle of Cristal they have.

And so all that remains is to figure out work. I know I can work as a freelancer from Tilos; all I need is a dependable Internet connection. But I would like to keep tied to my current position somehow. I am hoping to keep my favorite aspects of my job and hand over other parts to someone else, developing my skills in other areas. I need a change now that I'm into my seventh year at the company; it would be foolish not to challenge myself with something different.

So at the start of January, I tell my boss I'd like to step down but continue working with the company in a different capacity. Amazingly, happily, he takes it in his stride and we agree to try to find a way to make it work.

This is what technology is for—freedom. It's a great excuse for Matt to buy new gadgets, like a little solar-powered charger for his mobile phone.

Back when I left for France, so many people said, "I wish I could do something like that." Just as in John Steinbeck's journey around America, *Travels with Charley*, people kept saying, "I wish I could go." But this time, as I'm preparing to leave for Greece, many people say, "I know someone who did the same thing!"

I've never been in such a good position to live on a tiny Greek island.

I go for the final test my doctor set up for me at the hospital: a scan. I'm shown through fairly quickly to a darkened room and lie down on a bed, and the technician prepares me for the examination. She then explains that she can actually see on her screen what's going on inside me—and that all looks healthy and I'm about to ovulate. I'm both amazed by the science and thrilled by the hope it gives me. So, I'm okay, maybe! I'm supposed to come back with Matt and see the doctor soon so he can show us the full results from both of our tests.

I finish working on Vangelis's book and have it printed by the helpful people at ProCopy, then I box it up carefully and send it in three separate packages to Vangelis. In a few months, it will be on sale to visitors. His English friend coordinates everything, letting me know when it arrives, and filling me in on other island news of the olive harvest and the winter storms.

We both find everyone quite amenable to our changing the structure of our jobs, and miraculously it seems we will both be going there with plenty of work. Matt says he's got more than he can handle, including one guaranteed amount per month. Meanwhile, even though you'd think I'd be sad that the house deal is off for the moment, I'm rather happy to be in control again of this move, no longer at the mercy of his business dealings. I spread the word among my Tilos contacts that we're looking to rent a place for a few months.

At the same time, I get back in touch with the nice woman in the rental agency who I spoke to two years ago about letting my flat, back when I was going to Tilos the first time, and she agrees to handle it. I start thinking about what to take, I book the flights, I get zealously stuck into the logistics.

Everyone starts getting into the spirit of things. When I go into my bank to talk to the mortgages manager to fix a new rate, I make sure it's fine to rent out my flat, and inevitably we get talking about the move to Tilos. She seems excited by my plans and starts suggesting ways I could save on shipping by ordering office equipment on eBay once I get there.

Will I ruin Tilos by taking deadlines and work there, and with the inevitable harsh words that come from time to time in a long-term relationship? Will it no longer be my place to escape to? Will we live up to the demands of living in such a small community—will we pass muster? There's only one way to find out. It is seriously tiny, but it also has seemingly infinite space. It can take a long time to get to Tilos—it's not the most convenient place—but it's worth waiting for, worth the effort; better if the journey lasts for years, as the poem says.

Yes, I finally find the poem that James has been telling me about for a year or more now: "Ithaca," written in 1911 by Constantine P. Cavafy. The ultimate goal is to reach your island home, it says, but enjoy the adventures along the way, gaining knowledge from the places you find on the journey. I love it.

Everyone can find their own Ithaca or Tilos, wherever it is. Pick an island, any island…

When I started telling friends that we're moving to Tilos, they said, "What, forever?"

Who knows? Forever's a long time. It might not be the last place I ever live—I'd be surprised if it was—but I'd like to give it a try. For a long time I've been casually looking for a place to live, to really live, and I've taken the scenic route. Sometimes you've just got to commit and go for it.

I'm so excited thinking about being there for that first week, that first month, knowing we won't have to leave again. I'm looking forward to spending a whole summer in flip-flops. In a way, life did begin again when I returned to Tilos for that month of May on my own as a gift to myself.

Back in that dark winter before I decided to go there, a Buddhist monk friend wrote to me:

I'm glad to hear that you're working on staying positive and taking care of yourself. It may sound a bit like the "secret" but we really do go in the direction we're looking… Remember that your inner light, whether one calls it God or Buddha-nature, is always with you. Even spiritual practice isn't about trying to gain something we're missing, it's about learning to see and live in harmony with this infinite light and ability that's already there.

I hear of a house that's just become available to rent near Megalo Horio. It's next to a honey factory. I find the owner on Facebook, with a photo of the tiny house and the huge, wild, rocky mountain behind. I ask Manolis to take a look at the place, and he goes to see it one lunchtime, reporting back that "it is located in the earthen road, four minutes' walk from the main road, three minutes until the alone cypress tree and turn right one minute."

At the same time I find out about a flat available in Livadia. The flat is very convenient and new and perfectly set up for our needs, close to everything. But as soon as I start telling a good friend about the choice, he says, "You know which one you have to go for…"

Yes, we have to choose the little house next to the honey factory. You just know there are going to be goats sleeping on the roof and cats raiding the kitchen. We're not moving to Tilos for convenience, after all. We're moving to be surrounded by nature, to have the opportunity to live along an earthen road under a wild mountain near an alone cypress tree and have bees buzzing around the place. To experience a completely different kind of life. The fact that the earthen road leads to a secluded cove with pink sand seals the deal.

Finally, after exchanges of emails and bank codes, it's done:

we'll be arriving in Tilos again in early May and living in the house next to the honey factory. I will have sun-bleached sheets again and honey for breakfast. And I won't need to find a goat man to marry after all, as I'm taking Matt. All in all, things haven't worked out too badly.

~

Even though I've had months to prepare, my last days in the office are long and frantic, trying to finish things off, clear out years of paperwork, ready my office to be a virtual one, and let someone else inhabit this space. Only the excitement keeps me going.

We've had the going-away party for our friends at the Bull Inn, a pub now run by one of the old Park Tavern crowd, where the landlord's wife cooked up a Greek-inspired extravaganza. It was sad that Matt's colleagues from work didn't come along; they never come to our parties, although he always invites them. Still, he goes on a lads' night out with a couple of them the week after. We've had my office going-away party, which Matt came along to as well, dressed up in his linens and panama hat, already in Mediterranean mode.

We've packed up and waved good-bye to our box-loads of stuff, sending it away on an improbable journey to a tiny island that no one's ever heard of. The quote from the company I hire is so reasonable that I have visions of the boxes balancing precariously on the back of a donkey, swaying across the mountains of Albania, then being rowed across the water by an old man in a boat… We've dropped off bags and bags and boxes of stuff at the charity shop. I've cleaned the flat and touched up paintwork and we've moved into a hotel for a few nights to let the tenants move in. And in the midst of all that, I've had three days of a hectic trade show to attend.

I'm exhausted; I can barely move. But I know that soon I'll be able to relax in sunny Tilos.

On my last day at the office, as if it wasn't busy enough already, I've got to dash away during the afternoon to meet Matt at the fertility clinic at the hospital; the appointment had to be today, didn't it?! The last tests I had suggested things were still in working order for me, at least. The doctor will go over the test results for both of us today.

Matt is supposed to be meeting me there after he's been to the bank to get the keys to his flat. He finished work a few weeks earlier and has been swanning around town buying things to take to Tilos, a new computer and clothes, and it's ridiculous that this bank meeting has not been able to happen before now. Still, finally he should get the flat back and we can stay there for the last few nights instead of in the hotel. Then we can go up to my mum's for a few days as planned, and in a week or so we'll be off to the airport.

Before I leave the office, Matt sends me a message that

seems a little odd. I call as soon as I can escape from my desk and start walking to the hospital. There's no answer. I call again, and his voice sounds strange. I realize he's crying.

"I've been lying to you, Jen."

"I know," I say—and suddenly I do. I realize it's something I've suspected but never for a moment really believed was true.

Although he promised he would never lie to me after that first time a couple of months into our relationship, there have been a few tiny things that made me wonder. But it was only intuition that something wasn't quite right; there was never enough to question him.

There was one time when I thought he told someone that his house in town was the third one in from the left, not the second. It was just a weird moment; I thought—have I got it confused? It's not like he'd ever put in writing which house it was. His properties were his affair. He was making me happy; what else did I need? Why, I reasoned, would anyone make things up—knowing that if I found out he was lying, we'd never have a future? And how could he make things up? He knew people around town—I'm the newcomer to this town, not Matt.

"How bad is it?" I ask.

He wants to meet but I refuse until I know more. I make him spell out all the details.

The business? He never owned it.

I'd laughed with my mum that even though he'd taken me

to see the factory, he could be the janitor for all I knew. Not quite—it turns out he was the general manager, but he never owned it. That, I see now, was why I was never allowed to get to know his work mates; although when I met the guys that day at the factory, and when we ran into his secretary in town, and other business associates on a train station once, at any moment I could have said something that would have exposed his stories. It wasn't that they weren't nice enough people to show up at the parties we invited them to— presumably they were never invited. All those conversations we had about his struggles with keeping the business afloat, then…about selling the business…about buying the business in the first place. All made up, in glorious Technicolor. When he came home at night and made dinner and we'd sit and talk about our days… it was all a lie.

The flat? He doesn't own a flat by the sea, the one where all his things were apparently stored, which the bank had taken as security against a loan; the one he even offered to let to me the year before we got together. The other house in town, which he wanted to have as our base in England one day, which he rented out in the meantime to those tenants he liked—he doesn't own a house, or have tenants, or collect rent; even though he told the stories so many times about how he walked in to the sales office and surprised the sales agent by snapping it up so fast. Obviously he doesn't own anything in Paris or Dubai either. How had he managed to coordinate emails from the fictitious financial adviser Don, who was negotiating the deal on the house in Tilos for us— negotiations I was copied in on? I don't know—maybe Don did exist and he was lying to Don too.

You might wonder why I didn't question more, but it didn't feel too good to be true, even. Sure, I felt lucky that he was able to buy us a house in Tilos, luckier than I'd ever been, but then a lot of people wouldn't have "got" Matt, wouldn't have put up with his quirks and foibles. We'd had our problems; it hadn't been too perfect.

The freelance work he said he was taking to Tilos? He doesn't have any, even though he bought a new computer to do it on.

He must have been making things up since well before there was any talk of us getting together, and he's kept it all up in ever more elaborate detail for two years.

He has a few hundred pounds, and what's in his suitcase.

Which now he won't be taking anywhere.

Twenty minutes later, I keep the appointment at the hospital to find out the doctor's assessment of our test results, which is utterly surreal. I apologize to the doctor that due to unforeseen circumstances, my partner won't be able to attend. Matt insisted on the phone that he really did have children before, that that's something he didn't lie about, but according to the doctor, the reason we haven't conceived is probably due to his body and not mine.

"You should be able to conceive," says the doctor, "although because of your partner you will probably have to consider the cost of fertility treatment."

I am floating above all this, spaced out. Now I no longer have a partner so actually I won't need that fertility treatment, thanks very much. But I'm half-smiling as I leave. It seems I may be OK. And I am still going to Greece, after all. Nothing has changed that.

Perhaps unconsciously, I had protected myself in some ways. I'd rented a house in Tilos that I could afford on my own. Was it in case anything went wrong between us, maybe because of his dark moods as much as anything else? Maybe I'd protected myself emotionally too. Or more likely I'm too numb from the impact to feel much yet.

Back in the office, the last hours with my colleagues are bizarre, as we have a final tea-and-cakes session and they shower me with gifts, wishing the two of us all the best in our new life together. I can't bear to spoil the moment by telling them what's just happened. I am overwhelmed by the beautiful sentiments of the people I work with and realize how much I appreciate friends. There are so many hugs as people leave for the day, even though I'll be seeing everyone in a few months. I stay in the office late to finish up, dog-tired.

Obviously I'm not going back to the cheap hotel room we were staying in this week after moving out of my flat, or to Matt's flat by the sea that he was supposed to be getting the keys for today. I call a nice hotel and book myself a room to stay in for the night before heading up to my mum's.

When finally I settle in to my hotel room, have a shower, and change, I agree to meet Matt in the center of town. I haven't told him where I'm staying. It's horrible seeing him like that—he's clearly been crying all day and looks so pathetic and sad that I insist on buying him some food; it's weird going into Tesco and buying sandwiches the same way I did last night, now everything is so totally different.

"You know we could have been happy if you'd just told me the truth, don't you?" I say. "I even gave you an opportunity that night—do you remember—when I told you things didn't feel real…" But anything I say is only going to make him feel worse, because I am certain there is no going back after this, no trying to work things out. I could never trust him again. Still, I promise him that I will still speak to him and that when things have calmed down, I will consider again whether we could ever have a future together. He needs a counselor right now, a doctor, not a girlfriend. (Heavens, *fiancé*! Almost-mother of his children…)

Having exploded his life so spectacularly, he clearly didn't make any plans about surviving, so I try to talk him into going to stay with an old mate, so that he doesn't spend the last of his cash on the hotel room and then be homeless and penniless. I suggest he sell his new computer, and I give him a little money, which he insists he will pay back. I tell him that he can build up a life again, get another job.

The next morning, I get the hell out of town.

Once I do, I am numb and dazed. I feel completely sorry for this man who was so unhappy in himself that he had to pretend to be someone else, and I hope he will seek help.

But when people ask me during the next few days, gob-smacked, if I'm okay, the strange thing is—I am. I really am. I'm not upset. I'm so relieved that I can just leave this all behind. I've booked the flights and shipping and all that, so I'm able to continue with *my* plan—*my* dream, a dream that is real, not make-believe. If I wasn't going anywhere, deal-ing with Matt and the aftermath would have been horrible. Instead, I have a brand-new life waiting for me.

I spend some good time with my family, talking things through. I keep expecting it all to hit me and for the emo-tional crash. But it never comes. I'm not missing him because he was never real.

Maybe I'm too tired to feel anything else, though certainly a few tears fall every now and then, but life on Tilos is what I wanted long before he and I were together.

Full of excitement, I bring forward my flight by a few days. Then I leave for my new life, the dream life I have wanted for a very long time.

CHAPTER TWENTY

The Honey Factory

allen in the honey" is an expression Manolis once used to mean caught up in love. I fell in the honey with Tilos almost three years ago, and now I'm on my way to live next door to the honey factory.

Arriving at Rhodes airport, happy and still not believing that I've made it, I don't bother cramming on the first bus that arrives with all the Scandinavian tourists, but freshen up and wait for the next. From the bus stop it's just a short walk to the *Sea Star* ferry, and it's already in dock; a softly spoken man with a black beard confirms it sails at six thirty in the evening and it's fine to leave my luggage on the rack inside for the afternoon.

Unburdened, I go to sit in my favorite bar on Elli Beach, a few meters from the sea, drinking frappé coffee for the afternoon while I catch up on some emails.

The last few times I came here were with Matt. I tried to make sure he didn't get sunburnt. I look at my messages now and everyone's checking to see if I'm all right, expressing shock and outrage, asking what happened and how it unfolded. I can't wish he was here, not now. What went through his head?

The sun is streaming through the windows. My island is only a few hours away. My new life is beginning. I feel weightless, free, open to possibility.

Back in my early twenties when I lived in Athens, I was always happy traveling on my own, keeping my own pace. I tended to find interesting places on my own, as I wasn't afraid to do something a little unusual or get talking to strangers, or to change the plan if an opportunity for adventure came up. Greeks never let you feel too lonely anyway. One day I was the only person sitting on a bench in Syntagma Square and an old woman ignored all the empty benches and sat right next to me. Traveling, I usually found there'd be some local man keen to show me around; perhaps a fisherman who had no work because it was windy that day, someone who did odd jobs on the farms or in tavernas.

The waves get rougher and rougher, the wind picking up as the afternoon progresses, although the spring sunshine continues to make everything sparkle. For all the family and friends who are worried about me alone here after what's happened, I send reassuring responses. I post a Facebook message about the coming crossing to Tilos, saying it will be bumpy but beautiful, and think, as a metaphor for my life, a beautiful but bumpy ride seems to fit.

Settling in to a seat near the back of the boat, I see a familiar face: Pantelis from the seafront restaurant. He sits next to me and we chat, though I'm beginning to feel the lack of a night's sleep. While it's nice to know someone on the boat, it's hard making conversation the whole way; I took a very early flight and had to spend the night in the airport, mostly reading, closing my eyes but not really resting. I just want to get to Tilos and to the house I've rented. Rain and waves crash against the windows as the sun goes down.

It's dark when we arrive. I step onto the gangplank, and a beaming young face with smiling eyes leans forward and asks, "Barclay?" putting out his hand to shake mine and then grabbing my heaviest bag. Within minutes, Ntelos packs me into his car and drives me across the island to Megalo Horio, stopping first at the shop to buy anything I need. He and his family are from this village, and he makes honey with his father in the little factory next to the house that I have rented. He's friendly, relaxed, talking with pride about it being *isicho*, tranquil, in a way you wouldn't expect a young guy to.

We leave the village, then it's up a dirt track, through a gate, and we're at the house. I am beyond tired and it all feels so unreal.

It's a stone house with walls over a foot thick, once his

grandfather's, he seems to be saying. But it's just been reno-vated—no one has lived here yet—and it gleams immaculate inside: the shiny marbled tiles of the bathroom, the new appliances, the elegant varnished woodwork of the staircase and mezzanine where the bedroom is. Ntelos beams again as he shows me the screens on the windows, the Internet hub—things I'd asked about by email months ago. Outside is a big terrace with a garden and what looks like an old well and millstone. It's dark but I can see the white houses of Megalo Horio on the hillside. I'm amazed at my luck. After Ntelos leaves I go back outside and look up: hundreds of stars.

I thought I'd have a tin of *dolmades* and a beer that I picked up from the shop and fall asleep quickly, but I can't find a bottle opener so I eat my stuffed vine leaves and lie awake for a long while, listening with pleasure to the silence. The humming of the fridge is the only thing interrupting it, and I think about turning it off to soak up the profound quiet. There's just the occasional sound of a crow, donkey, dog; no cars. Ntelos turned on the lights in the garden, but I go outside and turn them off to enjoy the darkness too. I can see stars through the window by my bed.

Finally I fall asleep in the early hours and wake happily rested. When I lean up in bed, as I'd hoped, I can see the ruined castle of the Knights of St. John on the top of the mountain. From the bathroom, even—I wonder if it's entirely right to have such a glorious view from the loo. And from the kitchen window, I realize, I can actually see the sea at the end of the Eristos valley. I hadn't expected that. I go outside and look, amazed, at the fields around the house leading up to the mountain.

An older man arrives on a motorcycle and comes to say hello. I'm still in a daze and don't understand much of what he says, but he must be Ntelos's father, Pavlos.

"*Oti theleis, oti theleis,*" he says, pointing to the house. "Whatever you like—just ask."

It's sunny and fairly warm outside. I unpack the bags, then realize I don't have any soap and need a shower, so I walk to the village—down a steep dusty track, along another sandy track, with donkeys in the fields on either side: healthy, glossy, dark-coated donkeys, roped in the shade. One of these new neighbors is almost ready to make friends, coming toward me but a little too shy to be stroked. I continue toward the road to the village, stopping to inhale the aroma of a fig tree, and to look at the fields of olive trees filled with poppies and daisies.

I manage to explain to the lady in the little supermarket that I need something to open bottles and she hunts for ages on the dusty bottom shelf of the back aisle of the shop, riffling through endless plastic bags, until eventually, "*Na!*"—she finds them behind something else. We then figure out that I am looking for soap *"yia heria,"* hand soap, not the plastic bottles of shower gel.

Walking back, I am just about to pass a car when it stops—Rob and Annie, clearly surprised to see me. I heard from Pantelis on the boat over that they closed their bar, and they confirm this is sadly true. Two cars appear and one stops for the driver to talk to Rob while the other patiently waits behind, but eventually we break up the party so everyone can get on.

I work contentedly at my kitchen table for the afternoon, drinking coffee. Emails and texts continue to arrive with shocked messages about the Matt scenario, and everyone seems to think I am being very brave, but sadly I'm not feeling very much. On the walk back from the village, I was thinking about it. When I got together with Matt, the idea was that he was dependable, looking after me. But if he was lying all that time, that's no longer true and there's no point. Yes, we got on well, but I can find someone else I get on with if I decide to.

Whenever I think about Matt, I remember something else that he was making up, some other situation where he was lying, acting. All those times my parents and I sympathized with the stress he was going through keeping the business going... I feel angry that he deceived those people here in Tilos into thinking they were selling their house, and that he involved me.

There is also anger for something more personal: the fact that he took away almost two years at a point when I'd finally decided I wanted to try to get pregnant. And the doctor said, after looking at his tests, that we'd need fertility treatment. Although of course I am thankful that I didn't get pregnant, I have to wonder whether he knew all along that we couldn't.

It's the kind of thing I'd have thought could never happen to me. My head is spinning a little so I decide to walk to Skafi.

I pass a smiling farmer with tousled gray hair, and then his sheep, clanking their bells as they stand awkwardly at the side of the field waiting to see whether I have anything for them. Then I hear the dog, growling deeply and barking. But it's chained up, I see, and loopy as a fruit cake, wagging its tail and somehow managing to hold half a loaf of bread in its mouth as it growls.

A little farther along, through a gate held together with wire, pretty little goats leap off the path ahead as they see me coming. The mixture of rain and sunshine has brought out the smell of herbs growing on the slopes—oregano, marjoram, thyme. It's also brought out snails—translucent things, daintily making their way across the sandy path as I get closer to the beach, making me tiptoe around them. The beach is empty, of course; there's just the sound of water gently flowing in and out across pinkish pebbles. Even though the sky's a little gray, it's still one of the most colorful beaches with its red sand and blue water. On the hillside, there's a lone tree, self-consciously picturesque.

It rains again on my way back but the valley is green and lush, the gray mountains looming steeply in the darkening sky, a dramatic landscape. The farmer says hello again and comments:

"*Vrohi*!" Rain. I'm holding my jacket over my head as I didn't think to bring an umbrella. I reply saying it's good, though, and he beams and agrees.

The light rain stops as I get close to the house, and I spot what I think might be a small, brown owl flying out of a cave and into a tree ahead. Sure enough, as I approach, I see its little round face looking down at me from the branch, and as I pass underneath, the face swivels around to follow me down the path. As I get to the wire gate that keeps out the goats, a rabbit leaps away from the honey factory.

My first walk to Skafi beach certainly didn't disappoint. Nor does the view from the outside table, where I'm typing, looking over at the rugged mountains in shadow, blue sky, clouds slowly flowing between the peaks... the sound of birds singing. Tilos was waiting for me all this time and I never forgot it.

As dusk is falling, I go back to the village shop again for a bottle of wine. The evening bugle sounds from the army base across the way. I'm followed down the path by one of my donkey friends and have to shoo it away; it looks hurt, but I don't want it wandering onto the road. On the way back, in the almost-dark, a friendly sheep with big sharp horns runs over the road to me and I have to shoo that away too. Coming here really does feel like the perfect decision: my new neighbors a few inquisitive donkeys, figs ripening on the trees, a view of the sea from my kitchen window and the castle from the bathroom—and a friendly, honey-making landlord.

~

OK, that cockerel is a little bit annoying. It wakes me at five and then continues its pointless squawk-a-doodle-doo every couple of minutes, over and over… Can't it be locked on top of a hill very far away? An entire village awakened every dawn by one tiny creature seems excessive. But I find my earplugs from the flight and go back to sleep… and when I wake again after nine it's silent out there, just as it was late last night.

I lie for a while, enjoying it; I hear the vegetable truck man shouting "*patates, marouli…*" somewhere in the distance, then go and sit outside in the warmth for a while, think about getting some fresh vegetables. In the meantime I eat *gigantes*, butter beans in tomato sauce, straight from the tin. I don't have to worry about anyone else being hungry and needing their special omelette. The day is cool and gray at first, but the fresh air smells wonderful, and I can see the sun beginning to glint on the mountains.

I decide to walk to Eristos and hope to buy vegetables from the farms down there. As I leave my house, a rather overfriendly donkey follows me down the track again, and when it ignores my shooing noises, I change tack and stroke its chocolate-brown coat for a while instead. It's a lovely sunny midday, and the fields are full to bursting with poppies and other flowers in white and yellow and pink, the trees full of oranges and lemons, so many just fallen and rotting on the ground. A few farmers are going back and forth watering things and they wave as they drive past.

I'm drawn straight to Eristos beach, the sound of the water coming in and going out on the coarse sand. A couple are down there fishing, no one else. I read my book for a while, lying on the warm sand, dipping my feet in the sea occasionally.

Eventually I decide to tackle my shopping list, and wander into the hotel in search of olive oil—they make and sell their own. The old lady is watching TV surrounded by crates of supplies, water, and so on arriving for the season. She shouts up to her son, and it turns out he's just bottling the olive oil, pouring out the thick green liquid. Do I mind that it isn't labeled yet, he asks in his soft voice. It takes him awhile to find a euro change from my five, hunting around asking everyone and looking in his jacket pocket. Then he hands me some Easter biscuits in a serviette. I walk out beaming, turn onto the road, and there is the man unloading his vegetable truck with perfect timing. He shakes my hand and welcomes me back to Tilos.

"Can I buy some vegetables?"

"Of course, what do you want?"

"What've you got?"

"Everything!"

I have a look through the bags in the truck and choose a bag of *horta*, the green leafy spinach-like stuff, and some zucchini, carrots, oranges, and a cucumber, all for ten euros. It should keep me going for a while.

"How long are you staying—one week, two weeks?"

"Well, I'm *staying*," I say. "I have a house, I've got my work, we'll see…"

"Well, anytime you need to buy vegetables, I am here."

I walk back from the "shops" in the sunny afternoon very happy. This is exactly what I'd hoped to be doing. In an effort to find a shortcut home to avoid the donkeys, I scramble around humming hives, realizing that the path doesn't go all the way, and end up picking my way through the field at the back of the house in an undignified manner—just at the moment Ntelos is arriving.

"*Yeia sou*, Jennifer!"

He's brought me a bag of stuff for the kitchen, including some pegs, *mantalakia*, for putting out the washing. "Everything OK?" he asks. He waves and jumps back in his truck and drives off.

There's fruit, and then there are freshly picked oranges, bought off the back of the truck, so juicy it pours out of them as you peel them, and the ants are already marching across the patio to lick it up. And half an hour later, as I'm sitting reading my book, Pavlos arrives again on his motorbike with a jar of honey for me—made next door—and a bag of eggs from his own chickens. When I say I've been buying vegetables, he takes me to the garden and pulls up three huge bulbous spring onions for me and tells me to help myself whenever I want.

I think they are especially looking after me because I'm on my own. I like being on my own, but to Greeks it's sad not to have company. I haven't explained why my plans changed and I arrived here without my partner. I've somehow found the kindest family and the most beautiful place.

∾

I'm supposed to be working, but I've just been sitting enjoying the view. The sun is still high in the sky, though there's a breeze and clouds hanging onto the tops of the mountains—it's cool enough for jeans and a sweatshirt and socks now, but it's warm on my face. The sunlight streams through the grassy meadow and glints off the tops of trees. The village that clings to the mountainside is still, white, timeless. The sea at Eristos looks flat and calm. A long-haired brown goat just came nibbling at the edge of the fence but looked up, surprised, and scampered off when he saw me. Little birds are twittering, crows cawing, a pigeon cooing, and every now and then there's the sound of a farmer shouting at his animals. A dog barks. I could just sit here and watch and listen for—oh, a year? A lifetime? Who knows?

Funnily, I feel more relaxed and content than I have for a long time, partly because of what happened with Matt. I have such a tendency to push myself all the time in my work, to tell myself I could be doing better. But right now I think it's a good idea just to look after myself and not worry about anything. Be happy in the present moment. Perhaps it's something I should do a lot more.

People say I'm living the dream, but I don't think anyone realizes how much that's true. Adventures in Greece were what I fell back on a long time ago when I couldn't find work after university. I fell in love with this country way back then. I've wanted to live in a house in the country near the sea for a long time. Now it's time to live my dream, on an island much like those I used to dream of every winter.

Matt used to treat me to all the things I'd hesitate to buy for myself, things I didn't really need but which made me happy. Maybe I'd have hesitated over moving to Tilos too if it wasn't for him…

The family seems to care that I have everything I need. It's hard to express how utterly at home I feel. When it gets

CHAPTER TWENTY-ONE

The Birds and the Bees

On the first of May, just a few days after I arrive, Ntelos's father Pavlos brings me a wreath of yellow flowers. He says his wife Maria and daughter Evgenia have made it for me to hang by the front door. It's traditional to make wreaths of flowers for *Protomayia*, the first of May, a special day in the Greek calendar.

"*Kalo meena*, happy month! And *Kali Protomayia*, happy first of May!"

It's May again, almost two years since I came to Tilos for that month as a gift to myself. I came here in the time of snakes and flies. I came then looking for some kind of happiness. And now I'm here to stay, in a house adorned with flowers thanks to my new, welcoming Tilos family.

I walk up into the village, wandering through the tiny whitewashed alleyways. When I come back, I notice a beautiful pink rose has bloomed, a *triandafillo*, or thirty leaves. I don't notice—Pavlos points it out to me later—that a goat has been in and munched the tops of all the flowers on the other side of the path. That's me, the one stopping so much to smell the roses, she doesn't notice the carnage seconds away. But I wouldn't have it any other way.

The top of the hill with the ruined castle glows honey-orange with the first sunlight when I wake up. I look at it through the bathroom window as I am brushing my teeth, scanning down the hill to the white houses of the village nestled in lush green trees, then down farther to a chocolate-brown donkey standing across the track.

I eat oranges and indulgently thick yogurt and honey for breakfast. From my kitchen I can hear the hum of bees in the hives outside, and sometimes a bee comes inside to buzz around while I'm working in the kitchen. All the paths here are full of flowers at this time of year as well as thyme and oregano, wild fennel and other herbs, and the bees love it. I take huge pleasure in hanging up my washing in the sunshine and the wind with only the sound of bees, crows, and crickets. I work at the computer all morning, and at lunchtime I gather in the clothes smelling warm and fresh.

Both Pavlos and his son Ntelos come by the honey factory

every day to potter around; it's like a big shed, it seems, where they tinker with this and that and can leave all their stuff lying about, old crates and hives, plastic tubs and metal drums. Pavlos also comes into the garden and waters the many flowers he's planted, as well as the sapling of a lemon tree that the goats have all but destroyed. He doesn't want to disturb me when I'm working, but if I want to take a break, I go out to chat a little while. I'm trying to learn at least one new Greek word a day through my chats with Pavlos. Being here on my own surrounded by locals, I'm more likely to absorb the language and be immersed in the culture.

Today he brings handfuls of *mousmoula*, which I find out are loquats—they look a little like shiny apricots and taste a little like mango.

"Thank you for the honey—it was delicious! I had yogurt and honey for breakfast." The truth is I'm eating half my body weight in tahini, yogurt, and honey these days as I sit at my desk.

"Ah, good, let me know when it's finished and I'll bring you some more."

Maria comes over later in the car bringing jars of home-made preserves and fresh eggs from their chickens. The house seems to come with an inexhaustible supply of eggs, honey, onions, lemons, and other fruit.

"Thank you for the wreath—it's beautiful."

"We're glad you like it! We're happy you're happy.

Is there anything you need? Tell me! Don't be afraid to ask…"

In the afternoon I decide to go to Livadia to buy a few things I need. I am planning to walk the four miles to work off some of this food, but when I stop to watch some fat, healthy hens clucking away in the long grass, a truck pulls up and the man inside asks if I want a lift. There will be plenty of times when a lift isn't on offer, so I jump in with less grace than I'd hoped, and together with his young son we drive down to town. The sun is shining on the colorful hillsides; nothing along the way has changed from last year.

I've arrived far too early, a rookie mistake; it's only three thirty and most things are still closed. I wander around a bit in the still of the afternoon and say hello to a few people who ask how long I am staying. At a new shop a woman from Rhodes chats to me in English; she's just opened a few days ago and is trying to get a feel for what people want, so if there's anything I need I should let her know. I try to explain the concept of an adaptor plug to no avail. I find a kitchen knife, but there's no sign of that organic muesli I used to buy, only things like Coco Pops, and I balk at paying six euros for a bottle of Nivea.

At first it feels a bit strange in Livadia; I wonder what I should be doing. Just over six months ago, I was staying here with Matt. But then I stop, sit on the shore, and simply look at that vast blue bay and the white pebble beach, the way I did that first month when I came to stay here alone and spent my lunchtimes thinking I could look at this blue bay for the rest of my life… And I fall in love with Livadia again.

I go to browse the used books at the Cat Bookshop. On the way back, I see that Nikos's *ouzeri* (an informal sort of restaurant for drinks and *meze*) has been set up ready to open, just as they were planning when I last saw Vangelis. People are gathering down by the quay, getting ready for the arrival of the big ship *Diagoras*. I sit on the rocks for a while, looking down at the impossibly clear, blue sea. The excitement of the ship coming in is infectious, and I think about all the times I waited for a ship, knowing I had to go home. This time, I don't have to leave, I muse, watching that huge ferry with its thundering sound, like a whale entering the harbor, so close to where I am sitting. I look forward to taking ferries to other islands and coming back here. The ship opens up and disgorges locals, tourists, truckloads of heavy construction equipment, and a priest. Yota from the bakery drives by, and when I wave at her she grins and blows a kiss.

I go for a long walk around the bay. On the way back, I see the other Maria, whose room we stayed in last year, picking flowers with a friend. My Greek is still terrible but at least we can exchange a few phrases. Then I find Keith, the Scot who lives here most of the year, sitting outside the seafront café wearing his trademark cowboy boots and a faded straw hat, with his collection of pipes. He's been spending the spring hunting for orchids and watching the birds, and trying to identify them, although it's getting harder to remember them all, he says.

I start off down the road toward home and see the man who runs boat trips sitting outside at a big table with some people, celebrating a birthday. I knew there would be so many people to see in Livadia, a shock to the system after my few hermit days in my rural house. And just as I turn to leave, there's a familiar face: Manolis coming back from swimming.

We have a big hug; it's been awhile since we were in touch. We go to the seafront café where I sip a frappé and he tucks into his crepe with chocolate sauce and banana. I tell him about what happened with Matt. Manolis just listens, then when I make noises about getting back to the house, he insists on giving me a lift.

When I'm back at home, sitting on my terrace, a bird of prey soars overhead. They seem to come over at appropriate moments, as if checking up on me—the thrill of seeing them still sends shivers down my spine. There are clouds suspended on the tops of the mountains across the way toward the monastery.

When the truth about Matt all came out, he said it was because he felt he wouldn't deserve me as himself, so he had to invent someone else. But then a couple of things made me realize he hadn't just lied to me; he lied to his secretary too, and he had been lying to John and other friends a couple of years ago.

It's possible he even believed it all on some level; surely he couldn't have pulled it off otherwise. He wasn't just eccentric as I'd thought; he was psychologically damaged in some way. In elaborate and highly convincing detail, he invented a whole fantasy world. You have a tendency to trust people who are good to you, but I'm happier on my own than with someone I can't trust.

I'm so thankful I protected myself, rented a house I could afford on my own, booked the flights myself, and was able to continue with the plan I had long before he and I got together. And he didn't ever jeopardize that, it must be said. He's even insisting on paying me back for half the shipping costs, and his generosity over the last couple of years did help me save money for coming out here. He hasn't tried to get on a plane to see me—he has left me in peace, even though he says he is sad to have destroyed our love. It's strange not to be more emotionally affected, but I feel like I never knew him at all. I keep thinking it's like a film when there's a glitch and the sound goes out of sync with the visuals; when suddenly I'm reminded that the story I've been following with such attention is of course fiction; it's all just fake and I lose interest. I can't watch it anymore.

And maybe I'm better off on my own, doing exactly as I please. As when I came back to Tilos before for a month on my own, once again I need some time to myself, to let time do its remarkable healing thing. I'm certainly counting my blessings, and I know it's going to be a good summer. There won't be anyone to complain that the walks are too long or the temperature too hot. There have been times over the last couple of years that I've envied single friends being able to do exactly what they like, not thinking about what's for dinner or what we're doing later, not having to be anywhere if you don't feel like it, stretching out in bed and sleeping in. I'm remembering all those things now and making the most of them. I can have a quiet evening of working on a manuscript then reading some more out on the terrace with a glass of wine and something to eat—just *horta* with lemon juice and feta—and when it gets dark, looking up at the stars.

Happiness is easy sometimes.

There's a bird in the bedroom! I thought it sounded close. I looked up from where I was working at the kitchen table and saw it on the wooden railing of the mezzanine bedroom, a tiny, delicate wren-like thing, sitting on the balcony. It must have flown in by mistake.

I go upstairs to try to coax it down but it hops off in the wrong direction, so I close the bedroom curtain so it doesn't fly at the window, come down and open the two kitchen doors wide, put some bread out to try to coax it outside. After a couple more failed attempts to shoo it toward the door, I go outside for a while to let it escape without being frightened.

I'd had visions of this kind of thing happening a few months ago when I thought about renting the house: there'll be goats in the kitchen, I just know it! And in fact I did find a goat outside my kitchen door the other day, in spite of Pavlos's best efforts to keep them out and stop them eating his rose bushes; they'd found a way in through the back of the building and we had to seal the gap. I stand on my terrace and look down the valley.

Last night, after spending too many evenings as a hermit in my little house because it is pitch-black all around after nine o'clock, I ventured out and made the ten-minute walk into the village. I'd practically run out of food, so I called in at the little shop and got into a long conversation in Greek with Irini who runs it. She carefully checked the dates on the tinned food I was buying, and told me that for bread I must go to the supermarket—the slightly dustier shop in the village that has more than one tiny room, and one aisle devoted entirely to pasta and shoes.

Irini said she was pleased to meet me, and asked where I was staying. I explained I was just outside the village. It turns out she keeps goats near my house. There was a tense moment when I told her that two years ago I'd stayed in

Livadia for a month. The two villages are only four miles apart, but there is a fierce rivalry.

"But… Megalo Horio is better," I quickly added. "I like it better."

"Yes, *kori mou*, it is better…"

I learned it's her name day today, and there's a *paniyiri*, a festival, at the little church in Eristos—aha, that's the church I passed on my lunchtime run, where the priest was putting up bunting! I must come to eat something, said Irini. While we were chatting, several other people came by and joined in the conversation, including an Albanian called Artin and an Australian who I'd met once before. We went up the road to the *kafeneion* for a beer.

There I got into conversation with Vicky, the lady who runs the elephant museum and whose English is excellent from speaking to visitors; she translated everything into Greek for the benefit of her husband, the traveling barber, and the rest of the men sitting around in a rough circle drinking ouzo and eating *meze* and flicking their worry beads. I mentioned the festival.

"Irini—Irene in your language," said Vicky.

"Yes, but I think Irini sounds better," I said. "It means peace, doesn't it?"

"Yes!" she said. "Ah, and there is a song—'Goodnight Irene'…"

She asked where I was living and when I told her the house

next to where the Koumpanios family make honey, she told everyone else.

"*Kali anthropi*," was the general consensus. Good people.

When I come back into the house, there's no sign of the bird so I sit back down at the kitchen table to continue with my work, and a sudden panicked fluttering of wings erupts from behind the computer. The bird starts flying around in circles again. And a bee has now joined it. Thankfully just at that moment when I'm wondering what to do next, Pavlos comes by on his motorbike, cigarette in hand as always; he is off today to gather oregano to dry out in the sun and sell. He never stops doing things, this man. I tell him about my bird-in-the-bedroom problem, laughing.

"Where is it?"

We go into the house and I show him the bird still flying around the rafters from the window to the wooden railing.

"Oh! There it is! *Ela…*"

Pavlos follows it back and forth across the bedroom, lunging here and there, and within five minutes he has captured it in his hands and set it free outside.

"It's just a baby," he says. He shows me the birds' nest in the eaves of the factory, and then points out a beautiful orange rose that has just started blooming in the garden around the house. "We don't use chemicals, *farmaka*, on the flowers in the garden because the birds and the bees eat them."

Now the bird's gone, I can go to Irini's name day festival.

I ask for advice on what I should wear to the *paniyiri*—is it OK to wear jeans? He says that's fine. And reminds me that the big festival happens in late July, Ayios Panteleimonas, with food and dancing. "We'll go together!"

"Thanks so much for getting the bird out of the house—otherwise I couldn't have gone!" I'm laughing about it again.

"I like the way you are always laughing. It shows you're a good person."

I put on jeans and a lacy but demure top, and walk down to the church in the valley. It's a whitewashed church surrounded by fields, and colorful bunting strung all around flaps in the wind, while loud traditional music is piped through speakers. Most people are sitting at long tables in the shade, except the young kids who are running around playing football. The barbecue has been set up in a corner, one guy turning the goat on the spit, another stoking the coals for the big pot of potatoes. And there's a round dance floor in the midst of it all. Beyond the fence, there's nothing to be seen but trees and mountains.

Manolis comes to say hello, and I find a couple of English people I know also. They say Vangelis is selling a lot of books—they keep seeing him in the square talking to people, then he goes away and comes back with a book. He'll probably sell fifty a week in the season.

I go over to wish Irini "*Khronia polla*," many happy returns, for her name day. There are, of course, many Irinis here today named for the saint; a name day in Greece is at least as important as a birthday.

Eventually, I go to sit and watch the dancing: Nikos the taxi driver is leading a group of children. He arranges a line of kids in all shapes and sizes, well-fed and bossy young girls, a skinny boy with thin arms sticking out of a huge football shirt, a bigger boy with glasses in a tracksuit, carrying a red handkerchief to lead the line. They join hands in a circle and start jumping around to the haunting, lively sounds of the fiddle-like instruments, vaguely moving in the right direction until, predictably, one of the girls tries to snatch the red handkerchief and there's a discussion about who's doing it wrong, and it all breaks up while the taxi driver's back is turned. Nikos, tall and lanky in jeans and a shirt, steps up to take control again.

"*Ela pedhia mou, pameh!*" Come on, kids, let's go!

Holding a tree branch in one hand, he takes the back of the line and gets the dance moving around again. They take two steps back and to the right, one forward to the left, moving up and down to the rhythms of the music. Watching and smiling at this very special scene, I think about how badly I want to take Greek dancing lessons. This daytime festival is so simple and beautiful. Eventually Nikos, who has been providing music from his car, has to drive off to take a fare. The music system is set up properly and the adults take over the dancing, plates of goat and potatoes are handed out, bottles of retsina emptied, people leave and people arrive. After a couple of hours, unfortunately, I have to get back to my desk to finish my day's work, but from my house I can hear the music continuing well into the evening.

CHAPTER TWENTY-TWO

Greek Dancing and Moonlight Shadows

There are bee-eaters outside again this morning. I saw them first when I went for a run down to Eristos (startling the donkeys, which were having a dust bath), and I ran right under a flock of them: kingfisher-blue bellies, orange on top, sharply triangular wings and long thin beaks. They sit on the power lines and make an amazing sound like the wind whistling around a house. They swoop down to the hives and come back wrestling with bees in their beaks, until they swallow them, and dive and swoop again.

I feel like I've been here forever already, even though it's less than two weeks. I wake up rested, then go outside and potter around. I work in the kitchen with the doors open, looking out at the view. I go out onto the terrace again to peel a juicy orange from the two and a half kilos I bought from the farm, looking down beyond the honey factory and the green trees toward the deep blue bay, then watch an ant meander across the terrace hopefully. A couple of them valiantly staggered under the weight of a scrap of peel yesterday.

This morning, as I was sitting at the kitchen table that doubles as a desk, there was an earth tremor. I'd never felt one before. At first it felt like a very heavy vehicle was driving up the track, but that seemed less likely than an earthquake. I know we get them here. The house rocked gently for about thirty seconds.

On weekend afternoons, I choose a beach and lie in the sun, reading, watching the vivid blue sea, listening to the wind and the waves, until the late-afternoon haze falls over the green slopes of the mountain and the meadows filled with flowers, and the bay is gleaming silver.

On Sunday, Manolis and I drive to Eristos and walk over the northern headland to Ayios Petros. Going to see St. Peter also means you're going to die, in Greek as in English. And many pieces of plastic rubbish, *skoupithia*, wash up from the Mediterranean and come to die on this particular beach for some reason. But it's still one of the most spectacular walks. High up above the huge bay of Eristos, I see a small group of abandoned buildings. They don't look like ordinary houses, too functional. "A small Spinalonga," says Manolis. A leper colony, from before the war.

I am then distracted by a pair of falcons circling high above, and the pink flowers of the *pikodafni*, or oleanders, that grow in the dry riverbed, and the strong fragrance of herbs around here, *faskomilo*, or sage, and *thymari*, or thyme.

We surprise a few lovely long-haired goats, which stand haughtily on a dry stone wall for a few minutes looking at us then scamper off down the slopes. We follow the stony goat tracks that wind down to the water, which is a deep, deep blue reflecting a cloudless blue sky, and calmer than it's been for days. The plastic bottles and buckets tend to wash into one end of the beach, along with heaps of driftwood: it's sad. Manolis also points out a pen-shaped object filled with liquid: a chemical, used to find fishing nets in the dark. "It's a problem."

But at the far end it's clean and we find a little piece of heaven, empty and beautiful. I'm in the water almost immediately. Manolis takes a while longer to put on all his gear. He catches up with me and points out a small sandy-colored flat fish, good for eating. I watch the fish for a while: hundreds of some of my favorites, little blackish ones with forked tails, which I learn are called "small monks" because of their color. And a couple of the electric-blue and orange ones, and the *melanouri*. Then I take off my mask and look up at the sloping hills, still so green and yellow with gorse in this season. Close to the beach is a little stone chapel. You can imagine arriving here on a little boat and feeling safe because of that church, even if you were going to see St. Peter.

I go back to shore after twenty minutes as the water's cold and my fingers are turning numb. While I'm drying off and warming up in the sun, Manolis tells me it's exactly two years since we met, when I came to stay in Tilos for a month after that emotionally difficult winter back in England. I came here and this little island made me happy. Ever since it was a refuge in my mind, and a temptation: wondering—why wait? If you knew you only had a year to live, how would you live it? And here I am, feeling that a rocky journey can sometimes be a good one.

I fall asleep with the sun on my back for a while. When I wake up, I feel like going for another swim. No wetsuit or mask this time, just plunging in gleefully, diving down and seeing the blue from underwater, feeling the life and energy of the sea. Walking back from the beach, Manolis picks me some *faskomilo* to make into tea. Apparently it's good for the kidneys and lowers the blood pressure. I'm not sure that's what I need exactly, but I love the smell of it.

As we walk back past the old threshing floor, I remember when we walked this way two years ago and I said wistfully how great it would be to live here; he brushed off the notion, saying it's very difficult. But I persisted with my ridiculous notion of coming here anyway. That's one of the reasons he likes me: my spirit, he calls it, optimism and energy perhaps.

My shoulders ache a little from the swimming and my skin is salty. It's been a good day. By the time we get back to the car, the rays of sunlight are spilling over the top of the mountain that's now in shadow. Manolis has brought me a jar of octopus he caught and prepared in vinaigrette for me; he kept it in the cooler in the car as a surprise.

⁓

I'm walking down to Livadia at lunchtime to visit the post office when, a mile into the journey, I'm offered a lift by Vangelis's English friend and invited for a coffee in the square with him and his wife. They call Vangelis and he joins us, confirming that all is going well with the books. I recall it's his birthday soon, and ask if he'll be dancing, telling him about the festival—and he mentions the Greek dancing lessons that his daughter goes to. Lessons?! Yes, tonight in fact, at six o'clock at the junior school in Livadia.

The bus happens to be waiting in the square so I drink up my coffee and leap on it to go home and finish my work quickly. In the afternoon I walk back to Livadia, arriving rather warm exactly an hour later, so I have a quick dip in the sea to cool off before heading to the school.

There's a small group of women gathering in a classroom, and together we push back the little desks and chairs. Intended for small Greek children, the lessons on the walls are about my level. For a small fee everyone gets to practice the steps to a dozen different dances—or learn them for the first time. I recognize a few of the women, including Eleftheria from the Megalo Horio supermarket. Thankfully we start with a slow and easy dance, and as they get more complicated, I can step aside and watch, perhaps join in midway. No one minds as it's also a bit of a social occasion—a great opportunity for me to meet some of the local ladies as they have a gossip. Eleftheria tries to translate some of the jokes for me.

Most of the women know what the dance is just from the first few bars of the recorded music. It's pretty good exercise: they make it look easy but the moves are intricate. Many dances involve putting your arms on the shoulders of the people on either side—"*Omos!*" shouts the teacher—or holding hands so that they cross in front of the people on either side of you. Often they start with a simple, slow curtsey step to the right and a beat where you bring one foot to the other; but then there'll be a change of pace and some very fancy footwork indeed, a little leap, and somehow I end up on the wrong foot. But when I master a few moves, it feels fantastic. Finally I'm really learning Greek dancing, after all these years of watching and wanting.

At the end of the hour, Eleftheria says she'll give me a

lift home if I meet her in the square in half an hour, as she has some errands to run first; but somehow we miss one another and there's no bus at this time before the summer season. It's no problem; I'm happy to walk home. It's the last stage of what I dub my Tilos Triathlon: an hour's walk, an hour's dancing, and an hour's walk home again (with a quick swim somewhere in the middle)—little wonder I sleep so soundly.

Dusk is falling as I make my way up the hill out of Livadia. There's the last red glow of the sunset ahead, and absolute peace on the mostly empty road, just the occasional noise of goats. Along the way, as night takes over, I overcome my skittishness about darkness and get accustomed to it—it's so beautiful. The mountains are dark, and because there is no light pollution and the sky is clear, the stars and the moon are incredibly bright. As the moon rises, I realize with a thrill that I can see my shadow clearly in the moonlight.

Gradually all the hillsides are lit up by the moon. I turn a corner and the cluster of lights of the village comes into view ahead. Eventually I'm at the dusty turn-off to my house, and I shine the torch to check where the donkeys are, as they tend to spread out around the place and trail their ropes.

But otherwise I'm walking by the light of the stars and the moon.

They don't slow down long enough for me to tell if they are swallows or martins, to see if they have red cheeks, but I think what we have is a mix of both: glossy blue-black backs, white bellies, forked tails of which some are long and thin and trailing and others more trim and stubby. They shoot across so fast, doing their daredevil turns in the sky.

What's the point of being freelance if you can't take the day off? Never let it be said that I am not a good boss who rewards hard work. After an hour or two at the computer, I walk to the village. I have decided to check whether the Elephant Museum has postcards as rumored.

In spite of that gleaming, new, unfinished stone-and-glass building on the hillside near the cave a mile from my house, the museum is still in Megalo Horio in one tiny room between the church and the road. When I arrive, Vicky the curator is just wrapping up a talk to a small group of English visitors, and is showing them the postcards.

"Ah, and look, here is the pelican! You see? This pelican was injured and was taken in and nursed back to health by some people in Eristos."

The tourists lean forward to see the photograph and smile at the happy story. A woman looks at her husband, perhaps wondering whether they will go to see the lovely pelican.

"And then," continues Vicky, "a scorpion bit him! And he died. Now, if you like I will show you inside the church…"

In the uneasy moment's silence I buy a few postcards and

sneak ahead of them across the mosaic courtyard in front of the church, take the steps up behind the *kafeneion,* then walk back down past Irini's tiny shop.

"Where've you been, *koukla?*" she asks, using the familiar term of endearment literally meaning doll.

"Just working at home!"

"I thought you didn't love me anymore…"

A few steps below I find young Yorgos sitting on the bench, a nice surprise. He's wearing a dark sports top and dark stubble which suits his short black hair and dark eyes. (There are actually more eligible young men on this little island than you'd think.) I only usually see him in Livadia, standing outside the restaurant on the seafront; when I stayed for a month, his "*yeia sou,* Jennifer" and few words of chat became part of my happy routine.

"Are you working up here?"

This he confirms by pulling out of his satchel a thermometer and blood pressure gauge. I remember how his eyes lit up when he showed me photographs of his elderly patients before. "Yes, I go round to see all the grandmothers and grandfathers. You want me to test you?"

Cheeky. "It's OK, I drink *faskomilo*…" Yorgos talks fast but clearly enough that I can understand a lot. "Are you working at the restaurant?"

"No, it is closed. The cook died."

As if on cue to remind us that there's life in Tilos yet,

a hardy-looking old woman with a stick ambles over to sit down on the bench, and Yorgos offers her a little flower bud, which she laughs at and throws on the ground. I would like to understand her better but it's difficult, so I say good-bye.

"*Prosekeh, siga-siga!*" says Yorgos. Take care, take it easy. So I do.

I continue to the supermarket, not too hopeful of finding bread today, since yesterday they were rearranging the aisles and everything was in delightful chaos. The bread comes in sacks on the bus from the Livadia bakery. But I find my favorite kind, a round one with seeds on top, and wander off down the road, a spring in my step, breaking off bits of chewy loaf. I watch the bee-eaters, all fiery orange, electric-blue, and yellow, like a sunset. I take pictures of the poppies, the daisies, the roses. This season is windy but full of colors.

It's time to treat myself to a good brunch—Pavlos's onions from the garden, which are the most delicious onions I have ever tasted, big white bulbs with long green tops that turn so sweet when you fry them in oil; some fat olives chopped up, a little fresh tomato; and then when it's all cooking, a couple of eggs that Maria brought me yesterday from their hens. I eat outside as the sun is now hot, with the bees buzzing around; one lands in the egg yolk and does a sort of comedy slide and buzzes quickly away as if embarrassed.

Here at Bee Central we are unfortunately coming to think the bee-eaters have rather outstayed their welcome. According to Pavlos, they are now officially *Ena Kako*, a Bad Thing, like the goats, because the bees are scared to come out of their hives. So I have taken to shooing them off the electricity line running above the hives. Enough is enough.

I talked to Ntelos this week and asked if it would be OK for me to stay for the year, and he said, as usual, of course, whatever you want, which is wonderful. I also asked Pavlos if I could try growing some things in the garden here and he said yes, of course. So now I'm going to have to learn.

It's so warm and sunny I go for a walk to Skafi and watch the wildlife, trying to get a closer look at a golden oriole. Where the other day there were snails on the path when it rained, now there are lizards darting out of the way. It's a season of change.

⌒

Back when I waved good-bye to my wooden dining table and six big boxes of belongings and my bike, labeling them all "The Honey Factory, Megalo Horio" and the name of this tiny island that no one's heard of, I couldn't imagine ever seeing them again. At one point the shipping company said the shipment could arrive even before I did, which would have been embarrassing—but of course they didn't know Greece very well, didn't know that even if it did arrive, there would most likely be a strike and the stuff would sit in a warehouse for a while. Eventually, after chasing up, I find out from somebody in Athens that they've been waiting for me to call with my phone number (even though of course the shipping company had my phone number on all the documents). Still, I'm amazed it's made it this far.

I'm actually enjoying living without all that stuff, to be honest. It's amazing how little you need. I'm also not much looking forward to unpacking Matt's belongings.

If the shipment is ever to make it to the island, however, it will probably come on the big ship, and I will have to make sure I'm around to receive it. So I'm trying to keep an eye on the times the ship arrives, twice a week. Saturday's arrival comes and goes so it takes me by surprise when I get an email on Sunday morning from Rob and Annie across the valley.

"Jen, are you waiting for something to be delivered? They've been trying to find you…"

It is quite funny that my things can find their way from one end of Europe to the other, from one fairly small town to a very small island; and yet they make it to the island and can't find me.

An hour or so later, a huge truck rumbles up the dusty track, backs right up to my garden path, and a hunk of a man with flowing chestnut locks jumps out. Somehow, miraculously, on a Sunday morning, my boxes have made it all the way from a gray day in England to this wonderful blue-sky day in Greece. And not that I'm complaining about the removals man who took them away, but the removals man at this end is far more charming.

Between us, he and I unload the perfectly intact boxes in about two minutes, we exchange some pleasantries, and he's off to finish his deliveries. Immediately, I'm a woman possessed as I tear the bubble wrap off my bike and check it's OK. I just need to find the key to adjust the handlebars back and the pump for the tires, and I can go for a bike ride! Now, where would I have packed those…? Surely somewhere easy to find? Never was a woman more frustrated. Eventually I give up and go to meet some neighbors in the valley, who seem to be doing work on their house and probably have tools. The Italian man very helpfully sorts me out with what I need. His wife is English but they have lived here for years, though they're not here all year round, and I discover that they used to live in the apartment I rented for that month in Livadia; her father painted the mural on the wall of the terrace. Small world—very small island. Later that afternoon, I wave to them as I cycle by, grinning.

So that's it: I've got books and clothes and kitchen stuff and shoes and my bike, and a big wooden table to work at.

"Why did you bring all these things?" says Maria, mother of Ntelos, when she comes to take a look at how I'm settling in and sees the huge unpacked boxes. "We have these things—if only you'd asked me!"

"It's OK," I try to explain in Greek, "but thank you! I

was letting my flat so I had to move all my things out of it."
I think of all the other stuff I piled into the attic or left for
the tenants, all the masses of things that went to the charity
shop and to friends. How did it all fit into a one-bedroom
flat? "Otherwise I would have had to sell it or throw it away."

"Ah, so you don't live with your mother, your *mama*?"

"No, I have my own flat." I'd forgotten, but Greek families
are so close that very often people live under the same roof as
their parents until they're married and have a family of their
own, unless they move away for work.

"When is your mother coming?"

"At the end of May—in just over a week! She's coming
with her friend." I'm sure this must seem to Maria like my
mother is coming so soon because she couldn't bear to be
parted from me, but actually we've seen quite a lot of one
another lately. She's visiting now mostly because she got a
good deal on a flight and has other places to travel later in
the summer.

"That's good, *koukla*, then you will have company. When
your mother comes, we will make goat stuffed with rice, our
local specialty. Usually we make it for Easter, but if your
mother's coming, it's a special occasion."

CHAPTER TWENTY-THREE

Enjoying the Open Road

Living the dream involves regular power cuts in May. They're only short, but it's a good idea to keep both of my computers fully charged, I reckon; and after it happens a couple of times, I make sure I always have some work downloaded to be getting on with in case I don't have Internet access. The power can go off locally because of someone doing some work up the road, but apparently it can also be cut off to the whole island if one of the cables is affected by a rockfall or even a fishing boat. We have a generator that can power the whole island, but I hear it can only be used on application in writing to Rhodes, which isn't much use when you need the power right away. Sometimes the water is off for an hour or so too.

But minor inconveniences don't bother me. Not only do I have my dream island, but I am also feeling somewhat superhuman after the strange ordeal I've been through, and I'm looking after myself because of it. If I feel like doing nothing but sitting in the shade and eating halva, or watching the pink sunset on the mountains, that's what I do. I love having the outdoors at my fingertips: I run to Eristos then jump in the aquamarine sea for a long swim, dry off on the hot sand, and walk home.

Like that first month of May when I came here alone two years ago after a winter of heartbreak, this first month alone on Tilos has healed my bruises. I know now there's no going back to Matt; I can't even imagine it. My life here feels full in a way it probably wouldn't have been with him, and I have a chance to integrate more with the community. Maybe it was always meant to be all about me and Tilos.

I spend the week working, gradually unpacking (and repacking Matt's belongings and hiding them under the stairs), cycling to the beach and then back loaded down with vegetables, interrupted only by my Greek dancing lesson and occasional forays to the village. I am hoping to learn enough Greek dances to be able to join in a little at the summer festivals.

When I feel like I've been tethered to my desk for long enough, staring at my computer screen, a hike with long views in every direction is the best antidote. And Manolis has promised to cook me dinner, so I set off walking to Livadia on Friday night with a good end of the week feeling, the sun dipping down behind the mountains. This walk across the island is such a good space for thinking and getting things in perspective and feeling the freedom of possibility. I pass a couple sitting at the side of the road outside a chapel, who smile at my fumbled *kalimera*—uh, *kalispera*! Good day, I mean good evening! (I've been thinking in English all day.) I like living in a place where people always say hello. I stop to watch birds circling very high, hunting.

As I enter the town I pass a restaurant on the corner and wish *kalispera* as usual to the man who's cooking; the smell of the food makes me hungry for some meat, which I haven't had much of lately, since the butcher is in Livadia. Suddenly, I *need* a pork souvlaki. But Manolis is cooking some special fish for dinner, so I resist.

Walking down to the sea, I see Vangelis sitting upstairs on his own in the *ouzeri*, and I wave. Then I think, hang on, what's the rush? And I go back and ask if I can join him for a bit.

Even though the place has just opened, Vangelis says Nikos already has a regular lunch crowd. In the summer, when the Greeks come, it'll be busy. As Vangelis has told me before, the Greeks, especially those who live abroad, like to order fish when they're by the sea and they don't look at the price.

"How are things going with the book?" I ask.

"Very good! I will have to print some more, I think."

"That's no problem. Don't worry, I'll look into it."

The restaurant is cozy, with a beautiful location up here, looking out to the sea and the mountains, and over the port. "It's exciting coming into town and seeing people," I say. "Some days I only talk to the donkeys."

Vangelis likes the idea that I talk to the donkeys. "These are not Tilos donkeys by your house though—Tilos donkeys are smaller, and more"—he searches to show me the color—"not blue exactly…"

"Gray?" My neighbor's donkeys are chocolate-brown and furry, and they look all embarrassed when I catch them rolling in the dust to get rid of the flies.

"Yes, gray. There are now not many original Tilos donkeys. One time, every family had a donkey. You know why?"

"Ah, I think I do! Pavlos showed me the thing for the olives, the olive press, and said the donkey walked in a circle and pulled the stone around… ?" Pavlos had finally asked the other day if I knew what that stone thing in the middle of the garden was that looks like a stone well with a flat stone top.

"Yes! And also, for the work in the fields, the donkeys bring back the fruits… But after the war, when the people leave Tilos, they kill the donkeys… Now, one man he have two and he try to breed them. I remember right over the mountain there, you know Gera? Up on the top of the mountain was the OTE, the telephone station, and they had a donkey to carry the diesel and the water up there to keep the telephone going. It was in fifty-eight, maybe."

"You have so many more stories—you'll have to expand the book!"

"I think maybe in the winter, yes, after the treatment, I would like to write something more. I think of things." He's still got to get through another round of chemotherapy and has to wait to get it covered by the insurance. His friends are worried.

"How are you feeling?"

"OK, you know?" He shrugs. "Ah, I didn't think I would get sick like this, but what can you do?"

The wind's picked up and Vangelis is cold and needs to go inside, so I kiss him on each cheek and then dash off to Manolis's place for dinner.

Manolis has filleted a fish called *loutsos*, "the Greek edition of barracuda," and grills it so the skin lifts away and the flesh is lean, delicate, and delicious. He serves it with tomato salad and crusty, cake-like, freshly baked bread. The wine I've bought at the last minute at the new shop around the corner, on the other hand, is atrociously bad, half sweet and half sour. Manolis teaches me a new phrase, *i sapouni halvas na to fas*, "You'll eat it whether it's halva or soap"—so we drink a bit; he can use the rest of it to make vinegar.

After, we wander down to the seafront café and stand outside watching the sea while people come and go. We try to talk, but beyond our beach adventures, Manolis and I have never got on swimmingly; I find him a little too serious. I drink a bit too much wine, wishing for some lively company, although I know I'm being ungrateful; he's the most devoted friend you could wish for really. When he drives me home, he gets out of the car when I do, stands around talking in the warm evening. I say I've got to go, give him a quick peck on the cheek, and dash inside.

Since I've stopped going to the beach with him so much— usually if I'm working during the day, I want to escape to the sea on my own without plans—he has taken to emailing me photos of the daily beautiful, dead octopus he's speared. Another one bites the dust. Sometimes he emails saying, "Today only two fishes, I am not lucky every day." That's life, I think. Thankfully, some days the fishes win.

~

What I love most about Tilos is its wild, empty spaces; it's mainly rocks and goats, I think as I enjoy the open road on my bike. Ayios Andonis is one of its wilder places at the north of the island, where the waves often crash on the shore and the wind blows across its empty wasteland. Cycling home, I stop to say hello to a bunch of piglets, gorgeous little things, all poking their noses out toward me, hoping I have something for them, and the mother watching over them… Forget what I said the other day about needing a pork souvlaki. Will I ever eat meat again?

While I'm having a shower, Pavlos and Maria come round after cleaning out the chickens. Pavlos is watering all the flowers, while Maria deadheads them. When I come out, she goes off to the car and brings me yet another handful of fresh eggs.

"I took your chair!" says Maria as she takes a break and rests her legs. "Have you been for a swim?"

"Not today, just a bike ride, but usually I swim every day."

"I haven't been for a swim for eight years! I don't like it, I get cold. Ah, this is the best time of day here," she says as the sun goes down behind the mountain and everything turns mellow. "The view—it would be better without the factory in the way but it's OK, and sure the trees have got so big you can't see the sea, but… Up on the roof is the best of course. I'm going to get Ntelos to bring some chairs for you tomorrow—or whenever he's around. We never see him!"

Sometimes I can't follow everything in Greek or it takes me a while to catch it all, so maybe I'm standing there with a slightly glazed look.

Pavlos says to Maria, "She doesn't understand you!"

"Yes she does—don't you? We're teaching her anyway. She'll understand soon. I wish I spoke foreign languages but I can't. When the foreigners come to buy the honey, I can't speak to them. Evgenia just writes the price for this amount. You're the same, aren't you, Pavlo?"

"Me, I speak seven languages!"

"Seven languages, eh?!" She laughs loudly. "Seven lan-guages… So, you'll have company on Tuesday?" My mum and her friend Hermi are arriving next week.

"Yes, I'll have to take the *Sea Star* boat and stay overnight so I can meet them on Tuesday. It will be lovely!"

Pavlos and Maria are happy that I'll have company, and they remind me we'll be celebrating with stuffed goat.

Am I just hormonal, is it all the exercise and sunshine, or do I just like Greek men? Sitting in front of me in the beach bar are a handful of tanned guys in jeans and shorts and T-shirts, tousled black hair, dark eyes, stubble, sitting around joking with one another, and I'm enjoying watching them far too much (from behind my dark sunglasses). Goodness, they are far too young; avert your eyes, my dear. But I suppose it's a good sign that I'm not turned off men for good. Maybe there'll be a chance to "fall in the honey" again. It's been an odd odyssey that's brought me here this year. And of course there's that other thing I still think about a lot: according to the doctor, I could still become a mother.

I'm waiting for the ferry to Rhodes. I'm happy about my mum and her friend coming to visit, looking forward to showing off Tilos, and I'm also pleased to be leaving Tilos knowing that I'm coming right back *home* again.

A few hours later after a pleasant ferry journey, I check into a hotel just a few minutes' walk from Mandraki Harbor—the harbor with the famous gates where legend says the Colossus once stood, now with more subtle statues of stags to welcome you. I go to Elli Beach to work for a while in the café, then back at the hotel I have a shower, put on jeans and a sparkly top, and go for a walk in town. I wander around some old haunts, amazed by all the shops after so long in Tilos. In the Old Town, I stop at a wine shop and taste some good wine and buy a couple of bottles to drink with Mum and Hermi. I can't believe they'll be here tomorrow. I look for somewhere to sit and relax but it's early. I walk back toward the hotel and from the kiosk buy an English newspaper, another thing I haven't seen for a month—although I can get news online, it's not the same as sitting down with the paper and reading it at leisure. I never used to enjoy it, but here it's a bit of a treat.

The New Market is mostly full of bad tourist restaurants, but I remember Indigo was a bit different. I walk past but somehow don't feel drawn in there either; I can't seem to settle, but that's me sometimes—I'd rather keep looking until I find somewhere inviting. And just a little farther around the New Market, I'm surprised to find a cozy *ouzeri* with a wooden bar and an empty stool or two. Perfect. There are no touts asking where you're from and trying to drag you in, no signs offering ridiculously cheap food and drink. In fact, it looks pretty much like an upmarket locals' place—it reminds

CHAPTER TWENTY-FOUR

Life and Love on a Greek Island

I'm locked out of the house with dirty fingernails.

I actually have blisters from working in my garden this Sunday morning in mid-June. I have soil under my fingernails.

After going to bed late and only a few hours' sleep—on the couch as it's cooler—I woke up early when the sun lit up the mountain. I've gotten used to making up with a little sleep during the afternoon anyway, as the locals do. And I went straight outside to get down to some gardening. Having never had a garden before, I've got all the enthusiasm of the newly converted. I watered all the flowers and plants, then took some of the seedlings for vegetables and planted them out, breaking up the earth first nicely and then watering them again. Then I watched a bit to see if they'd started growing yet. It's all very satisfying and I hope they take OK.

The rocket that we planted straight into the ground is already appearing, slowly.

My mum helped me set up the garden, showing me how to water the seedlings and so on. She grows all manner of vegetables in her garden, but there are certain things that work in England that don't work in Greece—I'll need local advice too on growing seasons and pests.

When she and Hermi were here, everyone thought Mum was my sister, as usual. She let me drive the hire car to get me confident again, having not driven a car for years, and we had some great meals out, the most memorable ones having nothing to do with the food at all, but with the way Hermi gave Vangelis an enormous hug and kisses, or furtively stuffed the tip into the back pocket of the cute waiter in another restaurant while the owner wasn't looking. We went swimming in Livadia one day, and I found a starfish and dived down for it to show them.

Maria, as promised, cooked up an amazing feast of the local specialty of goat stuffed with rice and liver. It was a convivial affair with a full table of people: except for Evgenia, who was at work, it was my whole Tilos family, being grandfather Pantelis, Pavlos and Maria and Mr. Honey-maker Ntelos, as well as his friend, a good-looking young coast guard, plus Hermi and Mum and myself. "*Then tros!*" complained Maria—"You're not eating!" as she heaped my plate with mounds of meat and rice sticky with juices. Meanwhile

Hermi showed off her shoulder massage skills to the very surprised coast guard at the kitchen table. Pantelis hasn't stopped asking when Hermi and Mum are coming back. I guess I'm quite boring company by comparison.

Meanwhile, the man with the deep voice I met while reading my newspaper in Rhodes sent me a rather nice message a few days later. When the time came for Mum and Hermi to return to the airport, I accompanied them. They protested that it wasn't necessary, but I think they guessed my ulterior motive. I met him again in the same place, and we ate together and talked for hours. He was good company, and I liked him a lot. I liked the sparkling eyes and the mischievous smile at the edges of his mouth. He helped me to find a place in Rhodes to get Vangelis's book printed for a reasonable price. I'm looking forward to telling Vangelis the good news. And I'm enjoying occasional messages from Rhodes…

I'm still thinking about all this, pottering around the garden in my shorts and bikini top and flip-flops in the mud, when a sudden big gust of wind slams the front door shut—locking me out.

I could walk to the family's house (thank goodness I am decently dressed—sometimes living out in the middle of nowhere, I'm getting rather blasé about dressing properly), but instead I figure out a way through the living room window, standing on a chair, carefully removing the screen on the window, and slithering through. At least now

I know how to take the screens off and replace them. I must remember to lock the windows if I go away. Or maybe it's not necessary.

Rewarding myself for solving the problem, and resolving to keep the keys on the outside of the door in future, I make an omelette with olives and feta and the feathery tops of the wild fennel from the roadside, and eat it with ratatouille from the fridge, then have a cup of mint tea made with leaves from the garden and a spoon of honey made next door. I'm giving myself a few of my favorite things this gloriously lazy Sunday. It's a luxury just going up to the roof to look at the sea; I sit up on the wall and I've got fields all around, nobody between me and that huge rugged mountain. Later I cut up some sweet melon, a gift from my new friend Ed nearby who in turn had received it from Grigori as a thank-you for fixing his scales. I make lemonade from fresh lemons.

And Pavlos brings strawberries; he's in shorts and sleeveless T-shirt and baseball cap, with his cigarette in its holder.

"Are you well?" I ask.

He gestures up to the heavens. "Yes, thanks to God!"

He waters the plants again, happy I did it earlier today. I'm just glad that finally I know how to say I watered them, *potisa*. He says the zucchini I've planted out look good. I hear his phone go off and he answers it: "*Ela*!" Then he heads off down the bumpy stony track without starting the engine of the *michanaki*.

There's something about looking up at that ruined castle on top of the hill every day that makes me feel like climbing up there on Monday lunchtime. The route starts off with shiny, proud road signs pointing the way to the Ancient Settlement, before becoming a little vaguer as I follow the steep road up the side of the village. One of the more beautiful homes has fresh goat skins drying on a washing line outside amidst the bougainvillea.

On a gate that is, like so many gates here, made of a few planks falling away from some wire fencing and fastened by another loop of wire is a handwritten sign in sort of serial-killer scrawl saying *"Kastro,"* or castle, in three languages. We are unfailingly international here, if somewhat informal.

I pick my way through rocks and scrub. The trail follows a vertiginous course, and I'm soon admiring the views over the village, the valley and mountains beyond. I pass the overgrown, abandoned buildings of the former village, from back when the people needed to be close enough to the castle to retreat behind its walls in times of danger. A few times I have to look carefully to find the path, to see if I should scale this rock or push through the bushes and undergrowth. I stop to take photos and get my breath back, and hear the brittle leaves of the drying bushes crackling in the sun.

About half an hour and those walls suddenly loom close,

and I'm feeling the welcome breeze across the top, and looking down all the way to the sea, calm as a swimming pool between Ayios Andonis and Plaka. Although I'm high up, the midday is so quiet I can hear the waves coming in. The view is amazingly clear of the volcanic island of Nisyros with a white village perched on top of the caldera, and beyond, the tiny island where they mine the pumice, Yiali, and beyond even that to the island of Kos.

The entranceway and steps to the castle are built of ancient, smooth, white stones, though used mostly by goats now, as is the chapel with its faint traces of frescoes, perhaps a couple of hundred years old, remaining. The whole place is completely overgrown, and every few minutes I walk into a big spider's web.

Later, I venture back to the village. Going to Irini's shop is an experience, and I am learning I need to put aside at least an hour to enjoy it properly. First I must apologize for not visiting for a while, then I must sit down and tell her my news. Artin pops in and jokes with her. The friendly priest with the long gray beard comes by in his black robes and asks about the halva but doesn't buy as he wants his halva plain, not with almonds. Gradually we get on to the business of my actual shopping, and I help her move some piles of things off the tin of feta so she can cut me a slice. I must taste the olives before I buy. The yogurt is out of date—do I still want it?

At the supermarket the aisles have been completely spruced

up and rearranged for ease of browsing, though I feel a sort of sentimental pang for the old days. It too is becoming more social, now that I know Eleftheria, and I feel I am no longer a tourist when her mum sees me looking at cheese in packets and says, "No, don't take that one. Why don't you buy the lovely fresh *mizithra* I have over here?" She goes to wash her hands and carefully cuts me a piece, wraps it in paper. I am going through an initiation. This week, the proper cheese: who knows what next? Mostly, of course, I don't need to buy things because I have bushels of vegetables and fruit.

Another day, Eleftheria's sister tries to help me in English and her mother interrupts: "*Kseri ellinika!*" She knows Greek. It's a proud moment.

I've been thinking about the messages from the man in Rhodes. I don't know if I'm strong enough yet to deal with the possible heartaches seeing someone might bring. I'm likely to have a few trust issues, shall we say. I need to get my equilibrium back. My very awareness of this seems a good sign that I am protecting myself still. It might be interesting to see him again and see how it goes. It's good that he's on another island, an hour or two away, so I preserve my island escape on Tilos.

Meanwhile, there's Manolis… It's good to have him in my life as a friend—but I think that's all we will ever be.

At the end of a long day, I am sitting outside, looking at the view. I am still working hard these days, but barefoot, to the sound of crickets. The sky is turning pink and I see a bird of prey—an eagle, perhaps, with a huge wingspan, high up, gliding majestically. I watch it for a while, remembering it's Tilos I fell in love with—Tilos that still takes my breath away after all this time.

I think the strength I learned during those days of Gifts to Self has made me less vulnerable. And the fact that I'm here, I've made it, gives me a quiet confidence. It might be interesting to start seeing someone and see how it goes.

Sometimes, though, I love having time to myself. It is heavenly to be on the beach on my own with just a book and the sea, with no one around. There's the summer stretching out ahead and it's refreshing to be learning things. Soon we'll be making honey at the honey factory.

The bugle sounds from down below at the army base, the soft call that signals the end of the day, maybe time for a glass of retsina at my wooden table on the terrace. The sky is now pale blue and lemon yellow and a dog is barking. The wind has dropped and the sea in the distance looks still. I'm not in any rush to go anywhere. Going nowhere can be a very positive thing. I sit for a long while as twilight comes.

The sun has gone down behind the castle, casting the hillsides in golden light.

The thing to remember is: there's always Tilos to make

me strong. Just being on this almost empty rock in the sea, looking at the moonlight on the bay or up at the stars and the Milky Way, learning to dance and listening to the silence, I feel happy, at home.

It's that magical moment at dusk when the lights come on in the village.

CHAPTER TWENTY-FIVE

Dancing the Summer Away on a Greek Island

This last week of August has been the final big week of the summer holidays, the last big festival of the summer, and very hot. I've been picking the remaining ripe figs and prickly pears as I walk past, sometimes eating the figs still warm from the sunshine. Nights are magical with the castle lit up above the village—a string of fairy lights leading up the hill to soft, honey-colored walls.

I walk the mile or so to Kamariani, a church on the otherwise empty hillside toward Plaka and the monastery. On such a hot night it's beautiful to reach the shore at Ayios Andonis and hear the waves. In the distance are the little lights of villages in Nisyros and Kos and Turkey.

The tables are packed with people and I wander around saying hello to people I know. The priest with his black robes and long gray beard makes sure everyone gets fed, then sits down to drink retsina and eat fried potatoes. Young Saeed from Afghanistan, in his cool trilby, is helping out by serving people. Dina from Kastro restaurant walks around with her grandchild in her arms. The first dance is led as usual by Fotis, a man so well known for being an enthusiastic dancer that the musicians include some words about him in the song.

Eleftheria's mum from the supermarket is dishing out food from the huge cauldrons of goat in tomato sauce and potatoes. "Have you eaten?" she asks as I walk past. "*Ela*, here," and she piles up a plate for me.

I'd thought by now that the man from Rhodes would have come to visit me on my island, I think as I walk home on my own, but he can't seem to find the time. It's been lovely getting to know him and spending time in Rhodes together, but I don't know if it's going anywhere. I wonder what I should do about it. I look up at the sky full of stars and hear someone coming up behind me on a scooter—it's a friend from the village, offering me a ride home. Don't worry about all that other stuff: let it all fade.

Next morning I pick up my post and head up to the *kafeneion*. Sofia's husband, dusting off a crate of beer bottles, asks me how I am and now I realize why there is so much stating of the obvious about the weather—"*Zesti, zesti!*" Sometimes it's too hot to think of anything else—all you can summon the energy to say is "it's hot." The café is empty and I head toward my favorite spot in the narrow corner with a view over the valley, which gets a tiny bit of breeze.

He shouts for Sofia. I tell him not to worry—I'm not in a rush. My toes start burning when the square of sunlight creeps closer, and I move them.

When Sofia arrives she laughs. "My husband calls me and says, 'It's a *kopella poli gnosti*!'" I am "very well known"! "How are you, *koukla*? Where've you been? Did you know about the festival last night?"

"Yes, I was there! Not for long though. How are you?"

"Oh, I cooked, I worked, didn't get to bed till five…" Finally, as an afterthought she asks, "Did you want anything?"

I ask for an iced coffee and it arrives just perfect. After a while, I hear them eating their lunch in the next room.

In the evening I meet my friend Anna off the bus from Livadia. She texted to say she's heard there's a *koupa* tonight, another traditional night of dancing. But as I walk up to meet her, I pass Artin and his friend sitting on the terrace, who both say there's nothing tonight. Irini in the shop and then Sofia confirm this—the *koupa*'s tomorrow. We are slightly over-dressed for the Megalo Horio *kafeneion* in our dancing finery, me in my sparkly dress and Anna in her figure-hugging short number, but at least we amuse the others and we are caught up in one conversation after another. I go in for another bottle of retsina and Sofia warns, "You won't be dancing tomorrow if you get drunk tonight…" So I grab a big bottle of water too.

Sofia and her sister keep laughing at my high-heeled shoes that tie in a bow around my ankles and say I'll never be able to dance in those anyway. "Tomorrow!" they cackle. We will be remembered always as the women who got the day wrong.

⌒

Koupa, the cup, is an old local tradition, an informal night of dancing in the village to raise money for the church or for a couple who want to get married. As with all the festivals, in times gone by it was also an occasion for men and women of the villages to get to know one another.

At eight the tables in the church square are still empty, the older ladies stoically sitting around what will later be the dance floor, while the men are warming up with a drink or two inside the *kafeneion*. In fact it sounds like they might have been warming up for a while. There's singing (some of it tuneful) and music and a bit of dancing, so we settle onto the terrace overlooking the church and the mosaic pebbles of the square. The singing gets louder and the ladies down below still sit quietly.

"I don't think they're going anywhere," says Anna. "I'm not sure if they'll actually make it down the steps anyway." But then there's a stirring, and suddenly the procession is on, the group of older men playing their instruments and singing in their deep voices, shoulder to shoulder as they make their way down through the archway, down the steps, and into the square, where the church windows are open, offering glimpses of the nineteenth-century iconostasis inside.

And the dancing starts. Anna and I both go to the dance classes, though she knows much more than me. With the combined enthusiasm and a nip of the grape liqueur *souma* from Stelios from the village, whom I met at the previous *koupa* and who joins our table, we have ourselves a lively evening. I find out he's the son of the traveling barber and Vicky from the museum; at the last *koupa* he had to leave early, as he works as a fisherman, but not tonight. When in the early hours we've had enough of the haunting sound of the dances—though plenty of old folks are still going strong—Anna gets a lift down to Livadia, and Stelios persuades me to get on the back of his motorbike and sample the delights of the makeshift driftwood and bamboo bar on Eristos beach. I try not to worry as we vroom off down the dark road.

As we arrive, I hear a message come through on my phone—it's from Anna: "I think he likes you!"

I grin—though I don't believe it for a minute—and kick off my shoes as we walk down the sand under the stars.

⌒

A few days later, a special service is being sung in the church, the beautiful rising and falling voice of the priest amplified across all of the village and valley at eight o'clock on Saturday morning. A cockerel is still crowing somewhere. Pantelis, sprightly grandfather of my landlord, Ntelos, frequenter of *kafeneion* and festivals, later sits down in the shade with me and says well done for dancing at *koupa*, then explains the church service was for Ayios Fanourios.

I look him up and find out Fanourios is much loved and prayed to as the Orthodox saint of lost things, causes, and people. His name means "revelations," and when you find what you are looking for, you bake him a cake, a *fanouropita*. I like him already.

Perhaps I'll have to learn how to bake that cake.

The story continues on my blog: www.octopus-in-my -ouzo.blogspot.com.

Food for a Greek Island

~~~~~~

The best of Greek food, for me, is simple, traditional peasant food, food from the land. I don't like food that's been messed with too much. Good bread, ripe tomatoes, local cheese and meat, fish and octopus, wild greens, fresh lemon juice, tasty olive oil, thick, acidic yogurt, and hearty stews and bakes infused with herbs and garlic. So the following are simple tips on how to prepare a few basic side dishes to conjure the flavors of Greece.

TZATZIKI WITH AUBERGINE

After our first holidays in Greece, my mother started making her own Greek dips.

Now you can find them in most supermarkets, but for a zingy taste and natural goodness it's far better to make your own. *Tzatziki*, made with yogurt and cucumber, isn't just a dip to eat with bread; it goes well with salads and fried potatoes, fried calamari or souvlaki. It's heavenly with grilled aubergine.

Remove the seeds in the middle from several small cucumbers and chop or grate the flesh into julienne strips as finely as possible. With your hands or a spoon, squeeze all of the water out of the strips (into a cup, and drink it!). Using a metal spoon, mix the strips vigorously with half a kilo of thick strained Greek yogurt, about 2 tablespoons olive oil, 1 tablespoon lemon juice, 1 clove pressed garlic, and some fresh herbs, preferably dill (*anithos*), but fresh mint (*thiosmos*) is also good. Leave to stand in the fridge.

Slice the aubergine (about a quarter of an inch thick); you can sprinkle the slices with salt and leave them to sweat for an hour, then clean off the salt, so the aubergine absorbs less oil, though it's not essential. Brush with olive oil and grill close to the heat, or dust with flour and fry in a generous layer of olive oil over a medium-low heat until golden-brown on both sides, and then drain between paper towels. Arrange on a plate and serve with fresh herbs and the *tzatziki*.

Fried Cheese (*Saganaki*)

You usually eat *saganaki* as a starter or side dish (or very occasionally in the early hours of the morning after returning from an Athens nightclub).

Take some hard cheese such as *kephalotyri*, *graviera*, or *kasseri*—if you can't get these, choose something slightly rubbery in texture, like halloumi or pecorino, not a cheese that will melt at the first sign of heat. Slice off a rectangular piece about the size of a saucer and just less than a centimeter thick. Dampen the cheese and dip lightly in flour, then fry in a heavy pan in olive oil so that it quietly sizzles at a medium temperature, until golden-brown. Drain the oil off the cheese and serve hot with a liberal squeeze of lemon quarters and perhaps some fresh ground pepper and parsley. Perfect with salad and bread.

It's called *saganaki* after the little two-handled frying pan it was traditionally cooked and served in. Sometimes—this idea originated in a Greek restaurant in Chicago, apparently— they'll splash ouzo on it and the waiter will set it alight so there are flames still dancing as he brings it to your table in a blaze of glory, shouting: *opa!* OK, it's a little cheesy, so to speak, but it's fun. When you cut it into bite-size squares, the cheese should ooze a little.

Potato Balls (*Patatokeftedes*)

I first ate these in the restaurant in Megalo Horio in Tilos. They make a delicious *meze* and might be a perfect comfort food for the broken-hearted.

Cook half a kilo of halved or quartered potatoes in salted water, then drain and peel them. Mash with a potato masher or fork, and then push through a sieve into a large bowl. Add plenty of a fresh herb such as dill or mint, torn into smallish pieces.

Mix a tablespoon of melted butter with an egg yolk and

add to the potatoes with a handful of chopped spring onions, 2 tablespoons finely grated feta, 1 tablespoon lemon juice, and salt and pepper to taste. Mix with a fork and refrigerate.

Place a baking tray or two in an oven preheated to around 375°F. With cool, dry hands, shape the potato mixture into half-finger croquettes, flatten slightly, and lightly dredge with the flour. Brush the heated baking trays with olive oil and arrange the potato balls with plenty of space between them. Brush with olive oil and bake for up to 20 minutes or until brown, turning once. Drain between paper towels and serve warm.

You can use a similar technique to stuff zucchini flowers: mix very finely chopped zucchini, fresh herbs, egg, spring onions, a grated cheese like graviera, and seasoning. Stuff into the yellow zucchini flowers—this is perfect toward the end of the season where you get fresh ones every day—and fry in olive oil.

Aubergine Salad (*Melitzanosalata*)
Put three medium-size aubergines in the oven at a medium temperature, then turn off the oven once they start to shrivel, which will take about an hour depending on the size. When they've cooled, remove the tops, skin them, then cut into small pieces into a bowl. I love anything that involves getting my hands messy, so I then smooth the mixture with my hands. Press 1 garlic clove into the mixture, and crumble half

a block of creamy feta in there. Add salt and pepper and fresh chopped parsley, the juice of half a lemon and a slurp of olive oil, and mix it all up with a fork until smooth-ish. You can roast the garlic with the aubergines, which gives it a delicious smokiness and takes away the harshness. You can skip the feta to make it lighter and just add the lemon and olive oil and fresh ground black pepper. Eaten at once, it's absolutely delicious—also on toast in the morning for breakfast.

About the Author

Jennifer Barclay grew up in a village in Saddleworth on the edge of the Pennines in the north of England. She blames her family for getting her hooked on travels in sunny places, a school teacher for helping her fall in love with Greek language and culture, and a small newspaper ad for luring her to adventures in Greece  Photo credit: Malena Block

after university. She then lived in Canada and in France and traveled in Guyana and South Korea before wondering if she might be trying to avoid growing up, and returning to England for a while. She now lives in a village again—but not in England—and for much of the year works barefoot, to the sound of crickets. She is the author of *Meeting Mr. Kim: Or How I Went to Korea and Learned to Love Kimchi*, and her travel stories have appeared in various magazines and online publications. She is often to be found at www.octopus-in -my-ouzo.blogspot.com.